Just Education

What is and what should be

Just Education

What is and what should be

edited by

Michael Golby and Allen Parrott

EXETER SOCIETY FOR CURRICULUM STUDIES

ExeterFairwayPublications
EX4 4RT

Published by

ExeterFairwayPublications

EX4 4RT

mjgolby@aol.com

ISBN 978-1-5272-3481-9

Cover Design by Michael Golby
Typesetting by The Artful Bookman
Printed by ImprintDigital.com

In Memory of

Martin Bloomer
Maurice Holt
Kelven Smart
Ted Wragg

Stalwart colleagues and supporters
of our Exeter Society for Curriculum Studies
and for
The Great Educators of Today and Tomorrow

CONTENTS

Preamble   1

Section I

Political Contexts

1   Mike Golby   Ted Wragg's Ten Steps   21

2   Allen Parrott   Five Big Mistakes   29

3   Andy Hannan   Education Futures   39

4   Roger Darke   Working the System   45

5   Allen Parrott   A Thinking Minister of Education! 59

6   Michael Bassey   Education as the World Warms   69

7   Mike Golby   Seismic Shifts   83

Section II

Lessons from Practice

8   Stella Darke   The Primary Curriculum:
                       for Better or Worse?   91

9   Will Taylor   Into Teaching   105

10 David Atton   Each Way Bets and Individual Needs   129

11 Gordon Brown   On Assessment   137

12 Paul Niklaus   Community and School: a case study   145

13 Allen Parrott   Community and School:
                       a lifelong education vision   151

14 Gail Parfitt   Re-visioning the Past for
                       Our Future Learners   165

15 Maurice George   Geniuses were also welcome:
                       Oxford in the fifties   185

16 Paul Ernest   The Changing Knowledge Market
                       of the Universities   189

17 Gordon Brown   Keele Experienced   203

18 Mike Golby   International Comparisons 1 Finland   209

19 Rosemary Richardson International Comparisons 2 China   213

Section III

Teaching as a Profession

20 Allen Parrott   George Bernard Shaw was Wrong!   223

21 Mike Golby   Teaching as a Profession   243

22 Colin Richards   School Inspection Revisited
                       and re-envisaged   255

23 Mike Golby   Maurice Holt: educational leadership   265

Section IV

Awakenings:
for Justice in Education

24 Mary Wilkinson   Education for Justice:
                           what do the people want?   275

25 Mike Golby   Pursuing Education   281

26 Colin Richards   Three Views of the Curriculum   293

27 Mike Golby   Philosophical End Piece   297

Section V

Conclusions
and Recommendations

311

The Editors and the Exeter Society for Curriculum Studies thank the University of Exeter Graduate School of Education for use of Campus facilities and access to Research Seminars

Our Authors

David Atton's most recent post was headteacher of a large urban comprehensive school. There he led the school through many of the challenges discussed in this book.

Michael Bassey is an emeritus professor of Education of Nottingham Trent University. A life-time of teaching, training teachers and research leaves him appalled at the way in which recent governments of both left and right have micromanaged schools. His late wife, Penny, was head of a primary school from 1991-2001 during the tempestuous years when the national curriculum, local management of schools, and Ofsted inspections began to impact on primary education. He says that it was her experience that turned him from researcher to polemicist. Now aged 86 he describes his three lovely grandchildren as his stake in the future.

Gordon Anthony Brown graduated from Keele in Maths and Physics and a Diploma in Education (with Commendation). He has taught in six different local authorities and in Istanbul. His experience has been in a range of secondary schools including technical high schools and comprehensives. His roles have included head of Maths departments, senior teacher and deputy headteacher. He has served as a teacher representative on LEA committees, as President of his teachers' professional association at local and county levels and as a long term governor in two large comprehensive schools. Gordon is Chair of the Exeter Society for Curriculum Studies.

Roger Darke began his career with one year as an unqualified teacher in Birmingham and then attended Alsager College of Education, gaining a Certificate of Education in 1971. For nineteen years he taught primary children in an area of social deprivation in the south west of England before becoming a full-time trade union official. In the mid-1990s he gained a Diploma in Industrial Relations from Keele University. He ended his career as a senior official based in the union's headquarters.

Stella Darke began primary school teaching in Birmingham in 1970 following a three-year teacher training course. After a career break bringing up young children, she returned to full-time classroom teaching in Devon. In 1990 she embarked on a Master's degree course at Exeter University and went on to complete a PhD in 2002. Her doctoral thesis substantiates the idea that theory should be developed through practice and teachers' professional research, a view in which she remains a firm believer.

Paul Ernest taught mathematics in a London comprehensive school in the 1970s. After lecturing in Education at Bedford, Cambridge and the University of the West Indies, Jamaica he was appointed to the University of Exeter where he is currently professor emeritus. At Exeter he established and ran the doctoral and Master's programmes in mathematics education. His research explores questions at the intersections of philosophy, mathematics and education, and currently he is writing on ethics in mathematics and education.

Maurice George is the son of two factory workers who left school at the age of 14. Having passed one hurdle - the 11 Plus Exam - and after National Service, he researched the Oxford entrance system and was accepted, much to his surprise. He graduated from University College, Oxford, with a B.A.(M.A.) in French Literature and then attained a P.G.C.E. from the University of London. He has worked in the education services of Zambia and the U.K. teaching adult students. He counts himself lucky in the benefits bestowed upon him by his 'time-slot of free education'. His favourite pursuits include Information Technology, Green Party activities and L.G.B.T.Q. issues.

Mike Golby taught in primary schools, in a teacher training college and as a central academic at the Open University. There he was responsible for a substantial part of the influential course *Curriculum Design and Development*. He moved to Exeter University in 1976 with responsibility for a taught Master's degree in Curriculum Studies, which flourished. He retired as a Reader in Education and continued in support of the Exeter Society for Curriculum Studies.

Andy Hannan taught at what are now Birmingham City and Plymouth universities. He undertook research on multicultural education, primary teacher education, higher education (innovations in teaching and learning, widening participation, and external examining), and the effects of television on the behaviour of children. From 2013 until 2017 he was Devon County Councillor for Priory & St Leonard's in Exeter, acting as Education spokesperson for the Labour Group. He has served as a governor of three primary schools.

Carole Newton has spent over 40 years working in Education. The major part of her career was in non-selective state secondary schools teaching mainly English to all ages and abilities from Year 7 through to GCSE and A Level. After service as Head of Year and then as Head of Department she became Deputy Head at a Community School with special responsibility for curriculum development. She also has long experience as an external examiner for a number of different exam boards. Carole believes passionately in access to free, lifelong learning for all and has a particular interest in community education based on the original concept put forward by Henry Morris.

Paul Niklaus began teaching Maths in a secondary modern school in 1963. In 1974 he experienced a merger with a local grammar school to create a comprehensive school. He went on to promote comprehensive schooling within the local authority in association with Maurice Holt. He strongly advocated primary school liaison and community involvement. He became Assistant Principal of his school in 1997. Paul was Chair of the Exeter Society for Curriculum Studies from 1981-84 and Honorary Treasurer from 1984 to date.

Gail Parfitt taught in primary and secondary schools and in adult and community education before working with schools on whole-school development and evaluation in Hackney and Islington. She then moved to Exeter University in 1990, where she taught Educational Studies at under-graduate and post-graduate levels, becoming Subject Chair in 1993. In retirement as an Honorary Research Fellow, she has continued in support of the Exeter Society for Curriculum Studies.

Allen Parrott started his career as a full-time adult education organiser in two community schools - in Devon and Leicestershire. In the 1980s he was the Dean responsible for adult and community education in a successful tertiary college which combined sixth form, further education and adult education provision for a large rural catchment area. In this role he attempted to put into practice the community education vision which he and Ray Flude had set out in *'Education and the Challenge of Change'*, a book published by the Open University in 1979. In 1996 he became a Lecturer in Education at Exeter University. He finished his career as an education consultant employed to help improve teaching standards not just with teachers in educational institutions but also with senior doctors in various health contexts.

Colin Richards taught in primary schools, a college of education and a university department before joining HM Inspectorate. He became Staff Inspector for Curriculum 5-16 and later Ofsted's specialist adviser for primary education. Since leaving Ofsted he has been visiting professor at three universities and has published a large number of articles and letters related to policy and practice, especially in relation to curriculum and inspection. He is emeritus professor at the University of Cumbria and relishes the epithet 'an old-fashioned HMI' bestowed on him by one of his critics.

Rosemary Richardson began her career in the NHS. This included planning and co-ordinating several public health and health education projects and liaison with a wide range of health professionals and local education authorities. Her further studies concerned initial teacher education and, later, an MEd and PhD at Exeter University. She took part in curriculum planning for pre- and post-graduate nurse education programmes in a university and was responsible for planning modules for an MSc course in public health.

Will Taylor graduated with a B.Ed from Exeter as a mature student. After five years at a comprehensive school he moved on to become head of English as a grammar school merged with two other schools to become a 13-18 comprehensive school. Seconded for an M.Ed in Curriculum Studies in 1987 he went on to conduct research for Lord Young of Dartington, seeking a model for an Open School. Other research led to responsibility for the Governor Support Centre at the School of Education and to EU-funded work in Mongolia and elsewhere.

Mary Wilkinson has worked in a variety of positions at home and abroad. As a primary headteacher Mary developed an approach to teaching early years mathematics modelled on the principles of the Emergent Language Programme. She has been a school Governor, Primary Adviser, Maths (Primary) Adviser and Ofsted Inspector and worked as a primary consultant at home and in Oman and the Caribbean.

'It is a question of whether we grasp the real nature of our society, or whether we persist in social and educational patterns based on a limited ruling class, a middle professional class, a large operative class, cemented by forces that cannot be challenged and will not be changed. The privileges and barriers, of an inherited kind, will in any case go down. It is only a question whether we replace them by the free play of the market, or by a public education designed to express and create the values of an educated democracy and a common culture.'

Raymond Williams *The Long Revolution* (1961) p155

Preamble

The Exeter Society for Curriculum Studies is an association of education professionals based at the University of Exeter. Members of the Society have lengthy experience across all sectors of the education service from pre-school to university and further education extending over the past forty and more years.

As school and college leaders, as educational researchers and of course as parents and grandparents we have experienced at first hand the ever more severe effects of successive waves of educational reform. The Society has participated in and monitored education in schools and colleges since 1979.

Since then we have held termly conferences and seminars and attracted distinguished speakers from academia, politics, and the world of practice.

For many years we had been concerned about the mis-match between the brief and impulsive nature of governments and the evolutionary nature of effective change in education. Our thinking was brought into sharp focus in the run-up to the General Election of 2015.

Not for the first time, we held a General Election hustings with regional parliamentary candidates. This event dismayed us for we found our candidates struggling to articulate their views on education policy. These were people in places of real potential influence over the direction of change in education. Yet they had real difficulty in expressing themselves and seemed unfamiliar with the broad parameters of educational discussion known to us as professionals.

For example, our guests were ill at ease with discussion of the balance between 'vocational' and 'academic' education. We do not blame them for this unfamiliarity with educational discourse. Rather the opposite. As a professional community we have not articulated our thinking well, even internally among our own colleagues. It is unsurprising therefore that parents and others have often remained in the dark over educators' aspirations for their children.

We think it is now necessary and urgent that professional practitioners reach out to policy makers, who cannot specialise in all aspects of politics; to parents who have their own children's interests at heart; and to the general public, which is vulnerable to soundbite politics and deserves a better knowledge of what is at stake in their schools. The teaching profession has lacked a voice in public debates and needs now to speak.

So we offer here a considered professional view of education in practice. Though not every author will agree with every view expressed here (that would produce mere blandness) every contribution has been thoroughly discussed and reflected upon by the group. We seek not agreement with our every proposition but discernment that there is much here to discuss and to decide for the future.

We ought also to say here that we align with no particular political party and with no particular teachers' professional association or other interest group. If we assert any political opinion, it is because our educational experience backs it up.

It must also be noted that when we employ the term 'national' in connection with educational policy, for instance in the case of the National Curriculum we refer to England. This is also where our experience lies. Note also that on occasion we refer to Ministers of Education as a generic term encompassing both Secretaries of State and their juniors.

Our major thesis is that neither 'state control' nor 'the market', the two main drivers of education policy since 1976, can deliver the excellence and equity in education so conspicuously lacking in today's Britain. We argue for a renewed vision of the educational process. This does not mean a restoration of the social status teachers may have enjoyed in the misty past. We cannot remember such a time. What it does mean is that we need a balanced understanding of education as a social and political engagement working for fuller lives and the greater common good in a just society.

It is obvious in any such vision that teachers must be accorded the space to make their own independent judgments about the conduct of their work, their lessons, their teaching styles and their assessment of their students' learning. This does not risk classroom anarchy, self-indulgence or a licence to do anything that comes to mind. For one thing, teachers work together as school staffs and, a proper legacy of the recent past, there will be legitimate curriculum guidance including that from local and central government alongside input from school governors and local communities.

But this is to look ahead. We feel it necessary before going further to offer a brief account of how we have arrived at today's crisis. While reminding ourselves of landmarks in our careers, this may be of particular use to 'new readers'.

To begin at the beginning

For us, the beginning may be dated from the *Education Act of 1944,* the Butler Act. This legislation, looking forward to a post-war era of social reconstruction and greater opportunity, was enacted while German bombers were still overhead in Westminster. The Act raised the school leaving age to 15. In 1964 it was raised to 16 and ROSLA (raising of the school leaving age) became a hot topic in schools until and even after its introduction in 1972. Today, those leaving at 16 are required to start an apprenticeship or traineeship or spend twenty hours a week working or volunteering while undertaking part-time study.

The 1944 Act required local education authorities to submit proposals for secondary education and most aimed to introduce three main categories of school: grammar, secondary modern and technical though in the event few technical schools were established. This latter omission was to haunt the system ever after; technical and vocational education remained a weakness.

All the same, the 1944 Act set up a ladder of opportunity based on the equation IQ+Effort=Merit. The elements in this formula appeared at the time unproblematic but very soon became contentious.

Intelligence was supposedly measured by Intelligence Tests but these were soon discredited as 'measuring what intelligence tests measure', which is arguably 'the ability to learn certain kinds of things-abstract puzzles perhaps-given certain kinds of social and parental, support and a primary school curriculum prioritising passing the eleven plus'.

Effort is in reality as hard to discern and difficult to measure as intelligence. Also, like intelligence, effort is a function not only of 'character' but of social factors too.

Merit means 'desert' and rewards those who have put in effort on top of their intelligence. So to speak, they have added perspiration to inspiration. But it is not difficult to see that the equation favoured in practice those pupils already advantaged in one way or another, certainly through native endowment but also through the culture of home and the effectiveness of school. So there was injustice and inequality here, built in to the system from the start.

Meritocracy

This denotes a social system in which those with merit govern and are appropriately rewarded. To accept at face value the key concepts-

intelligence, effort and merit-is to approve and work towards a certain social and political order. Schools are seen as instruments for producing differentials in status, income, lifestyles and respect. The latter, 'respect', has come to seem crucial to the atmospherics and conflicts that now confront us. Our Section Four, Awakenings: For Justice in Education attempts to analyse the current situation in these terms.

Among our authors are many who owe their whole careers, their social standing-and their pensions- precisely to these crude and unjust mechanisms. Among some of us there are undercurrents of 'survivor guilt' and anger at the injustices of the selection system. This will be apparent to readers in several of our papers. There are also discussions of the concept of 'meritocracy' which has been appropriated from the work of Michael Young by recent politicians claiming it as an instrument of 'social mobility' and fairness. In Young's view it meant exactly the opposite! Allen Parrott discusses this further in Chapter 13.

The idea of the comprehensive school emerged from the confusions enacted in the system by selection for grammar schools at 11 plus. Under the tripartite system of secondary education in England between the 1940s and 1960s, approximately a quarter of children were selected by the eleven plus exam for entry to grammar schools, either 'maintained' grammar schools fully funded by the state or direct grant, quasi-independent grammar schools. Most of the maintained grammar schools were closed or converted to comprehensive schools in the decade following the Labour government's *Circular 10/65* which required local authorities to submit plans to introduce comprehensive schooling in their areas.

Delaying tactics since 1965 have left only a handful of local authorities running grammar schools including among others: Devon, Kent, Medway, Trafford, Buckinghamshire and Lincolnshire. There remain only about 160 grammar schools out of a total number of over 3,000 secondary schools. Nevertheless, there remains the possibility of expanding grammar school provision by the devious means of opening 'annexes' or 'off-site' premises for existing schools.

Moreover, in December 2018 government announced a *Selective School Expansion Fund* of £50m to provide 4,000 additional places at existing schools. Almost half of the grammar schools chosen to receive the funding are located in the home counties and only one school to benefit from the Selective School Expansion Fund is in the north of England. It will cost £12,500 to fund each new grammar school place under the expansion scheme, the figures suggest, which is more than double the amount that state secondary schools are given per pupil. The amount spent on each secondary school child in England was £6,200 in 2017-18. A disproportionate number of these privileged schools is in a Conservative held constituency. *(Independent 3 December 2018)* Damian Hinds, the Education Secretary explained that the existing grammar schools had been selected based on their action plans to improve access for disadvantaged children. More than half of the schools have committed to lowering the mark required to pass the entrance test for poorer pupils.

Is it necessary to spell out the contradiction in this statement?

How, then, to explain the enduring appeal of the grammar school?

Many of our authors are grammar school products. We may be able to help in answering this question. Despite compelling research evidence that standards in grammar schools are not higher for any category of student than elsewhere, *(Sutton Trust 2008)* grammar schools still enchant the public imagination. It is not, we believe, their empirical achievements but their spell that must be challenged. It is the imagery of the grammar school, the uniforms, the crests, the prize-giving and the 'house' systems- much of it borrowed from the public schools-that holds sway. The process continues with many of the new academies. It's as if being a high-quality secondary school now means looking like a traditional grammar school. In fact, also, being a high-quality primary school means in too many cases looking like a prep school of days past.

It is that quaint English blend of nostalgia and snobbery. No more needs to be said.

But comprehensive education is not a done deal

We must not be precipitate. All is not yet lost! However, we must recognise also that the basic principles of comprehensive schooling itself remain in contention. Does it imply 'mixed ability' teaching? Must the curriculum achieve balance between academic and practical learning? Must the comprehensive school be a local school? If so, how is it to achieve a social mix? How does the community participate? Such questions still detain us. Harold Wilson famously saw his comprehensives as 'grammar schools for all'. We have moved on. Debate continues!

The primary school

The abolition of the 11+ and the creation of secondary schools for all freed the primary school to seek its own destiny beyond that of the elementary school. Freed from restraint at 11 plus, primary schools could, if they wished, embrace 'child-centred' schooling. *The Plowden Report* of 1967 after extensive enquiry endorsed progressive teaching in general and sought to promote it up the age groups by recommending middle schools.

However, in some cases, primary schooling fell into incompetent or even 'politically motivated' hands. This proved disastrous and resulted in much reactionary comment accumulated in the right-wing press. In

1974-75 the introduction of some extreme, absurdly radical practices at the William Tyndale Junior School in the London Borough of Islington led to an increase in general concern and contributed to Prime Minister James Callaghan's *Ruskin speech* in 1976 calling for a 'Great Debate' on education.

Meanwhile in another part of the forest....

A slow beast was stirring, making passage from Chicago to the London School of Economics, manifesting from the American side in the persons of Hayek and Friedman and in England in Popper and Oakeshott. We are not economists and do not fully understand the complexities of the theories within this movement. What we do know is something of their surface features which have come to be influential, in fact fundamental in policy making from the eighties on.

The principles are retailed by Letwin (2017) as

- Economic freedom and social freedom (lifestyle, choice, expression) can only be secured by prosperity.
- Prosperity can only be secured by free markets and
- The state has no role in social justice.

This ideological case has not been fully won, even within the Conservative Party, still less in the country at large. However, the 'neo-liberal' line of thinking, if it can be so described, has been the default setting, the first option for policy for most of our professional lifetimes. It lay behind some of Tony Blair's Labour Party's policies such as the private finance initiative and the creation of the academies. The idea of creating market conditions, that is to say privatising public utilities like transport, water and power obtains some public consent. But the public is instinctively less supportive of inroads into public welfare like health care and education and the process may best be described as

8

one of creeping erosion of the public sector.

The neo-liberal project was reasserted by the Centre for Policy Studies, a Conservative think-tank on 24 June 2016, the morning after the vote to leave the European Union and described as '*a unique political opportunity to drive through a wide-ranging supply-side revolution on a scale similar to that of the eighties*'. Nigel Lawson, a former Chancellor under Margaret Thatcher, on 5 July 2106, a fortnight after the UK vote to leave the European Union, declared this the opportunity to '*finish the job that Margaret Thatcher started*'.

The implications of neo-liberalism for educators are serious. For, if the 'state has no role in social justice', then no more will 'state schools'.

But this has been to leap ahead. We must first acknowledge the major watershed in educational policy of 1988.

The Education Reform Act 1988

This legislation is widely regarded as the most far-reaching and important set of measures since the 1944 Butler Act. The impact on local education authorities is the surest indicator of its intentions. 'City Technology Colleges', precursors of 'academies,' and government funded 'Grant Maintained Schools' were provided for and taken out of local control. Local Management of Schools (LMS) allowed all schools to be taken out of the financial control of local authorities and handed to head teachers and governors.

At the same time a National Curriculum and an accompanying structure of 'Key Stages' and of national testing was established. In due course in 1992, Ofsted was established as in its own words '*a force for improvement through intelligent, responsible and focused inspection and regulation*'. *(Ofsted 2017 to 2022 strategy, Ofsted website)* The logic of this development is apparent. Once a uniform curriculum is established and parental choice foregrounded, a basis for comparison among providers is needed. Nothing more enthrals politicians in particular than standardised measurement and so we see a simplistic methodology based upon crude observational schedules develop.

The upshot is of course competition between schools for 'market share'; and, conversely, competition among parents for places at the most sought-after schools.

The effects of these radical reforms are now apparent. We are now faced with an extreme, close to chaotic diversity of provision. There are: local authority community schools; foundation and voluntary schools; academies; grammar schools; faith schools; free schools; studio schools; city technology colleges and private schools. Funding sources and governance are various. Notably, academies and free schools don't have to follow the national curriculum. Nor of course do private schools. Grammar schools may select their pupils.

Perhaps the most dramatic developments have occurred in the academies.

At January 2018, *7,472* schools were academies (*35%*), of which *6,996* had converted from maintained schools. Academies were teaching an estimated 47% of pupils. Academies constitute two thirds of secondary schools but only a minority of primary schools. The number grew dramatically under the coalition government from May 2010 and continued under the Conservative government of Theresa May.

In this gigantic explosion, and human nature being what it is, some spectacular malpractices have been uncovered. Many cases of excessive salaries paid to chiefs and managements of the rapidly developing multi-academy trusts (MATs) came to light. Much more was covered up in NDAs, non-disclosure agreements exchanging large cash pay-offs for silence.

Nor have the universities been exempt from the prevailing ideology.

It is another whole story and it is touched upon in Chapters 15,16 and 17. Competition, marketisation and corporatisation have left their marks even upon this previously immune phase of education. The whole concept of the university has diversified.

Seismic shifts

As this book was in preparation and in addition to the educational changes already mentioned, seismic shifts in popular sentiment and the political climate occurred. A number of profoundly shocking events raised fundamental questions of social justice across the whole polity. Some discern early intimations in the international banking crisis of 2007-8. Some in a scandal concerning MPs expenses. Gordon Brown's encounter with Mrs Gillian Duffy is another such precursor and it is discussed in Chapter 7.

Then the result of the British referendum to leave the European Union of June 2016 and the election of Donald Trump in the United States in November 2016 were generally regarded as anti-establishment protests and thus a challenge to all established authority including that of schools. Michael Gove's denunciation of 'experts' and the OED's citation of 'post-truth 'as the 'word of the year' in 2016 suggested deep-seated popular rejection of established forms of rationality.

Then the Grenfell Tower disaster of 14 June 2017 caused seventy-two deaths of residents. The Enquiry into this event is still to report and we make no assertions about its causes. Inevitably, however, the symbolism was compelling. A blazing tower populated by poorer people, including many ethnic-minority residents, in the Royal Borough of Kensington and Chelsea containing some of the most expensive houses in the world, and with the highest gap between rich and poor anywhere in the country. This terrible event could not have been a more telling emblem of social division and injustice.

In April 2018 it came to light that thousands of perfectly legal immigrants from the Caribbean, the 'Windrush generation', had been the target of government efforts to reduce overall numbers of immigrants. They like other immigrants were being met with a highly engineered and intentional 'hostile climate'. It was reminiscent of a similar hostility towards teachers as, in the words of Michael Gove, part of the 'blob' impeding ministerial intentions. This was government by the management of popular sentiment rather than by any approximation to rational debate. In any event, deep injustices needing decisive action were being starkly revealed.

Late awakenings

We confess to late awakenings to this broader and deeper crisis. *'What do the people want?'* cried one of our number in something approaching desperation at one of our meetings. We offer no panaceas here. However, we can at least address the injustices of which we are aware in education and about which something can be done. Fundamentally, this means we have to challenge the current disarray introduced by wholesale 'marketisation' in terms of its basic principles.

Education is a public good and it cannot be put up for sale without compromising its essential character. This is the subject of some discussion in *Chapter 27, the Philosophical End Piece.* Education must be a force for equality and justice, not an engine of advantage for some at the expense of others. In our *Section Five Conclusions and Recommendations,* we propose a number of urgent and immediate actions and recommend a pause for thought and a machinery for future deliberation. There must be an end to impulsive legislation and soundbite policy making.

A straw in the wind?

There is one straw in the wind, a hopeful note on which to conclude this Preamble.

In her Ofsted Annual Report 2108, the chief inspector Amanda Spielman said

> *'Across the whole education sector, a mentality of 'what's measured is what gets done' trumps the true purpose of education, and curriculum thinking-the consideration of what needs to be taught and learned for a full education-has been eroded.'*

Fine words, for which we should be grateful.

This book, then, aims to bring the experience of a generation of practitioners to bear on the issues arising from our recent history as sketched above. We do not want to turn the clock back. But we do want to see salvaged from the past those elements we think of lasting value. The writing of the book has concentrated our minds upon this question. We hope it will contribute to debate and to better policy making.

This book is organised as follows:

Section One: Political Contexts paints the big picture of the post war years since 1944 and brings into focus the dramatic scale of change across the whole education system. Fears of Orwellian 'state control' were followed in the eighties by neo-liberal marketisation. Latterly, populist sentiments developed, a very early harbinger of which, as we say, was Gordon Brown's exchange with Mrs Caroline Duffy during the 2010 General Election campaign. We don't know where these are leading.

Section Two: Lessons from Practice offers perspectives on work in schools and colleges as experienced by us as reflective professionals. Here practitioners present their understanding of their educational mission with the benefit of some hindsight. There is a sense of uncompleted ambition in much of this writing, a result of high ideals frustrated by both local circumstance and countervailing political force. We distil from this rich variety of experience the idea that teachers need and are entitled to occupy 'safe spaces' in which to work. That is to say, that teachers need professional autonomy if they are to contribute of their best.

Section Three: Teaching as a Profession takes up the idea of professionalism in teaching and attempts to define its scope and limits. What is going on when good teaching occurs? How can good practice be evaluated, safeguarded and developed? What forms of planning and accountability are appropriate? Crucially, what would a credible inspection system look like? And what can validly be learned from other countries such as Finland and China reportedly achieving better results than ours? It has become politically respectable to speculate upon the success of overseas educational systems, based on international measures of pupil learning, the PISA (Programme for International Student Assessment) tests in particular. A common inference is that teaching methods are a large part of the explanation for these differentials. We examine the validity of such thinking. We doubt that hard and fast conclusions can be drawn since educational practices are deeply rooted in host cultures. This does not mean that nothing is to be learned from overseas.

Section Four Awakenings: For Education

This Section is vitalised from our heightened alertness to social injustice consequent upon shifts in the general atmospherics of populism and social division. We ask what's education got to do with it? Have schools perpetuated the gap between the haves and the have nots? Have we in any way worked towards healing social rifts? What are the possibilities for the future?

It is clear to us that education must play its part in the struggle for social justice. We founder in the wake of the shocking disillusionment and alienation of many from the status quo in education. We do not hide behind the old mantra, 'education cannot compensate for society', which is a recipe for complacency. But nor do we see any single and immediate panacea. Rather, we strive towards a vision in which teaching is a civilising and fair contribution to the common good. Only teachers who comprehend this should be in authority in the classroom. Only legislators who support them should presume to intervene.

Schooling is at present underpowered for these herculean tasks. But schools remain moral communities and our best vehicles of civil relations across social chasms. What can be done in school, can only be done by an educated and trusted teaching profession. In this book we make a start on this forbidding agenda in calling for renewed perceptions of the aims of education and a revitalised faith in the teachers who are its exponents.

Section Five: Conclusions and Recommendations

Finally, we offer ways forward. Happily, we find ourselves in good company. Government itself has recognised that hectic change has had ill effects on children, teachers and families. Respected figures such as Tim Brighouse and Michael Bassey have supported calls for far-reaching reviews of where we are and where we are heading. Professional associations, long derided as self-seeking interest groups continue to make reasonable demands for dialogue. The Labour Party has proposed a National Education Service with as comprehensive an ambit as the

National Health Service. The embryonic College of Teaching, optimistic about teachers' professionalism, looks set to develop a medium for conversation like an oasis in a desert. The British Educational Research Association, historically heavily slanted academically toward positivistic research paradigms, is now actively engaged in promoting 'close to practice' research. (BERA 2018).

These are all good signs. They are reassurances that we are not lone voices in the wilderness. Our particular contribution here to the cause of 'real education' derives from our experience as professionals in a university-based community engaged over many years in critical reflection on the values that sustain us.

Our Proposals

Firstly, we propose an **Emergency Brake** on all but operationally necessary legislation and directives from the centre. Such a measure would allow for the suspension of the implementation of the most contentious of recent policies such as encouraging the expansion of grammar school places and promoting academisation, for example by means of the presumption that all new schools will be 'free schools'.

Secondly, we propose a full **Public Enquiry** into means and ends in the education service. It should draw upon the whole available range of experience and expertise from both within and without the education service.

We urge that the Enquiry should not become the site of political contest and point-scoring; that it should report within a realistic time, say around two years and that it should make recommendations as to priorities for legislative and other action.

Thirdly, we propose a permanent **National Education Council,** whose object would be to continue the work of the Enquiry beyond its first Report. The National Education Council should become a centre for ongoing research and guidance for government, teachers and the public.

The Enquiry we propose and the National Education Council to follow will cast a wide net. In what follows we signal our own concerns based on our own professional experience.

Section 5: Conclusions and Recommendations returns to these proposals more fully.

I

Political Contexts

Mike Golby

Ted Wragg's Ten Steps

Introduction

Mike began his career as a new teacher in a new primary school in one of England's new towns in 1962. It was all new. For him, for the staff, for the parents and for the children. The tabula rasa of a new school in a new town was a proving ground for a new teacher, especially so as the headteacher operated a laissez-faire regime, a school with very few rules and very little support for the classroom teacher.

A bright autumn morning in September 1962. 8.30 a.m. I find my way to the headmaster's office in the newly built Moor View County Primary School. The headmaster directs us, three newly arrived teachers, to the playground. There two or three hundred children mill around. The head blows a whistle and a degree of silence descends. The birds sing. The head announces a list of names. Those children - follow Mr Golby- I lead them, these ten-year olds, to an empty classroom. Forty and more desks and chairs. There is a general air of trepidation soon diffused in a spontaneous scramble for seats. I try to referee disputes, call for order, it's like fighting small bushfires. Very soon the headmaster arrives. He bellows for total silence.

Right, good morning, everybody. This is Mr Golby, he is your teacher this year. He writes my name on the blackboard, mis-spelling it. And departs. Carry on! He leaves. I don't remember much else of that first day. I suppose I had a few activities to hand. Colouring, a quiz, I don't remember. At any rate I don't think I saw the head inside my classroom again until well after Christmas except to bring messages, which we teachers understood comedically as 'spying'. We were left to find our own salvation. No syllabus. No text books. No reading scheme. No tests external to the classroom. No timetable beyond use of the hall for PE and Assembly in the morning.

The school building was spacious. The surroundings, where they were not building sites, were open and green. There was a large school playing field as well as playgrounds. In all there was a pervasive experimental, permissive, enthusiastic atmosphere. But there were very few established routines and practices. It had the feel, perhaps, of attempting to build a ship already at sea.

My salvation lay with my new wife, commuting to teacher training college in London in the final year of her teacher training. She it was who propelled us out that autumn to collect leaves and classify them on the nature table. Also, the 'projects' on 'the breakfast table', 'the shopping centre 'and 'the solar system'.

My own PGCE had been a survival course, the teaching practices exercises in control by adopting the effective local drills and routines. There was good theory though in the good fortune of meeting PS Wilson as a tutor. His book *Interest and Discipline in Education* was to be published in 1971, to my mind a modern classic in the philosophy of 'child-centred' education. I have always taken his precept that however trivial and inconsequential a children's interests may seem to be there is nothing else in terms of which they can be educated.

As to practice, Pat Wilson's contribution to my learning came after he had observed a PE lesson I was teaching in a freezing playground. I had the children running about, keeping warm. 'You seem to be making the right decisions there' was the remark. It went a long way, as the minutest encouragement from a respected mentor does.

While I had the enormous benefit of a wife who was also an in-house mentor my colleague Wayne next door didn't. Without ever observing him teaching in the classroom, it was evident that he was in continuous crisis. We shared a cloakroom in which our two parallel third year classes had their coat pegs. At the end of the day while I dismissed them with a level of formality, by name and individually, mentioning anything they had done well etc, Wayne opened his classroom door and released a tide of children who fell riotously upon their coats in a scramble to depart. Freed of them for the day, Wayne was then to be seen leaning against the wall or slumped at his desk lighting up a recuperative cigarette. We didn't discuss our work much, if at all.

When a visit of HMI was rumoured our classrooms suddenly became serried rows and lessons were rehearsed. The head expressed his regret at that to me but I lacked the confidence to go on a limb. In the event HMI did not arrive and we reverted to the standard grouping of desks into largely friendship groups.

What I have described here is no doubt an extreme case of the laissez-faire condition of primary schooling in the early sixties. There were neighbouring schools of a much more traditional kind and Pat secured a job at an extremely well-run and established school that made intelligent compromises between the old elementary tradition and the excitement of child-centred learning.

In those days of the early sixties there was a sense that sunlit uplands lay ahead for the Primary school. We breezed along with our project work ever more adventurously. My class ran a traffic census, counting the mini cars passing the school gate and recording their colours graphically against production figures supplied by British Leyland. I founded the school football team and encountered another shibboleth, parental involvement, in a big way over team selection. Also, I was plied with drinks on Saturday lunchtimes after school matches returning home to a late lunch, some Saturday socialising and, the TV high spot of the week, '*That Was The Week That Was*', with David Frost, Willie Rushton, Millicent Martin and, memorably, Frankie Howard. Along with 12 million others we participated in the satire boom, the Profumo affair and, soberly, the assassination of John F Kennedy.

After three years, with a new baby imminent and the Development Corporation unwilling to re-house us from our third-floor flat, we moved to Malaysia with the British Army Children's Service. Thus I ducked out of front-line participation in a period of intense debate on primary education. I followed it from afar but secure in an ordered and orderly British Army Children's School. This provided me with a structured environment in which to become a half-way adequate teacher.

It was of course co-incidental that within one year of my entering primary school teaching, the then Minister of Education, Sir Edward Boyle, asked the Central Advisory Council for Education (England) 'to consider primary education in all its aspects and the transition to secondary education'. The Council, under the Chairmanship of Lady Plowden, presented its report to the Secretary of State for Education and Science, Anthony Crosland, in October 1966 and it was published in 1967.The Plowden Report was the result of an extensive inquiry lasting nearly three years. Evidence was taken across the board, from academia, parental organisations, local authorities, teacher associations, teacher trainers et al. Volume 2 of the Report contains probably the most extensive collection of evidence on educational practice ever assembled.

The Report broadly endorsed progressive primary practice, promoted parental involvement and laid the way for Middle Schools in the belief that good primary practice could be extended up the age range; and for Educational Priority Areas (EPAs) in the belief that 'education can compensate for society'.

All the same, this definitive, epochal Report did not lay to rest all disquiets, and these continued right up to and beyond James Callaghan's Ruskin College speech in October 1976. There were 'scandals' such as those at William Tyndale and, in secondary education, at Risinghill School. The latter was derided by the *Daily Mail* as Raising Hell School and both were, as it happened, a mere taxi ride from Fleet Street. And both were pushing progressivism to the limits in the hands of zealous professionals, some of them 'politically motivated'. Callaghan worried about his grandchildren's education and thus became the first Prime Minister to make a speech entirely about education. He referred to 'the new informal methods of teaching, which seem to produce excellent results when they are in well-qualified hands but are much more dubious when they are not' and proposed a nation-wide Great Debate on education.

The Great Debate constituted a number of conferences across the country but of more importance were the initiatives it stimulated from the Department for Education(DES) and from Her Majesty's Inspectorate of Schools(HMI) .The DES Green Paper of July 1977 asserted 'there is a need to investigate the part which might be played by a protected or core element of the curriculum common to all schools' while HMI proposed a curriculum structure based upon an epistemology of the major fields of human enquiry. DES aligns with 'the basics' while HMI uphold a broad and balanced curriculum containing but going beyond the basics.

In early 1980 the University of Exeter School of Education published *The Core Curriculum* attempting to inform continuing developments. The tension between DES and HMI thinking was identified and Ted Wragg wrote *State-Approved Knowledge: Ten Steps Down the Slippery Slope.*

In that paper Ted Wragg prognosticated an Orwellian nightmare much of which has now leaked into everyday school life. The steps are as follows:

Step 1 Centrally Prescribed Broad Aims

Step 2 Centrally Prescribed Time Allocations

Step 3 An Agreed Syllabus

Step 4 More Precise Objectives

Step 5 Centrally Prescribed Objectives and Teaching Methods

Step 6 Centrally Prescribed Objectives, Teaching Materials and Strategies

Step 7 Centrally Prescribed Objectives, Teaching Materials, Strategies and Tests from a national Test Bank

Step 8 As (7) with Remedial Programmes

Step 9 As (8) with Publication of Results by School

Step 10 As (9) with Dismissal of Teachers Who Fail To Deliver

We know today that Ted Wragg's scenario has been more or less fully implemented. At the time, though, it was viewed more as satirical comedy than a serious prediction of things to come. It wasn't, and it has!

Roy Garland in a later paper in the Exeter publication summarises;

'A framework for judging the curriculum of state schools has been created and a rhetoric unfurled to justify it. An uncontested view of the curriculum is emerging that in the main has been generated by central agencies. A role has been found for teachers in discussing questions set by others. No matter how benign the proposals appear there is the scent of orthodoxy in the air and a disincentive to take risks', p 26)

Today we can see that the Ruskin speech marked a tipping point beyond which teachers were no longer to be trusted with the curriculum nor with much else including their teaching methods and the assessment of learning. Instead, they were to be cast as delivery agents for the central authority.

All of this would be fully Orwellian but for the fact that Mrs Thatcher came along. Her neo-liberalism diversified schooling and we now have a situation where the central writ is heavily modified by the liberties conferred on the private and semi-private sectors to go their own way. Latter neo-liberalism provided more freedom for some to do their own thing in education than most teachers enjoyed even in the sixties. The result is not only 'state-controlled knowledge' but the destruction of the whole idea of an 'educational system'. The same erosion of the public sphere continues to threaten other public services including pre-eminently but not exclusively the National Health Service.

Thus, education is caught up in ideological tides engulfing all that we knew as the public service. It must be doubtful if educational reform can be possible without renewed understandings of the whole machinery of governance. The traditional 'partnership' of central and local government needs to be revisited and the role of teachers as educated people restored to a central position in the education service.

Afterword

The blank cheque with which Michael Golby was presented in 1962 was never going to be cashed. He did not have the skills and lacked the even minimal support necessary to a beginning teacher. It was a predicament unique to its day. His new town ten-year olds were baby-boomers born in the fifties to a new post-war generation of parents. In the main they were from the inner-city areas undergoing massive redevelopment, areas of real urban decay. In the new towns they were housed in clean and modern homes, not tower blocks. The areas selected for new towns were in generally unspoiled rural environments with few local resentments. A considerable and proper, even idealistic, level of thought had gone into the planning of the neighbourhoods, each with their essential local facilities, shops, schools, clinics etc. The economy was in a (rather delayed) post-war boom. By 1957 Harold MacMillan was able to claim to the electorate 'You never had it so good.'

But for the education service there was one large reservation: a massive shortage of teachers. Consequently classes were very large, classes of forty and more children being more the rule than the exception.

With hindsight the local authority might have done more. The headteacher might have been more supportive and the teachers-mostly inexperienced-might have asserted their needs more adequately. As it was, given free rein the teachers followed their own noses. The result was an unacceptable anarchy.

Arguably, however, there were some benefits. What was done by a teacher was owned by, and the responsibility of, that teacher as his or her best attempt on the educational task in hand. There was no one else to blame for one's mistakes. The licence enjoyed by the teachers cannot be condoned. It could only become proper professional autonomy under a clear settlement of roles and responsibilities yet to be arrived at.

2 Allen Parrott

Five Big Mistakes

Introduction

Allen believes that the education policies of all recent governments have been based on fundamental misconceptions about the nature of education in general, the history of education in Britain and the future of education everywhere. Here he provides an overview or summary of where the policy makers have gone wrong. Because politicians and their advisors have allowed their educational thinking to be shaped by inappropriate metaphors from business practice, financial audit and competitive sport, they have made some very big mistakes. A fundamental change will be needed in the way education is conceived if these mistakes are to be rectified.

The five big mistakes in education policy over the past 40 years are as follows.

1. Over-centralisation

In the past forty years Britain has moved from a devolved 'national system of education, locally administered' to a highly centralised system. This transformation can be illustrated by one statistic. Following the 1944 Education Act and up until the 1970s, the Minister of Education had just three statutory duties. Today, the Minister of Education has more than two thousand statutory duties and the number is growing each year. History suggests that this is unlikely to be sustainable. The Tory government in 1902 set up local education authorities (LEAs) precisely because an 'isolated and unconnected' system had grown like Topsy across the country since the 1870 Education Act. Compulsory elementary schooling in 1902 was being provided by 2568 school boards and 14,238 voluntary bodies all answerable to Westminster, and this was proving impossible to manage. The quality of provision was variable across the country, teacher recruitment was difficult, and while one area might have too many schools another would have too few. Something similar seems to be happening today with the unplanned and uncoordinated expansion of Academy chains and 'Free' schools alongside 'bog-standard' state schools and a private school sector.

In the 19th century, following the Napoleonic wars, Britain developed a deep distaste for unfettered central power. Central government was expected to facilitate not to dictate. For most of the 20th century, the devolution of executive powers by central government, not only to the LEAs but also to the university sector and to Her Majesty's Inspectorate (HMI), was thought to represent an admirable example of how British politicians believed in democracy and were happy to trust the people they 'ruled over'. The French system by contrast was mocked for being micro-managed from the centre. The British used to smile at the thought of the French Minister of Education in his Paris office looking at his watch at 10am on Tuesday morning and being absolutely sure that all French 14-year olds were at that moment studying Virgil or differential equations, or whatever it might be. We're not laughing now.

For about 80 years LEAs provided the coherence, co-ordination and co-operation across local areas that a national state school system needs. They also offered direct support and educational expertise to individual schools and colleges. Sometimes they were led by inspirational and creative educators, like Henry Morris and Alec Clegg. They provided democratic accountability for their local populations. Most LEAs were not staffed by rabid revolutionaries, nor by time-serving bureaucrats dealing in unnecessary red tape, but by conscientious and professional public servants with educational expertise that schools and colleges found useful. The attacks on them, which started with the destruction of the flagship Inner London Educational Authority (ILEA) in the 1980s, were always based on an ideology - 'public sector bad, private sector good' - and on prejudiced media stereotypes, rather than on any compelling evidence of widespread poor practice. LEAs, or something similar, may need to be re-invented sooner rather than later.

2. Micro-managing the Curriculum

Even if the current over-centralised, top down approach to education policy and practice can be made to work administratively, it will remain essentially un-educational and therefore undesirable. The goals of education are manifold. The complex practices of teaching are always situated in a specific place, time and context. Every individual's learning is a journey of discovery and development being experienced for the first time. Education, by its nature, demands constant debate and continuous questioning about goals, content and methods. Such debates need to happen not in Westminster or Whitehall, but in the places and at the times in which the education is actually happening. Government policy certainly has an influence, for good or ill, on the overall curriculum and on everything that happens in educational institutions, but the essence of high-quality education lies in the relationship between unique teachers and unique learners in a unique context. Central government has to accept that it can never do more than advise: good education practice and quality outcomes cannot be imposed, nor ensured by fiat.

The complexities and uncertainties that are unavoidable in educational thinking and practice used to be well-understood by politicians as well as by practitioners. However much we may regret the fact and however many claims are made to the contrary, there are as yet no universal 'right answers' to the major curriculum questions of content, method and assessment. There is no uncontested 'evidence base' of 'best practice' in teaching that can be universally applied. Effective teaching and successful learning remain practical, professional issues which schools and teachers have to resolve on the ground and in the moment. Even the aims of education need to be a matter for local, professional debate in situ, with real life learners in mind. Society's need for skilled and knowledgeable adults is just one goal among many. Good schooling will also aim to contribute to each learner's personal development, in its widest sense. Qualifications are important, but for many people the intangible processes of education can be just as significant over a lifetime as education's more obvious 'products'.

3. The de-professionalisation of education: removing teacher autonomy

High quality teaching requires a high level of professionalism in its best sense. In every profession the contribution of individual practitioners, and exactly how much their collective contribution benefits society as a whole, will depend, firstly, on their being trusted to act in the interests of their clients, and secondly, on their being given sufficient freedom to use their professional judgement in order to do so. Removing that trust, or restricting that freedom, must inevitably lead to a reduced contribution from that profession. If the teaching profession is ever going to make its potentially enormous contribution to society, by enhancing the lives of future generations, high levels of trust and freedom for the profession will be essential. This means the restoration of a large measure of teacher autonomy.

It was widely accepted, even at the time, that the chief fault of the 1970s education system was the so-called 'secret garden' of the curriculum, whereby teachers often did their teaching behind closed doors and many were reluctant to be open about their curriculum choices or their teaching methods. It was unacceptable for the profession to misuse its autonomy in this way and it is understandable that some trust in teachers was lost. But the consequent removal of all teacher autonomy has perhaps been the biggest mistake of the past 40 years. As Shirley Williams wrote in 2009:

> 'Teachers had enjoyed a great deal of autonomy in designing their own curricula. Some lacked the ability to do it, others avoided boring or difficult subjects. What then happened was a lurch from one extreme to the other, from too much autonomy to virtually none. It is the heavy price England pays for a highly politicised system.' (The Guardian, March 3rd).

4. The de-moralisation of education: replacing moral values with money values

In 1980 Ted Wragg predicted that the state, after opening up the secret garden, would both remove teacher autonomy and intervene in every aspect of the curriculum, on a 'slippery slope to state-approved knowledge'. The de-professionalisation of teachers stems from precisely the Orwellian approach that Ted Wragg predicted. The National Curriculum and the introduction of Ofsted became the tools whereby successive governments sought to impose the state's will on the nation's schools. However, as Mike Golby has pointed out, educational change since 1980 was complicated by the dominant political ideology of neo-liberalism that deplores statism and wishes to 'shrink the state'.

Neo-liberalism sees no virtues or important values in the public realm: all its values reside in the profit motive and the market place. This means that at the same time as education ministers have been attempting to micro-manage the curriculum of state schools, they and their party have also been seeking to replace the public sector, including state schools, with the alleged virtues of private sector organisations and competitive market forces. Such confusion at the heart of government thinking has led to a decades-long lack of coherence in education policy and practice. It has also reinforced long-standing social inequalities. For example, private schools and 'free' schools were allowed to ignore many curriculum requirements that were at the time regarded as essential in the majority of state schools. The main result of the neo-liberal influence, however, is that money values have replaced moral values, as the starting point for educational debate and policy-making. Educational institutions have faced a never-ending wave of reform, in which the underlying thinking has been shaped by input-output metaphors and inappropriate models from industry and commerce and competitive sport. School subjects without any obvious link to future money-making have been downgraded or discarded altogether. Education has come to be seen as entirely functional and instrumental (creating a 'world-class workforce') and without any ethical or intrinsic merits (education of 'the whole person').

Criticisms of these reforms and any attempt to have a genuinely educational debate about the wider aims of education have been dismissed as special pleading and resistance to change by self-serving professionals (aka 'the blob'). Many teachers have been personally demoralised, in the usual sense of the word, by this turn of events and by the consequent loss of educational focus on creativity, criticality and personal development in the school curriculum and in their everyday professional work. Far too many good teachers have left the profession. The bigger picture is that the education system has been thoroughly 'de-moralised' in a deeper sense. Because education is fundamentally about doing good things for people, the starting point for policy-making, whether at national or at institutional level, should always be discussion and agreement on its moral purposes.

5. The de-humanisation of education: over-precise measurements of performance and expecting too much of technology.

Alongside de-professionalisation and de-moralisation, comes a creeping de-humanisation. A key feature of money values is that they can be precisely measured. The 'bottom line' is a simple figure, easy to understand, and very hard to refute if auditors and accountants have done their job. As money values have replaced moral values, policy makers have been seeking the same kind of precision in the educational context. But education is not simple and cannot be reduced to numbers, or 'metrics'. The most important aspects of education cannot be precisely measured. Accurate measures of educational performance, whether by schools, by teachers or by pupils, are impossible to achieve. Attempts to do so have led to excessive testing of children and oppressive inspections of schools. High stress for children and visceral fear of consequences for teachers cannot be the right atmosphere for a successful education system. They are anti-educational. The metrics often make things worse, not better. When tests and inspections have such high stakes for schools, incentives can become perverse and people will cheat to protect their jobs and reputations.

Also, when numbers rule so completely, humanity itself is in danger of being lost. Children become seen as learning machines. Teaching becomes 'delivery' of 'input'. Knowledge itself becomes reduced to information that can be easily measured. Tests become a mechanism to measure 'output' rather than to enhance future learning. Nothing should ever happen in schools that is not entirely respectful of human beings. This includes the work of senior managers and of Ofsted inspectors, as well as the conduct of teachers and learners. If it is to be a genuinely educational experience, a school inspection for example, even of a so-called 'failing school', should always be developmental for the people concerned as well as being a critical scrutiny of their performance. Any test of knowledge in a classroom or examination hall should be useful for the development of the learners concerned, even if it has such other uses as data collection for external authorities or as a selection mechanism for further and higher education institutions.

The justification put forward for the use of numbers, or metrics, is greater accountability and transparency. Taxpayers, it is said, have the right to know where their money is going. Parents want information about local schools to enable choices to be made. But the cost of collecting this 'data', in terms of real educational values and humanity, has been too high in recent years. The information gathered is itself often suspect. Governments should not pretend that the apparent precision of educational statistics, in school league tables for instance, represents anything that is precise and meaningful in the real world. The most recent Whitehall measure for ranking schools is known as Project 8 (P8). After some detailed mathematical calculations based on pupil tests at age 11 and their GCSE results in 8 subjects, most schools will receive a score between -1 and 1, with 0 being average. An under-performing school is one with a P8 score below -0.5. Transparent? Meaningful? These numbers may appear logical and rational to statisticians; but they have nothing to do with the personal development or education of real-life, embodied, uniquely individual human beings.

Even more de-humanising is the focus on 'efficiency', which has also been imported inappropriately from business practices and auditing procedures. The holy grail for some politicians would be the replacement of inefficient (and expensive) human teachers by efficient (and cheaper) teaching machines. 'Companies across the UK are developing chatbots, artificial intelligence platforms and holographic teachers...with a promise their products will teach children more effectively and cheaply' (The *Guardian*, March 27th 2018). Even though some of the research findings on these machines and these programmes are apparently showing some short-term success in the relatively simple business of transmitting factual knowledge, it is absolutely certain that over the longer term they will not be successful in the complex business of educating human beings. Human learners require human teachers. Technology and artificial intelligence will only replace human teachers when humanity has allowed itself to become machine-like, disembodied and completely disconnected from the natural world on which its evolution has so far depended.

Afterword

The implication of this piece is that a comprehensive re-think of British education is now essential. The re-moralisation and re-humanisation of the entire system might take some time, but there is no doubt that such a reversion would immensely benefit teachers and learners alike. More immediately and practically, the proposed National Education Council could be asked to identify the various challenges that society will need to face in the next decades (see Chapter 6 by Michael Bassey below) and to articulate the major education reforms now needed in order to face them. These reforms may well include: some new form of administrative decentralisation, some new guidance on the National Curriculum (see Chapter 26 by Colin Richards below) and some new measures to support and enhance teacher professionalism (see also Chapter 20 by Allen Parrott below).

3 Andy Hannan

Education Futures

Introduction

Andy Hannan writes as an educationist with experience in schools and teacher education. Here he discusses the political interest in educational policy. He does so with particular reference to his experience as a county councillor.

As a politician active in the world of education myself, albeit in local government, I am acutely aware of how badly let down schools, further education colleges and higher education institutions have been over the past generation. To give you a flavour of my own views and the issues I have addressed as a county councillor, here's the text of a speech I gave in July 2016 to a NUT rally of teachers striking not for better pay but for more investment in education with better learning conditions for their pupils and better working conditions for themselves.

The State of Education

I'm a Devon County Councillor, representing Priory & St Leonard's in Exeter. The County Council still has considerable responsibility for Education locally, and as one of the seven Labour councillors in a 62-strong council I have the task of leading for the Labour Group on Education issues.

In my three-and-a-bit years as a councillor I have been Vice-Chair of a task group on Educational Outcomes, which investigated what schools were doing with their Pupil Premium money and tried to identify good practice and ways in which the local authority could support and promote this, and Chair of a task group review on School Exclusions.

Both groups visited a sample of secondary schools selected so as to represent a range of types and to demonstrate how different outcomes could be obtained with similar pupil intakes, in terms of reducing the attainment gap between disadvantaged and more privileged pupils and with regard to reducing the incidence of both permanent and temporary exclusions.

My conclusions from these investigations and from my understanding of the political context within which schools operate, are as follows:

1. *Fundamentally government is hell bent on undermining the ability of local authorities to oversee and support schools, as well as to hold them to account.*

2. *All this is supposedly to free schools from the so-called tyranny of local authorities, to promote school autonomy, whereas it is instead giving more and more power to the Secretary of State.*

3. *Following the 1944 Education Act the Minister of Education had just three statutory duties and this figure stayed low for many years. Nicky Morgan now has over 2,000 and will soon have nearly 3,000.*

4. *Unaccountable and unelected Multi-Academy Trusts (MATs) and the equally unrepresentative Regional Schools Commissioner are the chosen replacements for local authorities.*

5. *In reality this government promotes a toxic mix of centralisation and privatisation.*

6. *Having supposedly abandoned forced academisation it instead uses a combination of coercion and financial incentives to convince schools to abandon their local authority – to jump before they are pushed.*

7. *The laughably titled White Paper 'Education Excellence Everywhere' is instead intent on making the world of Education into a market place where executive headteachers and MAT managers drive forward their enterprises, all at the state's expense.*

8. *This has created a system where the managers of schools are increasingly intent on maximising educational scores to impress Ofsted. They do this by narrowing the curriculum, intensifying the work of both teachers and pupils, and excluding pupils who do not respond as they must.*

9. *Increasingly schools refuse to admit the most vulnerable children or exclude them either formally or informally – with Elective Home Education increasingly being offered as the escape route for children who do not perform or comply.*

10. *Our research showed that children with Special Educational Needs and Disabilities disproportionately suffered from this, both those with and without statements being much more likely to be subject to temporary and permanent exclusions than others.*

11. *Recently there has been a marked shift away from temporary towards more permanent exclusions, which in effect creates an underclass of the under-educated and negatively labelled.*

12. *Teachers, of course, are caught in the middle of all this, with workloads and the consequent stress increasing and the children they teach becoming more alienated from a narrow curriculum and less personalised pedagogy.*

Comment

Although there are good reasons why we should be suspicious of politicians who think they know best about education, there are some occasions when they do seem to get it right. I think the foundation of the Open University, the establishment of Sure Start children's centres, the London Challenge programme of inter-school collaboration and investment, and, more recently, the Pupil Premium funding mechanism designed to benefit those children from disadvantaged backgrounds, are good examples. And leaving education to the professionals is not necessarily always a good thing – low teacher expectations of those from 'poor homes' and using 'cultural deprivation' as an excuse for low levels of attainment or poor rates of pupil progress are traps some teachers are unfortunately prone to fall into.

Although I agree that education should be about more than doing well in tests and examinations, and that it needs to foster the imagination and problem-solving and creative skills, not just the memorisation and regurgitation of facts, it has to be acknowledged that schooling is partly about social control. Education tends to reproduce social hierarchies – certification is all about differentiation, with the clever trick of making those who 'fail' accept that this is no more than they deserve.

Education is at least partly about power. For those who succeed it develops social and cultural capital which can be invested in rewarding careers. Those whose parents do well benefit from the advantages they can bestow. Challenging such a process of stratification is a difficult business because those who benefit most have the most power to defend their position. All this means that politicians will always have a role in education, it's a kind of politics in itself since it involves social and cultural reproduction. Education doesn't in itself create jobs, except those within it, but educational outcomes do affect the distribution of occupational opportunities and life chances.

Clearly the trick is to open up the possibilities for change, for enhancing opportunities for all, for breaking down barriers that prevent the disadvantaged from succeeding. There should be a good local school for every child across the age range. Education should be enabling, liberating, empowering. Better still there should be a more equal society in which outcomes and rewards are more evenly distributed, in which a less competitive schooling system would be possible.

Let me add some brief further observations:

- Strangely the national curriculum is no longer required in all state-funded schools. Academies and free schools are not obliged to follow it, which of course undermines its purpose.

- Local authorities have provided advice and assistance to schools through improvement programmes and targeted help on various topics, but the funding for this is under threat, especially through increasing academisation.

- The responsibilities of local authorities are increasing at the same time as their power to influence what schools do is decreasing.

- Ofsted inspection is now much more about monitoring 'the data', about outcomes rather than school policy statements and lesson observations. The surveillance is thus less visible, but at a deeper level.

- The intensification of schooling is damaging both children and teachers – there is a mental health crisis in our schools.

- The high level and recent increase in school exclusions, both nationally and locally, suggests systemic failure.

So, how do we get closer to the sort of education system we would like? I favour the idea of a Commission (Royal if that's what we have to call it) on Education, perhaps with separate elements on age-phases within the overall whole, to reveal the fine mess we've gotten ourselves into and give us a chance to arrive at a consensus about what needs to be done to put things right. Opening up the whole system to expert scrutiny and to critique from those involved could create a strong antidote to political bias and short-termism. Of course, political differences will remain, but let's make it difficult for policies to be introduced that don't at least refer to the findings and recommendations of the Commission.

Afterword

Andy Hannan brings his political experience to bear on the educational issues we are dealing with. In case we are careless enough to typify all political activity in education as malign, he reminds us that there are real examples of political initiatives for the better, for example the Open University and Sure Start. These, we should note, are examples of positive political action to widen access to education and to redress social inequality.

Andy identifies the tension between education as a means of liberation for individuals - what it can and should be - and its function as a means of social control - what it often is. Any national enquiry of the kind we propose in Section Five must address this apparent contradiction, especially in view of the disenchantment of many of the under-privileged with the status quo.

4 Roger Darke

Working the System

Introduction

No one writing in this book has had a wider experience of the education system than Roger Darke. A primary school teacher in a disadvantaged area, a school governor and chair, a teacher member of a local education authority and an officer of a teachers' professional association, in these capacities he has run up against all the interfaces making up what we optimistically call 'the system'. A keen sense of social justice runs through his work. He demonstrates here the complexity of our educational arrangements. Teachers, headteachers and their professional associations, school governors and local authorities jostle for influence across the system. Of late, of course, they have been destabilised by central government, a process that continues with an indefinite destination.

This paper deals with education during my time as a worker in the sector. It will also seek to cast light on some of the people I met and their attempts to change the direction that the service took during that time. It is not possible for anything that is a cost on the public purse to be totally taken away from those who 'sign the cheque'. However, I will attempt to cast a small amount of light into the decision making and the ways that those decisions are made. Socrates supposedly said that the ultimate evil was ignorance, but I wonder if he believed in the education of everyone, even the slaves/workers.

My wife and I recently visited the area of the country that we had lived in for the vast majority of our married and working lives. When speaking to an old friend I learnt that the local youth club with which I had been involved had been closed down. The local council had decided, as a cost cutting measure, to merge two clubs and because it only owned one of the buildings that housed these clubs it was in that one that the 'new' club would be situated. To someone who was concerned at the lack of funds in the local authority and who didn't know the area this might seem a logical and sensible decision. It did, however, set me on a train of thought and a trip of memories.

In 1971 I gained a teaching post in an infants' school in what was then a very small local authority. The authority was faced with the raising of the school leaving age to 16 and decided that instead of adding many facilities to their secondary schools they would add the extra year of pupils to infant schools, where they decided that it would cost next to nothing as small children took up less space. In fairness they were re-organising their secondary schools at the same time, down from two grammar schools and six secondary moderns to five comprehensives. The school I was going to teach in was due to become a first school of five to eight-year olds. In their wisdom the council also decided that the new 'big' seven to eight-year-old children might need male teachers who were not then to be found in the infant schools. Across the city three male teachers were engaged in preparation for the changes due to take place two years later. My post was in a very deprived area on a council housing estate.

Two incidents come to mind which are examples of the deprivation. The first was when a mother came to see me to apologise that her son had not been in school for the previous couple of days. She was embarrassed and told me that his shoes had fallen to pieces and she could not afford to buy new ones until her husband's wages had been paid. This was not because he was out of work but because the wages were so small they had no spare or extra cash. I told her that she should never let this happen again but to come and see me immediately because there was always another way to get her lad new shoes, even

46

from the school's lost property box. The second took place in the corridor when I was speaking to the headteacher. A mother came up to me and asked if I would teach her to read. She explained that she couldn't read and when I sent her son home with his reading book she was unable to help him. The head said that we couldn't do that sort of thing and the mother went off rather downhearted. I sought her out and said that whilst I couldn't teach her myself I had found a free adult literacy course that she could attend and, hopefully, learn to read. This she did.

Many years later I was, as Chair of the school's Governing Body, conducting some research on the level of deprivation in the area and found that it ranked in the lowest 5% in the country. The neighbouring area was in the top 5%. As this deprivation was a source of embarrassment to the local authority, the chance to bid for extra funds was not considered when the then Government offered authorities this opportunity, meaning that extra funds for the young people and a pay enhancement for the teachers, all to be paid for by the Government were denied. Luckily this small authority was due to be merged with the surrounding larger rural authority and two other urban authorities. Government research discovered that our authority was not the only one to fail to bid for the extra funds and, after the merger of the authorities in the area, the deprivation funding was made mandatory. The lack of knowledge and clear thinking by those who were on the small Local Education Committee added to the deprivation of the children and further prevented them from reaching their potential. It was such decisions as these that caused me to become more active in the teachers' union to which I belonged. This changed my career in education but never my belief in it.

I was advised by one Local Authority Advisor that I could never expect any real promotion inside the Authority and if I wanted a headship I would have to move to another part of the country. My name as a union activist was too well known. I did not let this annoy me because I had met many other people in the Authority whose ability and fair mindedness was very different from his. I was by this time a teacher member of the Education Committee. Three teachers sat with politically elected members as well as a few others from academia, such as Ted Wragg, and members of the church community. This was the era before and at the time of the Great Education Reform Act in the late 80s when LEAs made many important decisions regarding schools and further education colleges in their area. Although the composition of the committee was clearly governed by the largest political party on the County Council, I always found that they listened to what was said, even if their political views always governed their vote.

Some incidents come to mind from my time as a member of the LEA. There was once a debate on class sizes when one Councillor said that he could not understand what all the fuss was about. He had been educated in a class of 60 and it hadn't done him any harm. Luckily the others did not follow his advice and during a tea break another member of the committee came up to me and said that if that Councillor was an example of education in large classes then it was clear that they should be reduced in size! A more important example of bias against educational values was when, each year, the Committee debated at what level the 11 plus pass mark should be set. This was at a time when the pupil numbers in secondary schools were falling. Two of the smaller areas that came into the larger authority had not reorganised their secondary systems, retaining their grammar schools. Councillors from those areas were worried that funds that went to the grammar schools would be reduced as they were for all other schools. As funds were based on pupil numbers they wanted to retain the highest possible pupils in the grammar schools, without thought to educational considerations. Thus every year the LEA decided to reduce the mark necessary to gain a grammar school place. Despite a minority viewpoint that this was wrong they pushed forward with this policy. It, of course, ignored at least two major problems caused by the policy. Firstly, pupils that in other years would not have qualified to go a grammar school went, possibly being given an education not fit for their needs at schools that did not have curriculums designed for them. GCE was very different to CSE in its design and purpose at the time. A further major problem was the result that secondary schools alongside the grammar schools were subjected to a double loss in numbers and funding. You only had to look at many of those schools in years afterwards to see the effects those losses continued to have.

Although the LEA and then the County Council made the decisions on how the schools in the Authority should move forward, I believe that the role of the Chief Education Officer was and is of paramount importance. I was, and always have been, in favour of larger authorities for the managing of schools. I believe that it allows the best possible talent to be engaged in the management of schools across a large population. As a member of the Education Committee the CEO with whom I worked was excellent. What I noticed most about him was that although he would not always agree with you he would listen to you. He passed this method on to the Chair of the Education Committee who, I recall, once told one of his own party's councillors to be quiet and listen to what the teachers were saying because they were in schools every day and knew what was happening. This, unfortunately, had little effect on the decision making of the LEA and County Council. These decisions were always taken on a party political basis, with those in power winning the day following the party line.

I recall being asked to accompany two County Councillors on a visit to a primary school. The CEO briefed me that the school was in a very poor building and he wanted a report to go to the LEA on whether or not to build a new school. When we arrived I was appalled at the poor quality of the buildings. I said to the Councillors that if we had been RSPCA Inspectors and there were animals being kept here we would immediately close it down. Our report went to the Education Committee but it was a further three years before the school was moved into new excellent buildings. I wondered afterwards if the CEO had suggested me so that he could use my trade union position as a, behind the scenes, way of putting pressure on the Councillors from the ruling party to get something that they might not, in financial terms, be happy to consider.

In my role at a national union level I attended some of the Government consultations regarding what was called the Great Education Reform Bill. The Government was stating that they were giving authority to run schools to their local communities through greater powers to Governing Bodies. This was, of course, an illusion. Three hundred and sixty-five powers were taken from local education authorities and passed to the Secretary of State for Education at national level. I accept that some powers were devolved to a governing body. They no longer had to fill in a form to have a window repaired nor did they have to order their stationery through the authority's supplier. What they didn't point out was that both things now cost more because an individual school did not have the bargaining powers of an authority nor the financial 'clout'. Many unions tried to argue during this consultation process that there was little point in 'devolving' matters to a governing body that they had no control over. Salaries and pension payments were a very good example of this. At the time all salaries for those working in schools were covered by national bodies. Governors had to pay what was laid down in national documents. As these 'costs' made up a very large part of the 'devolved' budget, these national decisions put clear and overriding constraints on the supposed handing of decision making within the local community. This was a great example of the politicians saying one thing and actually meaning the opposite.

It was now towards the end of the 80s I was only teaching part-time because of my activities as a lay trade union officer and a member of the LEA. I enjoyed working with many teachers across two large rural counties. I witnessed the hard and excellent work being done in the majority of schools across those counties. I did, of course, because of my union work in representing teachers who had problems, meet with some who, by their actions, caused problems for themselves and for the institutions in which they worked. It would be easy to say that it was their own fault and they deserved whatever happened to them. However, like so many things in life it was never as simple as that. The teacher who was arrested on Christmas Eve by the police on the charge of sexually assaulting a pupil in his class is one example. It was very difficult to get a solicitor but I managed it. It later transpired that the young person had made about twenty such allegations against men in the area in which she lived, including her home's postman. She received therapy for the thoughts that she had, which were proved to be made up, and all charges were dropped against the teacher and all the others. That was not the end of it for him because the arrest and his suspension for his teaching job was well known in the area. He felt he could not return to his post and left the profession. This is not to say that there are not those who should not be allowed to be a teacher but as I once said to a politician who was saying that all teachers should be excellent that, with nearly half a million teachers in the UK, you have to accept that there will be a mix of 'the good, the bad and the ugly'!

My part-time teaching came to an end when I applied for and gained a post of a paid trade union official. I was now to cover seven local authorities. I never regretted this change and enjoyed the work but a bit of me was sorry. I had always wanted to be a teacher having taught my first fully prepared lesson at the age of 15 to a class of seven and eight-year olds at a Birmingham junior school.

One of the new CEOs that I met remarked on my accent, the 'slight' Brummie twang, and said that he had been an education officer in the city. I had done a year teaching unqualified in the city prior to going to college. In the late 60s there was a shortage of teachers and big cities could only manage if they employed unqualified staff. The school in which I taught had seven classes, one of which was taught by an unqualified ex-pupil teacher from North Wales, one by myself and one by the headteacher's wife, who was also unqualified. In the summer of 1968 the LEA had declared that for the following school year they had managed to get sufficient qualified teachers for their schools. Therefore all unqualified teachers received a letter ending their contracts. This had not really bothered me because I was heading off to college. All those years later I thought of the committee meeting when the CEO must have happily announced that Birmingham would have all qualified staff much to the political delight of those present. Unfortunately there had been a 'slight' miscalculation and I received a telephone call at the start of September saying that they needed unqualified teachers because of a shortage of qualified ones and was I available. I wish I could have attended the committee meeting where this 'reversal' of policy was discussed! I looked at my letter and guess who had signed it, the CEO who commented on my accent. Needless to say I did discuss it with him at a later meeting and said that although he had succeeded in unfairly dismissing me I would do my level best to ensure he never did it to one of our members! This is, however, an excellent example of incomplete information given to those in 'power' which leads to consequences for the pupils in the schools.

Some of the local authorities with which I worked would ask me to give talks to headteachers on the procedures which had been negotiated, disciplinary and capability being the main two. These were people whose actions would have a great bearing on the careers of teachers and the youngsters in the schools. When I spoke about capability I would always open my presentation by saying that if there was anyone in the room who believed that they only taught excellent lessons then they should leave now as they would not like what I was going to say or understand the reasons for my explanations. I said that in my career I hope that I had taught some excellent lessons, some not too bad but I had to admit that some had not always gone as I had planned. It was, I pointed out, how we analysed the failures and corrected them that was important.

National politicians, after the Chief HMI had said that there were thousands of incompetent teachers, decided to enforce a procedure for correcting this 'problem'. They wanted to introduce a system which included a level which was described as gross incompetence. Many will have heard of gross misbehaviour. This is when an employee does something that is immediately so bad that there can be no further contract between the employer and themselves; instant dismissal effectively results. Whilst many who heard the 'new' charge of gross incompetence knew about gross misbehaviour they could not see how someone could, during a lesson, become grossly incompetent. Lack of capability develops over a period of time. It could be tackled in many different ways. Luckily sensible people spoke to the Secretary of State and the Government dropped the idea.

When I left my teaching post, as you do, I had a leaving party with my colleagues. The headteacher said that if I thought that I was leaving the school I was wrong. She had recommended to the Governing Body that I be co-opted on to it, especially as I lived in the area, I became a community representative. A few years later I was elected as the Chair of Governors. Two things come to mind as I think of decisions that had far reaching effects, especially on the young people and their parents who had no say in the actions but had to bear the consequences.

The first came as the school was part of a re-organisation across the city when first and middle schools were being merged into primary schools and the 11 to 12-year olds were going to the comprehensive secondary schools. Many schools were being re-built, under PFI schemes, and ours was one of them. Our Governing Body suggested that as part of the new school there could be an office in the school that could be used by the city council to allow the residents of the estate to discuss their council homes and report difficulties. I had noticed over the years that many parents dropped their children at the school and if they wanted to report a problem in the house then had to, with their pre-school children, travel into the city centre to the council offices. By the time they reached the Council Offices their journey had been difficult and they were in no mood to be pleasant with the council official. They were usually described as difficult and often abusive. We thought that an office closer at hand would ease the job of the council. However we immediately hit a problem. The houses were owned by the city council but the school was being re-built by the county council. It proved more difficult to get these two entities to speak to each other than to sort out the Schleswig-Holstein question.

In the school's final term we received a letter from OFSTED telling us that it was to be inspected. As Chair of Governors I immediately contacted the lead-inspector to say that it was closing and surely it was a waste of money to have an inspection which could never be publicly reported. I was told that this didn't matter, we were scheduled for inspection and it would take place. The headteacher and I met with this lead-inspector and she spent the first thirty minutes of the meeting telling us of her experience, none of it teaching in a deprived area. She then said that her initial trawl of the documentation led her to believe that we were spending too much money on people and not enough on computers. I said that the need of the pupils was to interact with people and if we had a greater funding stream we would consider more resources such as computers. She brushed this aside as though she knew better than me. She had not, of course, enquired about my experience or that of the headteacher. The lead-inspector then had a meeting with the staff and another one with the Governing Body. Unfortunately a work commitment meant that I could only introduce her to my colleagues and then had to leave.

That evening I received a number of telephone calls from colleague governors. The inspector had been rude and condescending to such an extent that one governor had been in tears. I decided that the school had nothing to lose and I was not letting this bullying go unchecked. I contacted someone I knew in HMI and also asked the CEO to do the same. About a week later I received a telephone call from the lead-inspector who informed me that there was nothing to worry about but, as happened occasionally, her team was going to be inspected by HMI whilst at the school.

I put together a report on the area in which the school was situated and the problems which the staff encountered on a daily basis and sent this to the lead-inspector and the HMI who was also coming to see us. The inspection took place. The staff were happy with the way they were treated. I had an excellent meeting with the HMI and one with the Inspector who would write about the school's finances and the Governing Body. The Report, which only we saw, was a good one for the school and a testament to the work of the staff in difficult circumstances. I am not particularly proud of it, but this is an example of the phrase 'it is not what you know but who you know that matters'.

Prior to my retirement at the end of 2008 I met with many politicians both at local level and on the national stage, of all political parties. I found the vast majority of them to be courteous and to give the impression of listening to what was being said. I accept that since my retirement teacher trade unions have been labelled 'the blob' which has returned us to the era of trade unions in general being 'the enemy within' but my individual meetings did not suffer from such insults. What I do, however, recall was usually they might want to agree with what you were saying but if it did not fit in with their present policy it was rejected.

I was recently reading a book by Owen Jones entitled *The Establishment and how they get away with it* and it caused me to recall some research that I had done into teachers' pay. My research was into the correlation between stories of problems in the education service being in the national press and the, then, yearly negotiations on teachers' pay. This was in the days of the Burnham Committee, a committee made up of representatives of local authorities and teacher trade unions, supposedly independent of the Government. It was so independent of Government that there were always two civil servants at meetings and before the management side could make an offer the civil servants had to ring the Secretary of State to clear it. The Committee started its meetings towards the end of the calendar year in time for an April pay change. When I looked at education press coverage I found that either just before the Committee met or in the early part of the process there would be a release of 'information' regarding problems in schools. This led to the ability of the Government of the day and the local authorities' representatives being able to say however much they would like to see an improvement of teachers' pay there were more pressing problems that required the limited resources that were available. It has now been given the nomenclature of 'spin' and we have seen it in so many parts of our lives. Education has been subjected to spin and probably always will be unless we find a different way to discuss the needs of the service.

We perhaps can't even agree on a national level about what we mean by education. We can look at it from our individual perspective and we can debate it but how do we organise the system for the benefit of those within it? Malcolm Forbes is quoted as saying that education's purpose is to replace an empty mind with an open one. Whilst I may well agree with him and hope that in my days as a teacher this was one of the things that I sought to do, what really troubles me from my experiences in education outside the classroom is how a good education service is managed. Winston Churchill said 'Democracy is the worst form of government, except for all the others'. I still believe that sensible sized local education authorities and a governing body for each school provides the best form of management of the service at a local level. The present system, whilst I have not worked within it, seems to me to be built on a myth of local control. Some academy chains are bigger than previous LEAs, they cross different and sometimes large geographical areas and make no pretence of wanting local opinion or even having to stand for election on what they have achieved or not, as the case may be. It is at a national level that overall policy is made and there are other papers in this series that look at this but my experiences lead me to believe that it is only a long term plan without dependency on the next general election that will truly advance the situation of education in the UK.

Afterword

'A national system locally administered' was the standard description of the education service in England and Wales in the pre-and immediate post-war period. The partnership between central government, local government and the teachers underlay both the mechanisms and the spirit of administration.

This dispensation tolerated, perhaps even celebrated, diversity in institutional structures and even in curriculums until initiatives from 1980 onwards introduced new participants into the politics of education. Parents, firstly as governors of schools and latterly as 'consumers' in an education market came to the fore. At the same time central government in the form principally of the Secretary of State for Education came forward with, on occasion, dictatorial intent and effect. This all placed a squeeze equally on both local democracy and teachers' autonomy. No settlement has been reached that looks future-proof.

Roger has shown how good working relationships can produce benefits out of the miscellany of powers, viewpoints and interests pervading the education service. Are our present institutional structures sufficiently resilient to accommodate all the legitimate players in education: the students and parents; the teachers and their managers and leaders; local and national government?

It must be an early task for our proposed National Education Council to consult widely and to make proposals based on clear democratic principles for the future administration and management of the education service.

Allen Parrott

A Thinking Minister of Education

Introduction

In the Preamble to this book it is explained how this writing project began out of our on-going concern for quality in education. In 2015, when the Exeter Society held a General Election husting none of the regional parliamentary candidates was able to articulate a coherent view on education policy or on the overall purposes of the education system in England and Wales. Politicians cannot of course be specialists on every aspect of social policy or of national politics, especially in the period when they are still in their local area trying to become MPs. But it was still a shock for the Society's members to find out how little their local candidates knew about some long-standing educational issues and problems.

In a sane world, all politicians and aspiring MPs would be constantly seeking the views of professional practitioners or 'experts in the field' in order to inform their opinions and views on current policies and practices. But the education system had been so thoroughly politicised by 2015 that the then Education Minister, Michael Gove, positively refused to listen to the voice of teachers in the field ('the country has had enough of experts'), and he had done his best to persuade the media and the general public that the teaching profession was not worth consulting because it was no more than a self-serving, reactionary 'blob'.

It was a relief therefore for Allen to read 'Taught not Caught', a book published in 2017 by Gove's successor as Minister, Nicky Morgan, which not only showed great respect for many teachers in ordinary schools up and down the country, but which also made a very coherent case for the importance of educating the whole person (and not just the future worker or economic contributor). It is true that the education of 'character', which goes back at least to the ancient Greeks, is given an ideological 21st century spin by Nicky Morgan - grit and determination are mentioned more often than kindness and empathy, for example - but her book's message was nevertheless very welcome. Unfortunately, her book completely failed to address how or why the British education system in the 21st century has managed to lose its previous strong focus on the whole person or 'character'. Such an enquiry would have undoubtedly entailed criticism of her party and of several predecessors in her post. Hence, she only gets two cheers in this review.

Nicky Morgan, recently Secretary of State for Education, has written a book on 'character education'. In a gushing Foreword, Lord James O'Shaughnessy tells us that she was a brave minister who went against prevailing educational orthodoxy by seeking to place character development at the heart of the Cameron government's approach to education. That may be so. But surely most readers and most parents will regard the education of 'character' - or a focus on the whole person and not just on academic attainments - as simple common sense? How did the country arrive at a situation where it is considered brave of an education minister to believe what has been obvious to serious thinkers throughout history: that education is about the development of character as well as the attainment of knowledge and skills? The book itself would be braver - and deeper - if Nicky Morgan had explicitly discussed exactly how her thinking on education differs from received opinion and from mainstream educational thinking in her party. Particularly brave would have been some account of how her educational beliefs differ from the evidence-free thinking and policy-making of her immediate ministerial predecessor, Michael Gove.

The book has a number of omissions. Morgan claims that 'the English education system used to do character development very well' (p.124), but her book offers no explanation for why this is no longer the case. During the past seven years, the introduction of

EBacc and the government's continuing over-emphasis on STEM subjects are just two examples of how the overall curriculum has been narrowed, thus ensuring that schools in general are less likely to prioritise character education now than they were even ten years ago, let alone in previous generations. Also, Morgan does not address how her version of character education relates to so-called 'British values' or what it might mean for the PSHE curriculum in schools. Nevertheless, some parts of the book are well worth reading, if only because Nicky Morgan is a rare politician who is prepared to question, at least implicitly, the narrow instrumentalism of most education policy-making. Her book makes clear that there is an important national debate to be had about the purposes and the values of the nation's education system. In addition, she shows great respect to some educational 'experts', i.e. to many practitioners in schools up and down the country whose character education projects she visited as Secretary of State. In prose that is passionate and enthusiastic, rather than fluent or stylish, she describes how these professionals are attempting to put 'character' explicitly into the curriculum. In return, they and their successful projects provide her with a strong evidential basis for her beliefs. Nicky Morgan's educational credo is easy to summarise in three short phrases: education is about 'academics plus character'; character can - and should - be taught and learned in all educational institutions, from infancy onwards; schools that focus on character education will also do better in academic attainment and grades.

The book's opening chapter asks the question, 'what does 'character' mean?'. Very sensibly, Morgan does not attempt to provide a universal or comprehensive checklist of character traits which all schools should include in their curriculum offering. Such externally-imposed or 'government-approved' lists would almost certainly end up in a filing cabinet and would deserve to do so. Each school needs to have the debate and to reach its own consensus about the educational values and personal qualities it wishes to promote. As Morgan puts it, 'there is no one clear definition of character... no one easy list of boxes to tick' (p.16). The only way that 'character education' can become something real, something more than a vague set of aspirations and something that is part of the everyday experience of both learners and teachers, is if the concept itself is explicitly and regularly discussed, and therefore 'owned', by the entire school community.

Thanks to extensive quotes from sources in the university, secondary and primary school sectors, the first chapter is the best as well as the longest in the book. Recent research and thinking on character education are covered, as is the extensive vocabulary, some traditional and some newly minted, of educational values, personal virtues and character traits. For example, the Jubilee Centre for Character and Virtues at Birmingham University has updated a list of human virtues first identified by Aristotle, re-classified them in four categories - intellectual, moral, performance and civic - and showed how they remain relevant in today's world. Morgan also describes how different schools have developed and implemented their policies on character education. A Barnet primary school aims to develop positive traits of character to make every Year 6 pupil a 'Golden Child' (p.23), while a secondary school in Warrington has produced a booklet called 'Character Counts' which informs pupils that 'a young person's character is the summation of his or her values, attitudes and behaviours... Good character doesn't happen automatically, and it's too important to be left to chance' (p.31). This first chapter alone, because of its detailed exploration of the concept in many contexts, would enable any school or educational institution to initiate its own debate on 'character education' should it wish to do so.

The other nine chapters are considerably shorter and, on the whole, less useful, except in those passages where the author describes more good policy-making and teaching practice from the projects she supported and visited as Minister. Overall, the book lacks critique as well as depth. Morgan appears educationally naive. Her argument for having a better balance between a knowledge-based and a character-based curriculum is re-stated many times, but she seems unaware that there are some long-standing and contentious questions about the conceptual boundaries of education and about how desirable teaching and learning practices have to be distinguished from undesirable practices known as propaganda or brain washing. Just how far do schools have the right to 'mould' character or to 'impose' their values? Is this a matter solely for parents or does society as a whole need protection from 'rogue schools' and from unacceptable practices? Such issues need further exploration even among those of us who would largely subscribe to Nicky Morgan's credo and to her robust, common sense approach to character education.

Morgan shows some political naivety as well. In chapter two she professes herself to be a 'one nation Tory' in the mould of Disraeli. She deplores the gross inequalities in society and in education. But because she does not discuss any political or historical contexts, her writing on these matters comes across as disingenuous: 'my belief, though, is that we will fail to really turbocharge the social mobility which can be provided by education if we don't offer all pupils both a knowledge-rich, academically rigorous curriculum and the building of social capital (*i.e. through character education*)' (p. 39). She shows no recognition of the ways in which the past forty years of neo-liberal economic and educational policy have reduced social mobility and deepened if not caused the social and educational inequalities which upset her.

In chapter three, which focuses on how character education is related to mental health and wellbeing, Morgan comes close to the familiar political position of expecting schools to solve all young people's problems. 'As we see more and more young people reporting rising anxiety, depression, self-harm and behaviour problems, then it is clear there must be a place for a whole school focus on wellbeing and resilience to help to address these issues' (p 47). Well, yes, maybe. But if it is to be effective, any 'whole school focus' on wellbeing in all English schools would require a concomitant 'whole government focus' on wellbeing throughout the nation - and this in turn would require new government policies on, for starters: ending poverty, reducing inequality, providing social housing, increasing NHS spending on mental illness and positive health promotion and, not least, restoring professional youth work and youth clubs throughout the nation in order to complement the schools' provision.

In chapter five, on adult role models, Nicky Morgan recognises that schools have a 'hidden curriculum' which also contributes to character education. She points out that any educational institution's values are going to be picked up by students one way or another, even where there is no attempt to put explicit character education into the overt curriculum. But she seems unaware that this well-established notion of the hidden curriculum rather undermines her choice of title 'Taught not Caught'. Understandably, she wishes to stress the explicit teaching of values and 'character' over the unplanned, random 'catching' of values and ethos. But in real life, as her own evidence indicates, this is a false dichotomy: a school's ethos is going to be 'caught' whatever attempts are also being made consciously to define it or explicitly to teach it. Indeed, if she had called her book, 'Taught <u>and</u> Caught', she might have greatly strengthened this chapter on adult role modelling. She could have emphasised, for example, that everyone in an educational institution - adults and children alike - is learning about character from the role models they see around them. In educational organisations, the principles of good character, good conduct and how people behave to one another need to apply everywhere, at all times, up and down the institutional hierarchy: they do not apply only in classrooms. In other words, the whole school community including governing body members and midday supervisors, the senior leadership team and the caretakers, might usefully be part of an ongoing debate on what is meant by institutional ethos and, more specifically, on what their school's 'character education' policy might mean for them in their particular job or responsibility. In this way the school's ethos would combine educational and democratic values and would be 'walking the talk'.

Chapter six, 'Preparing for the Workplace', is the shortest in the book, which is surprising because it could have offered Nicky Morgan some telling examples in support of her argument about the significance of character development as an educational goal. Research over several decades has consistently shown that employers are just as concerned about the personal traits and attitudes that young people possess when they leave school as they are about their academic qualifications or practical abilities. These human attributes, or 'soft skills', desired by employers are often defined in the same kind of language as character education: the 'virtues' typically looked for include reliability, perseverance, confidence, communication, organisation, negotiation, leadership, teamwork, etc.

Chapter seven, 'Assessing Character', is the most problematic. Nicky Morgan has imbibed uncritically the modern orthodoxy that for assessment to be real and effective something always has to be measured. She tells us that one of Whitehall's mantras is 'what gets assessed gets done' (p.85), which is a weaker version of the ubiquitous

McKinsey motto from the 1980s, 'everything can be measured and what gets measured gets managed'. Yet the evidence of her own eyes, as she visits successful character education projects, compels her to admit that personality and a child's character formation over time cannot be meaningfully measured. A braver writer might then have acknowledged that both the McKinsey premise and the Whitehall mantra are wrong, at least in the instance of character education, because personal or character development involves the kind of truly human encounters and engagements which make precise measurement or assessment of the learning involved quite impossible - and quite irrelevant.

There will never be a valid, reliable, objective way to measure character education, just as there is no accurate or numerical way to measure other deeply human activities like love or friendship or empathy. But unfortunately, in the current neo-liberal and managerial Whitehall world - the world that has helped to make character education unfashionable in recent decades and therefore in need of Nicky Morgan's advocacy - no exceptions are permitted. The audit must always prevail, and something has to be measured in quantitative terms. So although she is prepared to acknowledge that internal dialogues, self-evaluations and self-critical assessments might be useful aspects of character education projects, she fails to appreciate that these are in fact the only kinds of assessment which have relevance in 'character education' or that the professionals engaged in such important developmental and potentially transformative educational work have to be trusted to do their good work in good faith. Because their work is quintessentially human and because it is always situated in a unique context, it is not reducible to a computer algorithm and cannot be successfully managed at a distance. The McKinsey motto has always been wrong for much that is important in education: not everything can be measured and not everything needs to be externally managed.

Fortunately, from her accounts of their work one can deduce that the real-life practitioners in the field of character education observed by Nicky Morgan can in fact be trusted. In her fervent prose they are presented to the reader as dedicated educators who would certainly not need external assessments, league tables, targets or performance indicators to motivate them. In this respect they are of course just like many thousands of other professional teachers. However, Nicky Morgan does not want to trust the evidence of her own eyes and she ends her chapter by calling for Ofsted to inspect character education projects in schools to 'assess the teaching to ensure they do *(sic)* reflect the traits and values each school has identified as important'. In its current form Ofsted offers entirely the wrong kind of inspection model for the evaluation of character education projects. Until Ofsted inspectors are encouraged to recognise complexity, nuance and uniqueness in a school's curriculum and until they are expected to engage routinely in long-term developmental dialogues with individual schools and teachers before coming to their inspectorial judgements, Ofsted would be more likely to do harm than to do good to Nicky Morgan's splendidly ambitious nationwide project.

Even though Nicky Morgan's book is too superficial and non-analytical to be recommended unreservedly, let me end this review on a positive note. She has undoubtedly achieved her stated aim 'to demonstrate not just why explicitly teaching character is both possible and necessary but also that it is already happening in many excellent state schools up and down the country' (p. 108). Moreover, she is a serving politician who has written a book with practical proposals that seek to improve the educational experience of all children and has justified her proposed educational reforms by looking closely at the good practice of professional educators and teachers in the field. So two cheers for Nicky Morgan!

Afterword

How refreshing to find a short, thought-provoking, non-academic book about the purpose and nature of education, especially coming from the pen of a serving politician! Fifty years ago, in the age of the 'Penguin Education Specials', there were more publications of this kind, written for a lay audience and for practitioners rather than for scholars and researchers. This current collection of papers by members of the Exeter Society for Curriculum Studies is attempting something similar.

We all need to consider how important a goal we think personal development, or the education of character, should be for a 21st century education system. More particularly, so does every politician especially if they have ambitions to become a government minister. A truly just education system would surely give personal development a high priority alongside other important educational goals, which might well include Blair's well-educated and flexible future workforce.

It is good to note that Ofsted's Chief Inspector, Amanda Spielman announced in January 2019 that in future school inspection will place less emphasis on exam results and more on conduct and behaviour. She gave no notice of what kinds of evidence would be sought to this worthy end and would be well advised to acknowledge the complexities Allen has pointed to.

6 Michael Bassey

Education as the World Warms

Introduction

All education must take a view on the future even though predictions are notoriously fallible. Many of us remember from the sixties and early seventies the considerable energies spent discussing 'education for leisure' on the expectation that spare time would become a problem in the future. It did become a problem but more in the form of unemployment than a utopian age of plenty in which technology would liberate us to a life of ease.

Notwithstanding the limits of our knowledge, we must take a best guess and prepare as best we can for what is to come. Michael takes up a fully committed position. He asserts the reality of climate change and the probability of deleterious social change.

Schools must be turned around from the present 'factory model' and their community role accentuated. Teacher education will require overhaul and Michael makes interesting radical proposals.

Michael offers practical ideas about how the school curriculum at both primary and secondary level could be altered and improved. His ideas on policy and practice include a strong focus on education for sustainable living and physical and mental health. He also introduces two key themes that are developed in later chapters: the potential of 'community schools' to enhance both children's experience of school and local democracy; and the potential of teachers, with their professionalism enhanced and trust restored, to provide appropriate forms of learning for each and every student.

The following words are how the great Labour election manifesto of 1945 described education.

'The great purpose of Education is to enable individual citizens to be capable of thinking for themselves, moral beings well equipped with the many and varied attributes that they learn in school and able to continue to develop and learn purposefully throughout their lives in a contented pursuit of worthwhile life, liberty and happiness'

The party manifestoes of recent elections have put forward various structural proposals for improving education but have been limited by the inadequate understanding that most politicians seem to have of schools and children. They tend to use the 'factory' model of education, in which teachers are seen as technicians in pupil factories with a government manual, regular inspection and pupil testing to ensure efficiency and measure progress. Competition in the future global economy is their justification for putting pressure on primary schools to improve SATs results and on secondary schools for better GCSE results in a narrow range of subjects. But is this right? My view is that the global ecology must take centre-stage, ahead even of the global economy.

Obviously, teachers themselves must be well educated and strongly committed people who deserve the trust of the wider society. This remains generally the case despite the many criticisms levelled over recent years. In addition, teachers need to be professionally trained so that their commitment is focussed on handling the characteristics and development paths of young people. But, sadly, professional training beyond 'learning from Nellie' on the job has not been recognised as essential in recent political quarters.

Beyond these familiar notions I believe today's teachers in training need to be prepared for their pupils growing up into a very different world – one that is being changed dramatically by global warming – and by a number of other factors.

In all this, schools should be joyful places as they go about the business of preparing young people for a future good life in terms of work, home and play. Teachers need to be warm-hearted professional firebrands, inspiring the young. They should be lighting fires, not filling buckets. Many of our politicians do not understand this since they measure the success of schools in terms of SAT results at 11, GCSE results at 16 and numbers of entrants to universities at 18 plus.

Governments tend to focus on the short-term, governed by the electoral cycle. But educational policy needs a longer perspective. My worry is that the government sees the future only as an extrapolation of the economic present with nations competing for markets for their goods and services, struggling to promote economic growth and needing a technically skilled workforce to engage in this global competition. Economic strands to the education debate have eclipsed all others.

What will life be like in 2050?

What will the future be like? Nobody knows of course, but teachers need to speculate. What will the world look like when today's five-year-olds are forty, hopefully in the prime of their lives? It needs to be thought about in order to provide a relevant education.

Google 'Year 2050 predictions' and look at 'FutureTimeline.net' for 2050. There is a long list of predictions.

Humanity is at a crossroads

- *Nearly half of the Amazon forest has been deforested*

- *Wildfires have tripled in some regions*

- *Traditional wine industries have been severely altered by climate change*

- *Fish body size has declined by nearly a quarter*

- *Hi-tech, intelligent buildings are revolutionising the urban landscape*

- *Automobiles are smaller, safer and high-tech*

- *There have been major advances in air travel comfort*

- *Continent-wide 'super-grids' provide much of the world's energy needs*

- *China completes the largest water diversion project in history*

It will not just be the wine industries that are affected by climate change! A very significant report on climate came from the Intergovernmental Panel on Climate Change (IPCC) in 2014.

This is how this body is described.

'The IPCC is a scientific body under the auspices of the United Nations. It reviews and assesses the most recent scientific, technical and socio-economic information produced worldwide relevant to the understanding of climate change. Thousands of scientists from all over the world contribute to the work of the IPCC on a voluntary basis. Review is an essential part of the IPCC process, to ensure an objective and complete assessment of current information.'

In a world now bedevilled by 'fake news' we can be sure that the utterances of this body will be reliable and trustworthy.

What do these world's scientists say? The IPCC's *'Climate Change Synthesis Report'* of 2014 identifies the following

- *Human influence on the climate system is clear, and recent anthropogenic emissions of greenhouse gases are the highest in history.*

- *Warming of the climate system is unequivocal.*

- *The atmosphere and oceans have warmed.*

Greenhouse gases (mainly carbon dioxide, methane, and nitrous oxide) in the atmosphere allow the Sun's radiation to pass through and warm the surface of the Earth, but the infrared heat that the Earth then emits is absorbed by these gases and warms the land, the oceans and the atmosphere. The IPCC states that there were 27 'units' of greenhouse gas warming in the year 1970 and by 2010 this had increased to 49 'units'. In 2010 this was due to: carbon dioxide coming from forests and similar lands 11%; methane from swamps and cattle 16%; nitrous oxide from agricultural fertilizer decomposition 6%; and carbon dioxide from the burning of fossil fuels 65%.

The IPCC makes these dire predictions for the year 2050:

- *Temperatures are expected to rise from somewhere between 0.8 and more than 2 degrees Celsius.*

- *More than one million species of plants and animals worldwide are projected to be extinct.*

- *Ocean waters are projected to rise one to four feet threatening the homes of 25 million to 40 million people.*

Sea level rise is already happening. On 19 May 2015 an article in *The Guardian* by Tahmima Anam reported that:

'Already in Bangladesh 50,000 people migrate to the capital city every month because rising sea level have made their villages uninhabitable and have destroyed their arable land.'

The IPCC is clear that we humans are responsible. By 2050 there will be more of us. According to the US Census Bureau, world population will grow from 7.4 billion now to 9.1 billion in 2050. And a recent United Nations report, noting the trend for populations to move to towns, expects that the overall growth of the world's population could add another 2.5 billion people to urban populations by 2050.

An alarming feature of world politics is these combined judgements of thousands of scientists are denied by some influential people including President Donald Trump of the USA. Google 'Global warming denier' and you learn in a Wikipedia article that:

'Between 2002 and 2010, nearly $120 million was anonymously donated... to more than 100 organizations seeking to cast doubt on the science behind climate change' (Goldberg, S Guardian 14 Feb 2013)

The fossil fuel companies, with enormous investment in oil, coal and gas, are prominent deniers that mankind burning fuel is responsible. Sadly, the *Daily Mail* and Rupert Murdoch are also deniers, so a high proportion of the newspaper reading public is led to have doubts about the cause of adverse climate change!

Apart from temperature increase there are other problems: pollution of oceans, air pollution in cities, plastic waste, soil depredation, key resource depletion, and water shortage. A report on the latter in the *Proceedings of the US National Academy of Sciences* says:

Currently, 150 million people live in cities with perennial water shortages. By 2050 demographic growth will increase this figure to almost 1 billion people. (McDonald R J 2011)

Various writers speculate about the future. For example: Ulrich Eberl's *Life in 2050* (published in 2011), Jacques Attali's *A Brief History of the Future: A Brave and Controversial Look at the Twenty-First Century* (2006), Laurence Smith's *The New North: the World in 2050* (published in 2010) and Elizabeth Kolbert's *The Sixth Extinction* (2014). Some are enthusiastic about the future and others despondent.

A future drastically different

Laurence Smith's book ends with the question: '*What kind of a world do we want?*' It invites all sorts of answers, but a more pertinent question for teachers is '*What will England be like for today's children?*'

Earth warming will have continued even if the sources of coal, oil and gas that produce greenhouse gases have been sealed off in the next ten years. As a result, our climate will change leading to major droughts as well as devastating storms. Trees will be torn down, roofs will be lifted, homes will be damaged, and sea surges will flood low-level land along our coasts. Some of this is already happening.

At present 60% of the food we consume in the UK is home-grown, but with warmer and wetter winters and drier summers this may be at risk, one reason being significant changes in pests, diseases and weeds affecting our agricultural production. Maybe our wine industry will improve, but other more important crops may suffer. Likewise, the 40% of our food that we import at present from other countries will be affected and it will probably become necessary for us to move towards self-sufficiency in food production and to adapt our agriculture to a changing climate.

As a nation will we be ready for such a time of adversity? Being in my eighties I look back to my childhood during World War II when my family lived in Orpington, a few miles south of London. The devastation then came from bombs. Some of the time we slept in air raid shelters. Every day I carried a gas mask to school. But it is not the horrors of that time I remember but the way that people pulled together, supported each other, and, as part of the war effort, opened up allotments on waste land and grew vegetables to feed themselves. I remember my father proudly pushing our wheelbarrow home with a pile of potatoes, carrots, cabbages and a huge marrow that he had grown. Walking home from school, if there was an air raid warning, we were told to go to the nearest house and ask to go into their air raid shelter. There were no worries of 'stranger danger' as there would be today. People invited strangers to take shelter with them.

I fear that fewer folk today are community minded. Recent research reported on ITV's Tonight programme reveals that more than half of the people interviewed didn't know the people living next door to them. More people seem to be competitive, self-centred, acquisitive, and out for themselves and their family than was the case in the past. We have become the 'me-first' society. Will Hutton in describes how in the second decade of the 21st century British society seems to be moving away from the 'justice, tolerance, freedom and democratic accountability' of the earlier post-war years.

> *'The simple pro-market, individualistic nostrums of Thatcherism, too little qualified or challenged by New Labour, have begun to metamorphose – egged on by a destructive, vengeful centre-right press – into a mix of crude libertarianism, scepticism of all things initiated by the state and distrust of the public realm. We do not act together: we look out for ourselves as individuals. Justice, equity, tolerance and proportionality are all in retreat and a more brutal, selfish and amoral society is emerging.' (Hutton 2015 p 33)*

This ethos has been pushed mindlessly by successive governments, of left and right, by encouraging competition and market forces in business in order to promote economic growth.

Preparing for a different future

Since the Education Reform Act of 1988 competition has also been promoted in schools. The constant testing of young people makes them and their parents increasingly competitive and promotes the 'me-first' culture. League tables do the same with the idea that one school is better than another and so 'my child should go there'. When we hear of parents moving home to be in the locality of a particular school because it is judged 'the best' we realise how far society has moved in the competitive stakes. I believe there are few teachers that actually want this state of affairs, and within their own classrooms I am sure teachers treat all their pupils as equally deserving, but they are aware of the external pressures demanding competition.

Parents who are obsessed with getting their child to the 'best' school don't seem to realise that in terms of primary education it is the calibre and personality of the individual teacher that matters, hardly the image and test results of the school. And, if we can accept Ofsted judgements, the state of play (in September 2016) is that 90% of primary schools and 78% of secondaries are judged to be 'good' or 'outstanding': so why do parents get fussed? There are community-building reasons for every child going to the local school.

What should schools do to prepare young people for life in the mid-century? Let's stay with present structures: with young people in school divided into classes: with primary schools having class-teachers and secondary schools subject teachers. I hope that soon today's instruments of government control – excessive testing, league tables, bench marks, floor standards, performance management, a detailed national curriculum and even Ofsted inspections - will be swept away. I hope that the pernicious Whitehall-based micromanagement of recent years will stop. I look for a local or regional structure that co-ordinates the links between schools and has small teams of local inspectors-cum-advisers who offer challenge and support to schools in the way that the best local education authorities provided in the mid twentieth century.

Fundamentally society must trust teachers to do the professional job for which they have trained and for which nearly all of them are highly committed: identifying the educational needs of young people and providing for each according to perceived need.

I hope that teachers will increasingly work collegially within their schools, meaning that they share ideas, and support each other. I hope that schools will co-operate with neighbouring schools rather than see themselves in competition. I hope teachers will interact with their local communities in devising curricula for their pupils based on simple and minimal national guidelines drawn up by a National Education Council of a kind proposed in our Conclusions and Recommendations below.

In particular I hope that parents and the nation come to recognise that they can trust teachers to do their best for every child and young person without the controls and sanctions that central government imposes today.

So, how should teachers respond to these ideas?

Primary education promoting community education

Beyond the obvious need for enabling children to read, write and do simple sums, and supporting their social and physical development, an important role for primary schools should be community development. Community matters since, when adversity strikes, the stronger the community the more people will be prepared to support each other.

As was mainly the case up till the 1990s, young people should attend their local schools and their school work should be collaborative. Young children should wherever possible walk to school. This contributes to their health and to community development. Attending the local school means that their school friends can also be home friends with whom they can play in their home locality. And their parents will meet at the school gates and, like their children, can then build local friendships.

Out-of-door activities like exploring nature, hiking and camping should be important ways of encouraging children to work well and successfully together, individually to be resilient, and to gain awareness of the beauty and the dangers of the natural world.

Secondary education contributing to the local community

I can't see it happening soon, but GCSE and A-level should be replaced, at the very end of schooling, by diploma assessments providing routes into apprenticeship, university, or work. The Tomlinson Report of 2002 – that was commissioned and then rejected by Tony Blair's government – should be re-examined.

I doubt whether the traditional academic subjects deserve the pre-eminence they get in the secondary school curriculum. Many of us have found much pleasure in learning history or geography or literature or physical and biological sciences, or social science, or languages, or music or art or drama. But whether these have fascination for all young people in our schools is questionable. How many youngsters actually learn little more than coping with boredom?

In preparing for the worst effects of coming climate change 16-19-year-olds should spend as much school time working in the local community as they do in the classroom or apprentice workshop. Student-led or teacher-led teams could support elderly people in their community, help young children with their reading in primary schools, grow vegetables, tend livestock, provide street theatre, enhance local environments, erect solar panels, plant trees, engage in other public projects, and through such team work learn democratic values and an ethos of harmony, co-operation, stewardship, self-sufficiency and self-worth.

Teacher education

What are the implications for teacher education? In *Education for the Inevitable* (2011) I have suggested substantial changes. After graduation from a degree course intending teachers spend at least a 6-month gap engaged in manual work in factory or on a farm and earning sufficient to support some travel around this country, or Europe, or the world. The importance of this is to gain some experience of the world outside school and college. All intending teachers then take an 18-month post-graduate course. (Yes, goodbye to the B.Ed). About half of the 18-month course should involve working in a variety of schools under the guidance of both college tutors and school-teachers. The other half, in-college work, should, as now, entail a strong element of pedagogic theory covering a range of subjects for intending primary teachers and on the degree subject for intending secondary teachers plus for everyone a focus on the teaching of reading, writing, talking and listening skills. There should be a good grounding in educational theory, especially child development. Much of this is actually happening now, although it seems to be too rushed.

But there is one more element that is needed in terms of a climate-changed future: theoretical and practical work on environmental futures. It is education for creating sustainable living. It is why the course needs to be 18-months long. It should embrace seminars on a range of books like Schumacher's *Small is Beautiful*, the Club of Rome's *Limits to Growth*, Illich's *Tools for Conviviality*, and Wilkinson and Pickett's *The Spirit Level* as well as more recent books on the future such as I have cited earlier.

Beyond the theoretical study, in practical terms, I suggest something quite novel. Everyone training to be a teacher should start their course in January and be allocated a patch of land with gardening tools and seeds in order to grow sufficient food to feed a few people during the coming year. It would be a fundamental lesson in sustainable living and self-sufficiency and I would expect it to have a major impact on their own teaching in the years ahead.

They might find helpful John Seymour's *The Complete Book of Self-sufficiency* (1976). He says:

'Self-sufficiency does not mean 'going back' to the acceptance of a lower

standard of living. On the contrary, it is the striving for a higher standard of living, for food which is fresh and organically grown and good, for the good life in pleasant surroundings, for the health of body and peace of mind which comes with hard varied work in the open air, and for the satisfaction that comes from doing difficult and intricate jobs well and successfully.'

This would be an excellent experience for teachers in training.

Envoi

I believe that rethinking primary, secondary and teacher education along the lines that I have outlined would help change us from a 'me-first' society to one based on the togetherness of communities. These ideas would help develop self-reliance in communities and the recognition that communities can act to resolve problems themselves when, and if, disaster strikes. They would encourage the local growing of food – on allotments, orchards and vegetable gardens – which would help sustain families. They would boost the morale of teachers and help them to 'grow tall in society'.

These thoughts would provide a better education for our young people than the present test-driven schooling that sees the economy as the prime goal for education and fails to recognise the coming challenge from ecology. I commend them as worthwhile ideas in their own right as contributing to the all-round development of young people, but also as a preparation for whatever climatic disasters lie ahead as the Earth warms up.

Notwithstanding the constraints put on their work I find that most teachers manage, as ever, to put enthusiasm, excitement and challenge into their teaching. I urge them to look into the future, recognise that today's demands on schools are quite inadequate for the likely challenges of the future – and take 'fire in the belly' beyond the classroom to demand change in the national system. Fight and fight again to win a better future for our children!

Afterword

Michael's perspective derives from a long career within which dramatic changes have occurred both in schools and in the wider national and international environment. That much is common ground among us all. We have witnessed an increasing pace of change in all parts of life.

Now Michael reminds us that we live in a global village in which our inter-dependence within and between nations is manifest. The greatest augury of this inter-dependence is surely global warming. Al Gore's landmark film of 2006, An Inconvenient Truth, begins with a scene of great and serene beauty. And then the realisation that environmental degradation threatens the whole of it. The same thought arises when we observe the frenetic reforms of the education service, so few of which address the imminence of catastrophic global warming.

Policy-making is shackled to short-term political advantage. And when initiatives are taken they are further restricted and even exacerbated by what Michael Bassey calls a 'factory' model of schooling. Conveniently practical as it is to see the world this way, as a continuous stream of quantifiable in-puts and outputs, much of the essence of education is overlooked. For example, the quality of relationships within schools and colleges is missed, screened out by the very measures employed to evaluate their effectiveness.

Michael's remedies are many. Less central diktat, more community involvement, self-sufficiency taught and practised in schools. More radical still are his suggestions for teacher education.

It is axiomatic that teachers must themselves be educated people, not robotic functionaries. For this reason, teacher education requires urgent attention in the Enquiry we propose and in the deliberations of the National Education Council.

7 Mike Golby
Seismic Shifts

Introduction

As this book was in preparation and in addition to the educational changes already mentioned, seismic shifts in popular sentiment and the political climate occurred. A number of profoundly shocking events raised fundamental questions of social justice across the whole polity. Some discern early intimations in the international Banking crisis of 2007-8. Some in a scandal concerning MPs expenses. I think Gordon Brown's encounter with Mrs Gillian Duffy another such precursor. It was an encounter between an 'educated' and an 'uneducated' person.

'She was just a sort of bigoted woman.'

History is not just one damn thing after another. It has always been the case that unexpected outcomes arise from minutiae. In our multi-media 24/7 news era, 'a week is a long time in politics' and small episodes can become charged with meaning and disproportionately contribute to a long-term course of events. The main way this happens is when a change in sentiment or the zeitgeist occurs. Retrospectively, small events can be seen as auguries of things to come. I suggest that something of this kind happened on 24 April 2010.

Prime Minister Gordon Brown, campaigning in the General Election, had taken to the streets of Rochdale. There he encountered Mrs Gillian Duffy, a lifelong Labour voter. She asked him a few questions about the national debt and immigration. He replied courteously, evading the immigration issue and she described him to reporters as *'a very nice man'*.

However, on return to his Jaguar he mumbled to an aide:

'That was a disaster-they should never have put me with that woman. Whose idea was that? Ridiculous' and

'She was just a sort of bigoted woman who said she used to be Labour'.

Unfortunately for Brown he was still wired up for sound by Sky News and within minutes his words were being broadcast nationally. The Labour Party quickly distributed Duffy's own opinions as expressed publicly to Brown: *'all these eastern Europeans what are coming in, where are they flocking from?'* as if in some extenuation. But this had no traction on opinion. He was forced to explain himself one hour later on the Jeremy Vine chat show, which he did not know was also being filmed and appeared with his head in his hands as if in despair. He was full of apologies and later he returned to Rochdale to apologise in person at Mrs Duffy's home.

Mrs Duffy was no agent provocateur. On first hearing Brown's recorded comments, she appears at once genuinely bewildered then saddened and then angry. She said

'He's an educated person, why has he come out with words like that? He's supposed to lead this country and he's calling an ordinary woman who's just come up and asked questions about what most people would ask him - he's not doing anything about the national debt and it's going to be tax, tax, tax for another twenty years to get out of this mess-and he's calling me a bigot. I thought he was understanding - but he wasn't, was he, the way he's come out with the comments?

It would be tempting at this point to discuss Brown's ineptitude in the wired media environment, Duffy's 'politically incorrect' remarks, whether the broadcaster set Brown up, the ethics of making immediately public a private conversation and the conduct of street politics generally. But here I want only to consider the way the idea of 'education' played in this small drama.

Education and social class

Until and unless 'education' is released from its class-ridden connotations of social superiority, the qualities of those who do not pursue traditional academic routes to fulfilment will remain disparaged and disrespected. This is, I must emphasise, not to say that all pursuits from pushpin to poetry are of objectively equal value. But it is to say that within the bounds of the legal and the moral what persons choose to occupy themselves with is a matter for them: and they are not to be judged by their choices in life.

There are of course complications. The lawyer, the doctor and the teacher are necessary to the functioning of civil society, as are other professions. They enjoy high status and financial security. But equally necessary are shop assistants and delivery drivers, occupations demanding their own skills and personal qualities. Pay differentials between such groups may be societally justified. But nothing justifies either the exaggerated respect for the professionals or their patronising near-contempt for their 'social inferiors'. That the one may be described as more 'educated', possessing more academic qualifications than the other, is neither here nor there.

Raymond Williams remarks

To educate was originally to rear or bring up children. .. (This) wide sense has never quite been lost but it has been specialised to organised teaching since the early seventeenth century and predominantly so since the late eighteenth century. When a majority of children had no such organised instruction the distinction between educated and uneducated was reasonably clear, but, curiously, this distinction has been more common since the development of generally organised education and even of universal education. There is a strong class sense in this use, and the level indicated by educated has been continually adjusted to leave the majority of people who have received an education below it. It remains *remarkable that after nearly a century of universal education in Britain the majority of the population should in this use be seen as uneducated or half-educated, but whether educated people think of this with self-congratulation or self-reproach, is for them to say. (*Williams, R 1976 p 95-96)

The term 'educated' has become essentially a term of approval, of status, an honorific. To deem someone 'educated' at any one time is to approve or rank them relative to their peers, the half-, the semi- and the un-educated. And this ranking is not merely descriptive, like say their ranking by weight or height. It is a ranking in respect and esteem. Of course, there are exceptions. The boorish possessor of an Oxford PPE degree is entertaining precisely because he is an exception. And there are the self-taught, the autodidacts who escape the elevating labelling of the educated. Tony Benn famously described himself in *Who's Who* as '*educated in spite of Eton*'.

Moreover, the criteria by which the honorific will be bestowed themselves vary over time. Not so long ago no one without the classical languages would be called an educated person. Later, when I was growing up in post-war Fulham an elderly neighbour who could not read called me an 'educated young man' because I could.

Like membership of the Order of Merit, to be educated is to have attained a rank. It serves as a recognition of esteem accorded to a (relatively) select few. No matter how many 'great people' Britain may claim at any one time, there will be room only for twenty-four in the Order of Merit. It's exclusive, a case of dead man's, very occasionally dead woman's, shoes.

A measure of the rarefied nature of the Order of Merit is that for every member of the Order there will be approximately 150 Knights and Dames. This latter is approximate because there are no published quotas; yet of course 'custom and practice' maintains a balance. And what we perceive in this social charade called the honours system is a hierarchy of esteem. Not to be honoured is to be disrespected. It resides in a pyramidical view of society.

It appears to me that the education system has this much in common with the honours system. It is a means of sorting the worthy from the unworthy. Not to be educated is not to be without the classical languages or without book-learning as the case may be, it is to be disrespected as a person.

Awareness of this historic legacy has intensified in the years following Brown/Duffy. Other much more substantial events such as the global financial crisis of 2008, the MPs' expenses scandal of 2009, the election of Donald Trump in the USA in 2016, the Grenfell Tower disaster of 2017 and the revelation of systematic, longstanding prejudice against the Windrush generation of British citizens have all pointed in the same direction: towards a populism taking us into untravelled country as a nation, perhaps as a civilisation.

The cumulative effect of all this has been that the whole pyramidical edifice of education is under question. The challenge to education is particularly serious in that schools and universities represent not only social authority but also the value of rationality. What future for schools and colleges in a 'post-truth' world?

We now have to account for the education of the future. What will an education that rejects its equation with social status look like? Isn't education a lifelong entitlement for all, not a one-shot window of opportunity for the few?

Education, we must repeat, is a public good and it cannot be put up for sale without compromising its essential character. Education must be a force for equality and justice, not an engine of advantage for some at the expense of others. In our *Conclusions and Recommendations*, we propose a number of urgent and immediate actions and recommend a pause for thought and a machinery for future deliberation. There must be an end to impulsive legislation and soundbite policy making. That way lies the deeper hole. We must stop digging it.

Afterword

Mike has adopted a challenging radical position. There is of course an extensive literature on the concept of education (Oakeshott, Peters, Hirst, Langford, Wilson etc) and he alludes to it elsewhere in this book. (Chapter 21 and Chapter 25). However, the search for definitions settles no disputes. In this chapter he has brought to notice the entanglement of education with social status and the somewhat deeper idea of 'respect'. Allen Parrott's and Gail Parfitt's arguments for lifelong 'community education' in Chapter 13 and Chapter 14 are visions of a future in which education is extended to include all manner of interests from the heads to the hands and the hearts of the people.

II

Lessons from Practice

8 Stella Darke

The Primary Curriculum: for better or worse?

Introduction

This paper provides an insider's account of change in primary education over a whole generation. While history was being made by the politicians, while the headlong decades passed in a welter of social, political and economic change, teachers like Stella Darke were picking up the pieces. Stella here recounts her personal experience in primary education from childhood to retirement and beyond. At her Birmingham primary school in the fifties she was a pupil in the elementary school tradition. The three Rs and the 11 plus dominated the scene. At her Teacher Training College, she learned about the 'project' method and investigative approaches to learning. Some of the thinking of the philosophers, psychologists, sociologists and historians of education became part of her own thought and practice. Entering the profession in 1970 she encountered the extreme variety, confusion and conflict of ideas and approaches characteristic of the time. But a constant factor was the idea of teacher autonomy. She valued this freedom to exercise her own professional judgment in her own classroom. When the National Curriculum arrived in 1989 it came as a considerable shock. It was too detailed, too demanding, too much at odds with what she believed to be the role of the teacher. Ofsted in 1993 added injury to insult. Far from being trusted professionals, teachers were to be inspected, their performance monitored, their schools ranked in league tables.

Stella retired in 2007. Since then, a grandchild's primary schooling has provided Stella with little or no consolation for ground lost. All of this is told in the first person, as witness to educational change by a teacher whose values survive the stronger for the challenges they have met. It will be for her successors to honour Stella Darke's struggles with their own.

The following front page headline appeared in the 3rd December 2015 issue of the Bromley Times, a weekly review of local news in the London borough:

'Secondaries are class act but primary schools must try harder'

Again, fault is found with primary education. Might the primary school curriculum be problematic?

Looking back sixty odd years I can only remember fondly my primary schooling. I attended a large, four form entry school, newly constructed by Birmingham City Council on the outskirts of the industrial city. Discipline was strict with the cane or slipper (perhaps a plimsoll) liberally used on those who failed to obey rules concerning social behaviour and attitudes to studies. The Three Rs were much in evidence with an emphasis on the 11+ examination in the last couple of years. Not all children gained selective school places but more than half did for which the school gained a good reputation in the north eastern suburb.

There was plenty of rote learning in the form of times tables, number bonds and spellings but opportunities to develop sporting, musical and artistic prowess existed in lessons and in less formal ways such as joining the school choir or representing the school in various sports. Art and craft lessons took place once a week with needlework for girls and woodwork for boys. Science was mainly nature study and history and geography were also woven into the curriculum, often in the form of comprehension exercises. Each pupil's School Report, usually given on an annual basis, listed the subjects studied with sufficient space for the teacher to give a grade and write short expressions such as good, working to capacity or could do better.

At teacher training college from 1967-1970, while time was devoted to developing my subject knowledge in the two areas of the curriculum I had chosen, the history, philosophy, sociology and psychology of education were important elements of our training as were professional studies where we were encouraged to develop a project based approach to the primary curriculum and investigative approaches to Maths and Science as could be found in the materials of the Nuffield Projects.

My first few years of teaching in primary schools felt a little like being thrown in at the deep end. There were huge variations in schools, the catchment areas they served, the head teachers and class teaching staff, the sizes of classes, the resources available, and the Local Education Authority Advisers with their particular areas of expertise.

Children in the urban areas in which I mainly taught were usually grouped into classes of around thirty five, sitting at individual desks or maybe at tables which seated half a dozen. The blackboard or roller board was a focal point in the classroom, although a carpeted area of my classrooms, as opposed to wooden floors, was reserved for children to sit for class discussions, story time, etc. Reading scheme materials and sets of resource books, often shared with other classes, were available too and the Three Rs continued to be essential elements of the children's learning. Sometimes I was required to produce formal schemes of work, usually based on a theme or topic which the school or I thought appropriate for the children's age and interests. I heard of some schools who were experimenting with open plan teaching and learning environments where teachers team taught, but I was not party to these innovations.

During this time I was allowed considerable autonomy to use my professional skills and judgement to engage pupils and develop their understanding of the world around them and their basic skills. I attempted to reflect on my practice in an informal way so that improvements could be made to my practice. (It wasn't until later in my career that I read Schon's *The Reflective Practitioner 1987*.) I felt that the relationship between myself and my pupils was of great importance and that teaching was '*not merely instruction but the systematic promotion of learning by whatever means*' (Stenhouse, 1975, p 24) I wanted my pupils to learn to be learners, to be fascinated by people, deeds, places, art, science and so on, and for their education to continue way beyond their time with me or their school lives, believing that my enthusiasm encouraged learning to take place. Children were highly praised for effort whatever their abilities. I wanted pupils to develop their confidence and self-esteem. Standardised assessments by way of spelling and reading tests were occasionally used for diagnostic purposes but keeping records of individual children's progress was not common practice in schools where I taught. However, this was before legislation was introduced to allow for the Local Management of Schools by headteachers and governors, and a National Curriculum.

I was teaching in the Junior Department of a large primary school in Devon when the folders of the National Curriculum arrived. I can still see them occupying a large shelf in my classroom, each folder containing many pages of close written text which I was supposed to assimilate and convert into meaningful chunks for schemes of work and lessons I prepared for my pupils.

In principle I didn't disagree with the notion of a National Curriculum but I had not realised until I was given the task of teaching this first National Curriculum just how cumbersome and unwieldy it would prove to be. The main aims of the 1989 curriculum were to promote the spiritual, moral, cultural, mental and physical development of pupils, and to prepare pupils for the opportunities, responsibilities and experiences of adult life. Core subjects of English, Maths and Science were established, and six foundation subjects, similar to those areas already taught in primary schools. From this one might assume that the new curriculum would be a useful tool, but the devil was in the detail. Each *Programme of Study* contained vast amounts of subject specific knowledge which primary school teachers were required, by law, to teach, and Attainment Targets by which teachers should assess pupils' progress.

I remember how hard my colleagues and I tried to make the new system work. As no-one wanted to prevent pupils from having the best possible education, many hours of our own and professional development time were devoted to creating a structure for the whole school with records of assessment that could be passed from one teacher to the next. Ideas such as a traffic light system which made use of colour coding for *'has been introduced to'*, *'is working towards'* and *'is fully conversant with the learning objective'* were formulated but I found it well-nigh impossible to implement any of this. Who could tell when learning was assured? Sometimes colleagues would disagree with me and vice versa.

To add to the difficulties I was experiencing, in 1993 the responsibility for school inspections was transferred from Her Majesty's Inspectors and Local Authorities to independent teams co-ordinated by the Office for Standards in Education (Ofsted). In my experience notice that an Ofsted team was coming created panic amongst staff. Lessons were observed and judged, systems and structures adopted by a school were scrutinised, results of nationally administered standardised tests (SATs) were used to assess a school's performance in raising standards and in relation to other schools, despite the many differences that might exist between year cohorts, schools and communities which they serve.

Some teachers may have felt comfortable with all this but, despite praise from all the headteachers for whom I had worked, I felt it was a stick to beat me, make me toe the line and castigate me if I was perceived as being poor at my job. Ofsted didn't offer help and support to a school or an individual teacher but expected a school considered substandard to design its own rescue plan which had to be agreed with the inspectors, with the threat that the school would be held to account in subsequent inspections which were likely to be only months away.

In 1997 this happened in the school in which I had taught for nine years. A large team which included Local Authority Advisers from a different county and some lay people invaded the school for a week. Everywhere you looked there were inspectors; my classroom became a lonely and scary place as they arrived with little warning and sat with clipboards in hand, taking notes without comment or smile. Under such pressure it isn't surprising that things can go awry and two long-serving members of staff had nervous breakdowns as a result.

The National Curriculum for primary schools saw many changes within the first ten years – Sir Ron Dearing's review in 1995, the introduction of Literacy and Numeracy Strategies in 1997, revision by QCA in 1999, a curriculum for the Early Years in 2000. Change was taking place at such a pace that teachers were hard pressed to keep up with them all. Professional training was cascaded from Local Authority Advisers, who had been instructed by subject specialists engaged by the various governments, to school's individual curriculum co-ordinators who in turn were supposed to inform their colleagues of new strategies, as if the politicians and their advisers could snap their fingers and change classroom practice in a few weeks.

I retired from teaching in 2007, two years before my 60th birthday. I had become disillusioned with a curriculum that was forever changing. In the previous couple of years our school had adjusted the planning so that for two weeks every term classes would be involved in integrated projects, in a style similar to the way I had taught thirty years before.

The teachers were concerned that the rigid timetable designed to accommodate the National Curriculum was having a detrimental effect on the children and that a more liberal, creative approach would improve motivation and enhance learning. I felt annoyed to be introducing strategies which I had used at the beginning of my career and knew to be successful, and that an enormous amount of my time and effort had been wasted.

I was sad to be leaving a job about which I felt passionate but felt I could no longer sustain the long hours of preparation, marking and record keeping required of me and maintain the high levels of enthusiasm and commitment that I believed my pupils deserved. As a Year 6 teacher I felt an obligation to assist my pupils to achieve the highest levels possible in the Key Stage 2 SATs not only for the children's sake but for the school as a whole and felt that I was transferring the pressure under which I was working onto them which was unfair.

In 2013 the structure of the Primary Curriculum was changed yet again and this is in operation today. Its aims are to introduce children to the essential knowledge that they need to be educated citizens and to *'the best that has been thought and said'* and help engender an appreciation of human creativity and achievement. As with the 1989 National Curriculum the devil is in the detail though.

As if three core and nine foundation subjects plus Religious Education isn't enough for 7-11 year olds, the 2013 National Curriculum document states that there is time and space in the school day and in each week, term and year to range beyond the national curriculum specifications and that the national curriculum provides an outline of core knowledge around which teachers can develop exciting and stimulating lessons to promote the development of pupils' knowledge, understanding and skills as part of the wider school curriculum.

This sounds like an enormous challenge when statutory elements of the curriculum are outlined for each year group following a linear progression as did the programmes of study in 1989, and teachers must set high expectations for every pupil, using appropriate assessment to set targets which are deliberately ambitious.

With a curriculum based on academic achievement whose benefits may only be found many years away, and the expectation that teachers will deliver the goods in a fashion akin to the rational model of teaching identified by Fish in *Quality Mentoring for Student Teachers: A Principled Approach to Practice*, published in 1995 there is a danger that developing rapport with children and playing a part in their cultural scene is forgotten instead of, as I believe, being at the forefront of teachers' minds and practices. I believe that we should be mindful of what PS Wilson said in his book *Interest and Discipline in Education, 1971*, that *'however ridiculous a child's interests may seem, there is nothing else in terms of which he (sic) can become more educated'* (p67).

Although the aims of the current national curriculum are stated I cannot find any description of why the subjects or their content have been included. Is this because the Philosophy of Education is no longer considered worthy of debate by the politicians who are in power? Certainly, it would appear that works of academics such as Dewey, Hirst, Peters and Oakeshott have been relegated to the bin. Should not all those committed to mass education seek an ideal of what it is to be 'educated' that encompasses everyone and benefits individuals and society alike?

In my view Michael Bassey's analysis of what it is to be an educated person is a good starting point. He suggests that an educated person is convivial, a social being feasting on the company of others, someone who plays an active part in their communities such as home, family and work, and recognises the benefits to be gained from such interaction.

Conviviality has a profound meaning concerned with the nature of human life. A convivial person is trying to achieve a state of deep and satisfying harmony with the world, which gives joyful meaning to life. Convivial people are striving for harmony with their environment, with their fellows and with their self. Striving for harmony with their intellectual environment convivial people seek to explore and understand the work of ideas and, where appropriate, to relate them purposefully to the world of action.

Striving for harmony with their fellows, they seek to co-operate with them; they neither exploit them nor are exploited by them; they try to live in concord with their fellows – to love and be loved. Striving for harmony with the self, convivial people have sufficient understanding of both their rationality and their emotions to develop their talents effectively; by using their talents harmoniously in relation to society and their physical and intellectual environment they become self-reliant and thus experience the joy of convivial life. (Bassey (1991) Presidential Address to the British Education Research Association)

My seven-year-old grandson began his primary education at a school in London in 2013. Initially he enjoyed every minute. He delighted in sharing his reading books with me and talking about the things he was learning. It was heartening to see his confidence blossom along with his understanding of the world he inhabits. However, now in Year 2, there is a marked change which concerned his parents. His bubbliness about going to school has been replaced with a far less enthusiastic response, feeling unwell at the start of the day or tardiness about getting organised for school. He told his mother that he didn't think the teacher liked him.

I don't know sufficient about the school or teacher and wouldn't like to pass judgement on either but perhaps the child's concern stems from the never-ending drive by teachers and schools to raise standards set by the National Curriculum and demanded by Secretaries of State for Education and Ofsted. Our grandson now has several hours of homework to complete each weekend and I notice in his reading record that notes are made about aspects of his reading that need improving. I know that he is a proficient reader for someone of his age but wonder whether the criticism is having a detrimental effect on his self-esteem.

In talking to a former teacher who was so disillusioned with her job that she decided to resign from her school two years ago and take up tutoring instead, I learnt that praise and encouragement, while still given by teachers, has to be tempered with comments which instruct the child where improvement needs to be made. The teacher referred to this as developmental marking and suggested that a primary school teacher would be admonished for not using this approach. Might this be the reason why our grandson thinks his teacher doesn't like him, remembering only the criticism rather than the praise? Only time will tell whether this is a hiccup or the start of many years of uncertainty and worry for him.

How will teachers in Bromley feel about Ofsted's conclusion that in the year 2014-15 the borough featured in the bottom 20% nationally for the proportion of pupils attending 'good' or 'outstanding' primary schools as described in the Bromley Times? Will this encourage teachers of schools labelled as satisfactory or less to feel good about themselves and continue to be enthusiastic in their work? In fact the number of pupils who attend 'good' or 'outstanding' schools is 77%, a statistic which also appears in the newspaper article but not in the headline and only in the second column. How statistics can be used!

I still feel a great empathy for primary school teachers and wish that they had a much better curriculum on which to base their teaching, one where the children were recognised as active participants rather than passive recipients. I wish that the skills of primary school teachers were recognised by those in positions of political power and their advisers, and that they were able to play a part in curriculum research and design. Without this I fear the status quo will continue for many a year and teachers and youngsters in their charge will be the poorer.

As Della Fish, writing about the development of a curriculum for the Royal College of Surgeons states:

> *Curriculum design and development is a complex educational practice. It is about both developing a policy framework, and implementing and evaluating it, such that the voices of those enacting it are influential in its refinement. This is a never ending process. Classical curriculum experts including Stenhouse, (1975), Skilbeck and Reynolds (1976), and Reid (1978), and more recent writers, like Kelly (2004) have all shown that professional judgement is at its core. There is no simple rulebook. Educational matters are values-based. All educational decisions involve collective practical reasoning about what is most valuable – firstly about the aim or goal of the curriculum, and subsequently about how best to achieve this. Developing a curriculum is a social activity and is context specific.* (Fish, D. 2004)

Afterword

Stella's paper is an insider's witness statement to the many fundamental challenges presented to the education service in primary schools over the past forty and more years. Central challenges have been offered to the profession and meeting them remains a continuing priority. They probe to the core the whole purpose of education.

First, is teacher autonomy a lost cause? No one suggests a return either to the impoverished elementary school tradition or to the romantic and unbridled progressivism in which every teacher and every school 'did their own thing'. Yet in practice there can be no alternative to placing trust in a well-educated and responsible profession.

Second, by what principles ought a national curriculum to be justified? At a democratic minimum, consultation is required. In what form? Colin Richards in Chapter 26 identifies three very different curriculums and in Section 5 there is further comment.

Third, how may teachers and schools become properly accountable for their work? The introduction of school governing bodies in 1988 opened up the possibility of local decision making and partnership with the local community. As it turns out, however, this aspiration so far as the curriculum, teaching methods and assessment go, has yet to be widely pursued. Instead, Ofsted has deployed simplistic and superficial instruments to measure and grade teachers and schools. It is true that much has been done, not least by teachers themselves to domesticate and make use of Ofsted inspections. The initial indignity of subjection to inspection of a heavy-handed and scrutineering kind has yielded to coping strategies. In some cases, schools have benefitted from the process. In many others they have been simply glad to have endured the ordeal. One may congratulate the profession as a whole for emerging with some good practice intact and some bad habits cast away. But we must never forget that there have been life-changing casualties too.

Overall, we judge the effects of the Ofsted form of inspection to have been generally dire. It is not the competence of the inspectors that is to blame but the entirely empirical model of the inspection process. There is insufficient room for non-measurable features of school, such as teaching style, the quality of the pupil-teacher relationship and the ethos of the school. Ofsted reinforces the tyranny of the measurable, tending to demoralise teachers and divert attention from the important and intangible to the trivial and the measurable.

The whole apparatus is part of a scenario in which 'standards' in education are 'driven up' by means of competition, principally for students. The poorest schools fail to attract 'consumers', that is parents, and they fail. Ofsted results are key features of the 'market' for education. That is why some schools erect celebratory banners outside on receipt of an 'outstanding' result.

And what, incidentally, about 'outstanding' as a category? At Garrison Keillor's Lake Woebegone all children are above average. That should be our goal!

To be utterly serious now. An ignorant, narrow and philistine understanding of education is at fault here. Education is emphatically not simply a personal service delivered to parents. The customer is not king. Nor is education simply a service industry in the supply train to economic growth. Of course, schools do fulfil some of these functions. But they are no more than people processing factories unless they also educate. The implications of this view suffuse this whole publication.

9 Will Taylor

Towards Teaching: Into Teaching

Introduction

Here Will Taylor takes an autobiographical approach to his formation as a teacher. Paradoxically, his own schooling provided him with an impetus towards teaching, albeit warily, shown here through a number of memorable critical incidents. It is also clear that educational vision is not separable from the political. Will's feelings about the eleven-plus derive from his rapidly developing sense of social justice. As a late entrant to teaching Will was receptive to the educational theory of the day in the shape of the foundation disciplines, especially the philosophy of education.

In the second part of his paper Will discusses his two substantial teaching posts and his subsequent activity as an educational researcher. His two secondary schools strike a set of illuminating contrasts. Each is a product of its history and its community: the first a well-established comprehensive school, the second still in the throes of reorganisation as such. Both schools were subject to the local influence of a major independent school. While the former was probably an excellent school in which to begin a teaching career the latter was not stabilised at the point where it could contemplate a form of organisation which some deem definitional of the comprehensive idea, mixed ability teaching.

Towards Teaching

I was born in June 1939 to a qualified carpenter who had recently been dismissed on completion of his work on half a street of tiny terraced houses. He had rented one of them in 1937, when he and my mother were married after a long courtship and engagement. On marrying she had been required to give up a responsible, secure job as a telephonist in the international exchange in London. After losing his own skilled job he worked as a railway labourer until conscripted to build airfields in East Anglia and subsequently into the army in 1941.

Not simply an only child, I was an only grandchild. Moreover, after my father had been conscripted I was the principal focus for grandparents and numerous great aunts. My mother was effectively a single mother. She read to me, she began to teach me to read, she encouraged me to learn.

My first encounter with education was a good one. In 1944 on my first day at the village school, a kindly elderly lady teacher asked if anyone could spell the word 'gnome'. I could, and she gave me a brandy snap, a delicacy I had never previously encountered. I never looked back. Very soon I became an avid reader. I joined the junior public library as soon as I was seven.

My primary school was governed by the 11+. I was among the top few in the strictly streamed classes of 48 or so pupils. In 1950, when I was ten everybody in my 'top' class 'passed' the 11+ tests. Surprisingly few arrived in the grammar school with me. It should, firstly, be remembered that 'passing' was a function of the number of selective school places available; and secondly that selective schools would also choose among eligible pupils. What my mother promised at the interview with the headmaster I know not. However, I eluded the filters that excluded so many of the classmates who also passed the initial 11+.

The Boys' Grammar School was two form entry, streamed A and B about thirty to a class with a small sixth form, a total of less than 400. I found myself in the A stream. I did quite well, often being in the top few in the regular marksheets that were posted in each form room. The school was competitive, disciplined and formal.

I enjoyed French and Art and sometimes English, I was already an avid and fluent reader, was quite good at Maths and most other subjects. In the second year the A forms dropped Woodwork and took either Latin or German. German was the choice I was offered. My progress in that subject was somewhat inhibited when on 3rd April 1952, the German teacher, who was my form teacher snapped, *'There's no need to sit there dreaming at the back Taylor, just because your father died yesterday!'* My dad had fallen off a factory roof he was building early the previous morning and died in hospital that afternoon. I think my performance in school dipped for a bit after that.

Three years later I eventually passed GCE German but not with the fluency I had in French, which was my best result.

The grammar school had a profound influence on my life, not entirely for the good. Aged 14 and questioned by a careers teacher, I announced an ambition to go to art school. *'No, we don't do that sort of thing from this school...'* was his immediate reply. Somehow, I was identified as a candidate for naval officer training. (I was a keen swimmer, I could row, and had enjoyed learning to sail a lugsail dinghy at a scout camp when 12).

I was eventually lauded as a working-class boy who had done well and been selected for Dartmouth Royal Naval College. This brought fame in the Daily Mirror, the local paper, and pride at my school and in my mother. All I had to do was pass a couple of A levels. The Navy promised to give my widowed mother money to keep me in the sixth form and that became a burden, a heavy millstone.

I remained an avid and wide-ranging reader and sought unorthodox artistic and cultural experiences that did not amount to an organised radical awareness. Rebelliousness was orthodox and self-indulgent along American themes explored by James Dean. I was early into modern jazz, which protected me from Elvis Presley.

In September 1955 following a very good set of O Level results, the contract with the Navy came into force and I joined the school Sixth Form aiming for Pure Maths, Applied Maths, Physics and Art, three of which were deemed most suitable for my intended career. Neither French, which I enjoyed nor English Literature, which I love featured as a goal. I had been shocked by a remark of my French teacher, *'I hope to God I'm not going to find you in my Sixth Form next year, Taylor!'* which wiped out an obvious academic progression. I now regard that as casual and ironic but it diverted me from a clear and promising set of options at a moment of some vulnerability

The A Level programme damaged my self-confidence, for I struggled. I protected myself from the difficulties I found by immersing myself in Literature and the Arts. My school, fearing I might fail to achieve the necessary A levels entered me for the Civil Service Examinations in which I did quite well thanks partly to an interesting question on TS Eliot. I also began to develop a deeper and more critical political awareness, partly through my contacts with students from a college of art and partly because of the turbulent public controversies relating to the real possibility of nuclear war.

I had begun to harbour serious doubts about my intended naval career early in 1956 but was conscious that my mother would have to repay the money they had given her. This became an increasing and troublesome burden. Suez shocked me and, angry, I found myself firmly with those who denounced the action and I nearly came to blows with a very good friend who supported the action as strongly as I opposed it. In the argument he pointed out that my attitude was inappropriate for one who intended to become an officer like those who were taking part in the action. He was right. I could no longer wish to obey orders without question at all times nor to issue such orders.

From then on I was sorely troubled by my projected direction. I rapidly embraced a latent radicalism seemingly suppressed for several years. Deliberate failure of A levels in the summer of 1957 would probably have led to release my mother from the financial obligation but now the Civil Service papers sufficed. In the end I passed in Pure and Applied Maths and Art, failing Physics. Before those results came out I was very depressed about the project to which I had assented. I was lucky to be rescued from a serious intent to suicide, one evening in early summer near St Ives, by a wonderfully warm and musky smelling art student from Corsham.

I fulfilled my obligation to begin my training in September 1957 but contrived my expulsion within a few months by going absent without leave at an early opportunity. That was complicated and led to arrest and eventually a hilarious train trip back to Dartmouth under escort. In so doing I also changed from local hero to pariah. That too was interesting, and in many ways distressing, especially for my formerly proud mother. Later still, as one of the very last cohort to be called, I refused National Service and became a conscientious objector. I accepted registration for alternative directed work, for I thought prison would impose too much strain on my already damaged mother.

When I emerged after two years and sixty days mostly working in the huge mental hospital in which my grandfather had died in 1955 I was unemployable within the expectations of my education. There were many more compliant young men with a couple of A levels. I had worked with essentially decent people, some of whom had strongly differing views from mine. Over the next few difficult years that pattern was repeated, with some exceptions.

I had certainly been enlightened by what I now regard as a modest grammar school and later by a small and interesting coterie of friends. That later, after a considerable period of turbulence, adventurous romanticism, and some seriously downwardly mobile excursions, I entered training to become a teacher must, nevertheless, be attributed to my secondary education and what I took from it. For a long time, I had resisted suggestions from well-meaning friends paraphrased as, *'Well, you could always teach'*, as an unworthy impulse. However, I eventually succumbed.

Reluctance to embrace the responsibility of teaching had to some degree originated in the apprehension that the turbulent course of my life had been driven by the rejection and substitution of a clear ambition by a so-called careers teacher who never taught me, nor had previously met me. That had almost led to a premature end. Such responsibility, including the influence of casual irony on unsophisticated minds, gave me pause.

I have volunteered the above somewhat embarrassing autobiography to explain the context of a tortuous approach to teaching as a career. Not only did I not grasp, but none of my teachers seems to have been aware of, either my unsuitability for what the school had volunteered me for, nor of my increasingly evident unease.

During the spring of 1967, when my wife and I were able to apply for a mortgage, qualifying through two year's work at an adequate rate of pay I tried again. I wrote to St Luke's College, Exeter asking for a preliminary discussion about my suitability as a candidate for the two-year Cert. Ed. course which was advertised. An entertaining conversation with the Principal led to an offer.

I carried quite a lot of educational baggage into that entrance. Moreover, I had absorbed, developed and considered certain attitudes and values that I still regard as important, among them

- a lot of decent, intelligent, highly skilled and admirable people are damaged by schooling.

- the hierarchical labelling of individuals is both wicked and wasteful

- spoken language is a major factor in classifying individuals

At the time that I entered training, 1967, there had already been a considerable furore over the then Labour government's decision to encourage comprehensive secondary education. *Circular 10/65* had resulted in great waves of protest from supporters of selective grammar schools who insisted that to reorganise thus would lower standards all round.

I embarked on a two-year course of teacher training at St Luke's College, Exeter. That mutated to a four-year B Ed course from which I emerged with distinction to become an English teacher.

I flourished intellectually and psychologically from the course at St. Luke's. I was being asked to listen, read, write, think and discuss. I still remember, exclaiming with joy, *'They're paying me to write essays about Hamlet!'*

I was able to undertake courses in English and Art that far exceeded the A levels I had been guided away from at 16, and that was joy indeed. Moreover, the series of lectures on education as seen through various filters - psychology, philosophy, history and sociology could be made challenging.

At the college I found myself quite unusual in appreciating the lectures on education. Many of the younger students, and indeed several of the older in my group, seemed to find them irrelevant to their preoccupation with the main academic subjects they intended to teach. To me it seemed otherwise.

I flourished in my English and Art lectures and the work I so much enjoyed, and I did very well. Yet it was from the history, sociology, psychology and philosophy of education elements that its rationale had to be derived. That was where we might seek to discover how society dared to compel all its young to participate in a process that would discriminate among them and have huge influence on the direction and purpose of their lives.

Some of the lectures were dull, but the ideas were not. I made good friends with Bill Josebury who taught us philosophy. We got on well and would argue and discuss in his study, or over exceptionally good cheese and onion rolls in the Clifton Inn, long after our timetabled afternoon sessions. He was a good and demanding thinker and often lubricated that with whisky from his desk drawer.

I was protected from imitating his excess by my need to drive thirty miles home in my rusty minivan and to some degree by the practice I'd had working with others with similar addictions.

I am grateful to Bill. He made me think. I developed principles and questions that held good for my teaching career. I would like to be able to say that I lived up to them.

The four-year B.Ed was a good course. I truly enjoyed and benefited from it. I emerged with what remains a set of perplexing questions.

- How can we propose education as essential for life and then decide that many, even most, fail?

- If, when setting out that procedure, we know that, by design, most will fail, how dare we compel them to do so?

- What, other than making them mutually suspicious, is a legitimate rationale for separating one group of children from another at 11 when they have been together before that time?

- Is it necessary to define three (or more) distinct types of people in our society – tribes, which, despite their common humanity, cannot occupy the same spaces? Could it be that, if that seems to be so, there is something wrong with the spaces?

- Is democracy visible in the arrangements our society makes, or tolerates, for its young. If not, why not?

- Who is or are more equal than others and why? Is it the function of something we could reasonably identify as education to define and maintain such distinctions?

I emerged with a B.Ed with distinction, with which I was pleased. Whether that self-satisfaction was justified was to be tested by the next phase, actually becoming a teacher!

Into Teaching

My first post, in 1971, at the age of 32, was as an English teacher in a Comprehensive school in a small and attractive town in South Devon. The school was an established Community College formed in the mid-1960s from the amalgamation of an ancient Boys' Grammar School and two single sex Secondary Modern Schools. Its sites were complex. The two former Secondary Moderns, either side of a main road to the west of the town, had been modernised and a footbridge across the road linked them. There were a number of dramatic new buildings. Lower School, was principally used and occupied by younger pupils and overseen by a Head of Lower School. Main School was used mostly for 14-16-year-old pupils and contained the administrative offices and the Headmaster.

More than half a mile away stood a fine Georgian building in the middle of the town and former home to the quite small Boys' Grammar School, which held the Sixth Form.

The school roll was swollen to 1700. Schools of that size were deemed necessary to provide sufficient A level students to attract well qualified teachers. It remains difficult to escape from numerical hierarchy in our land. A fleet of up to 32 buses scooped up and delivered pupils from villages around that area of South Devon collecting them, suitably improved, for return every afternoon.

It was a dynamic community school that had quickly developed a good reputation in the district. There were no other state secondary schools nearby and the neighbouring private school was ultra-progressive. The school was a good example of a Community College even if access to its facilities was rather restricted for some of those who came in and out on the only bus that visited their villages.

Two newly qualified teachers joined the English department in September 1971. My colleague was a published poet and Cambridge graduate with a PGCE, and I came with my shiny new B.Ed degree, an unknown accolade. Some of the existing staff had misgivings about the head's recruitment policies and one, the head of another department, made that clear when he asked me from which circus I had been imported.

In 1971 the promised (1944) raising of the school leaving age to 16 had yet to happen, which meant that a proportion of pupils might leave before encountering any examination, though CSE had been introduced in 1965 to meet the criticism that 75% had no school leaving qualification. Most subjects were taught in ability sets and there was little pressure for mixed-ability grouping. There were some classes comprising only those who would leave at 15 and wanted to.

The classes from that group that I encountered as a new and trembling teacher were predominantly male and lively, somewhat contemptuous of school and eager to be rid of it. They had 'failed' at education, that noble pursuit deemed essential to a proper human life by many of those who had most significantly succeeded.

I valued, as I still do, the idea of education as an individual and public good. In a tragic manner, that I continued to encounter throughout my teaching career, so, it seemed, did they. For they described themselves as failures, or worse as 'thick' or stupid. The clear aggression of many presented difficulties for a new teacher. It was effectively subdued very strictly and often contemptuously by well-practised colleagues.

Yet that aggression seemed to represent some spirited rejection of the experience of school placed upon them. They wanted no more of it – nor indeed did it of them at that date.

It was difficult to convince them that I was in any way on their side and much more importantly that I did not share the notion that they were human failures.

Driving them in tightly packed groups of 8 around the school roads and car park in a borrowed 40-ton Volvo tractor unit certainly improved relations. However, an apt comparison might be with the contemporary comment, by a young biker prone to death-inviting antics around the North Circular, who responded to a BBC question about an evangelical vicar who sometimes rode with them. *'I don't care what kind of bike he's got! He's still an effing vicar!'*

The incident also elicited a strident remark across the staff room from the teacher interested in my circus origins – *'Mr Taylor, would you mind moving your visual aid, the buses can't get in!'*

In the end I got on quite well with him. He liked to joke and invented a cynical collective noun for head teachers – *A lack of principals.*

I did establish a rapport and some sort of dialogue with the challenging early leavers. There was a lot of talking, which at the time I may have characterised as 'discussion', that revealed a wide range of useful skills and experience among the pupils. These were not people who should have been written off. Yet the mechanisms that had drawn them, compulsorily, into this net, had been organised to discriminate among them and deliver certain proportions of failure, for that was, and is, the language used in relation to a prolonged activity called education otherwise presented as essential to satisfactory life.

The generality of such pupils I met in my career as a teacher have not for the most part failed to grow to adult humans or to live, become parents, drive cars, work, love or otherwise survive. Some of them have, I know, continued to develop skills they already had and have succeeded thoroughly in the conventional measure of earning and possessions. Most will be well-balanced enough. Some will have encountered catastrophic traumas, some become criminals, some will have died. Some may even have become teachers. In short, they are reasonably representative of the human condition in this country.

Yet when I encounter one of them, whose face I may just recognise though he or she certainly knows mine, any conversation beyond greeting is likely to elicit a comment that recalls a sense of failure at school. Quite often that seems even to overshadow what looks like considerable 'success' and contentment in adult life. It is shocking to have made a career from imposing such a burden on so many, especially when trying not to do just that.

After the eventual raising of the school leaving age in 1972 the school generally continued along 'setted' lines, that is to say they were placed in classes according to their perceived ability. Most of my own teaching was with pupils following a full range of examination courses, CSE, GCE-O level and GCE-A level. There was a sense of hierarchy, but the ethos of the school was strongly comprehensive and inclusive. There were some discussions about mixed-ability classes but there was no real drive for radical change. My recollection is that most of the former Secondary-Modern school staff seemed to be against it. The raising of the leaving age meant that all pupils would be involved in examinations classes and all could leave at the same age. That provided a tenuous kind of 'parity of esteem'.

The English team found much to like in the opportunities provided in the CSE examinations and pursued it with enthusiasm, even considering using it across the board, given that a CSE grade 1 was equal to an O level pass. Governors were not impressed.

Meanwhile the Sixth Form was widening its scope and accessibility. The concept of the Community College brought adults to my A level classes, which was an enriching experience for all. I ran courses on film-making and alternative technology where we built a water-heating solar panel from scrap around the school. I still have scald mark on the back of one hand.

I also took over from the head as representative of the school on the committee of the prestigious local Arts Society, helping to select films for the BFI cinema. I supported the school's excellent orchestra by driving the bus the school purchased to events and competitions. I helped organise their visit to the town's twins in France and Germany, driving the school minibus with bulky instruments and students who felt sick in the big hired coach.

I was learning my trade and enjoying it. I prospered in the easy-going atmosphere of the town that influenced much of the feeling at the school. It seemed natural and easy to engage with pupils, asking thought-provoking questions and trusting them, sharing delight in literature or aspects of life and learning. It was a good place to be, for it seemed to be developing on behalf of its students. I also took on numerous other responsibilities in the school.

A good example of how easy relationships had developed quite soon comes from April 26th 1972. I went to meet a 4th year class and just as they began to arrive was summoned (via a breathless secretary) to the local hospital, where my wife was in prolonged labour to produce our third daughter and had demanded I return.

I wrote on the blackboard, *'Gone to have a baby, stay calm – back later'*.

Clearly substitute teaching cover was provided, but nobody minded my leaving at full speed.

In 1976 I was appointed head of English at a grammar school in another part of Devon and designate head of English for the new 13-18 comprehensive school to open the following year.

I was sorry to leave my first school, I had been very happy there, as had my family. However, I was encouraged to move on since I had started at 32, was now 37 and was, as the estate agents say, 'ripe for development'.

Looking back on the values I learned or developed in those early years and how they fit with those I claim to have gathered as a student. I am abashed how few were followed with sufficient passion.

My early support for comprehensive education had been confirmed. (I had done teaching practice in a Boys' Secondary Modern School and a Mixed Grammar School).

Even though there was setting by ability in that first comprehensive school there was a strong sense of community and friends continued to mix even if they were separated in classes for some subjects. The school and most of the pupils belonged to the locality. It was a genuine Community College with no local rivals. It is much more difficult to organise a heterogenous mix in urban areas where natural communities are often united by income level as well as proximity.

The department I had joined was interesting and dynamic. I do not recall any discussions that implied that any pupils were inferior human beings, nor was there much nostalgia for the grammar School.

Into the cold

The second community was different. The town had a rich tradition of educational provision enabled by local benefactors. There was a prestigious private school, for long an enormous presence in the town. The Boys' Grammar School name went back nearly as long and had worked for most of the twentieth century in partnership with a girls' secondary school before merging as a co-educational Grammar School in 1953.

The long-standing presence of a large textile factory in the town and extensive factory housing had changed the nature of a significant market borough and provided relatively secure employment, if comparatively low expectations. There was also an important engineering works.

The planned and much delayed reorganisation as a response to *10/65* was complex, and curiously comparable with private education, comprising 5-7 First schools, 8-12 Middle schools and a 13-18 Upper Comprehensive to be formed on the site of the former Secondary-Modern school. The pattern represented one that had existed long before in the town's history. It is important to point out that the same model had been established in state schools elsewhere in Britain with considerable success, notably in Leicestershire. Where my first school felt the influence of a private progressive school the second felt the weight of prestigious public school.

By 1976 reorganisation had been very much delayed but would finally take place in 1977, which explained my appointment. The original distinguished head designate had resigned in frustration and moved elsewhere. There had been much wrangling with the adjacent FE College over sixth form and accommodation, a problem that was never solved during the 13 years I was involved.

It was clear that there remained a good deal of local opposition to *comprehensive* reorganisation, including among the groups of staff from both the secondary modern school and the grammar.

Teaching at the Grammar school was not especially challenging. Some of the younger pupils were quite rude, seemingly identifying me as the enemy who was to destroy their elite position and throw them in with their inferiors. Others were apprehensive and asked how it was in comprehensive schools. It seemed there had always been antagonism between the secondary modern and the grammar school, even though most had attended the same primary schools. The spectre of my own school experience was not much help, though the positive experience of my first post gave me hope.

The new school opened in September 1977 with two hundred more pupils than it would ever have again, the result of a failure to complete buildings and changes in one contributing community. There was a degree of chaos.

An interesting event was the final prizegiving for the former Grammar School, held shortly after the opening of the new school in the presence of all pupils of the new. I had been deployed at the rear of the hall where some sturdy potential dissidents lurked. When the senior teacher on the stage announced that a certain individual had been awarded an Exhibition at Caius College one of them remarked to me, glancing at his programme *'Whazzat then? Is he a painter or something? Can't even spell 'keys'.* One of the others remarked that there had been no mention of a young man who had been recruited to the squad of a major football team.

I tried, *sotto voce,* to explain that this was all to do with the former grammar school that was now a part of this one. It was quite clear that, however it had been intended, these examples of a pursuit of excellence, presented as they were, did nothing to integrate the student body. Nor did it much help integration in the staff room.

Those were turbulent times. In the wider nation the Callaghan government was struggling. A right-wing backlash against comprehensive education was popular in the press and carried weight among the parents of actual and formerly potential grammar school pupils. A very popular song proclaimed, disgracefully ungrammatically, that *'We don't need no education'*, likening the experience to one of forced conformity and loss of identity.

The IRA bombing campaign had intensified and gave rise to occasional bomb scares in the school, usually by telephone and usually by pupils. They could not be ignored and the whole school would be lined up in the playgrounds to be counted, causing great disruption to lessons.

The English Department I was supposed to lead contained three former grammar school colleagues one of whom was my predecessor, now a deputy head. There was also a very senior and experienced woman teacher now in charge of the Sixth Form and a younger earnest and devout man. There were also three from the former secondary modern, its former head of English and two very able younger teachers, a man and a woman. Everybody knew more than me.

From a list of applicants so long that we virtually resorted to discounting any that used green ink we soon recruited a very good young woman teacher and a young man who moved on quite quickly.

Meetings were sometimes tense, the former head of English from the secondary modern made it clear that he would have been a better choice for my job. He may have been right. We were very dissimilar; opposites politically and by temperament. He was a strict disciplinarian who believed in corporal punishment. We gave him the title of Associate head of department and he and I consulted frequently. The weight of the deputy head and head of sixth form was significant, he seemed to want to keep the grammar school flag flying high. Later the department was augmented by the presence of an ambitious Director of Studies and a replacement deputy head.

Very early on, after prolonged discussion the department accepted a very short and simple list of concerns proposed by me, not precisely as a mission statement, as exemplifying five significant aspects of language in use. 'We are concerned with, *Listening, speaking, reading, writing and - thinking.* These were vital as a means of *learning to learn'*.

Professional development, indeed the notional 'professionalisation' of teachers was a genuinely interesting aspect of my work and my experience in the early 1980s.

James Callaghan's 'Great Debate' and Shirley Williams' reforms had not impacted upon the school. It would be fair to claim that the English department was alert to ideas and keen to investigate and I believe I can take some credit for that. We had spent quite a lot of time discussing the different English languages of our pupils after consideration of Bernstein's work on linguistic discrimination which gave rise to much discussion about the *defensive* use of the *'restricted code'*. Despite such highlights the department was quite riven by opposing opinions.

Even so, we were very disappointed when a lead role in the consideration of *'Language Across the Curriculum'* related to the *Bullock Report, A Language for Life* was officially forbidden to English departments. Other users had to take the lead. It was a good principle that was not followed with great vigour. We were permitted to join discussions and found it too easy to take over, for we were interested. The processes of analysing text books from other subjects for basic readability were instructive and revealing.

One finding was that the history books in current use required very advanced reading skills to access not particularly difficult information and ideas. Some subjects in a non- selective school effectively selected those who would take the more prestigious examinations by using unnecessarily complicated textbooks.

We agreed to encourage group work, and discussion, and considered how to make good use of quite large classrooms to vary desk arrangements. I favoured a horseshoe shape or near circle so nobody was looking at the back of anybody's head, the open centre of the curve contained, as it were, the matter of any discussion. We were all involved, teacher and pupils together. Where groups of four or five were working together it was easy enough to put desks together. I found that collaborative work worked very well as did several colleagues. However, I knew that some other members of the department much preferred classic rows and that one indeed was adamant against changing from his established practice. Nothing was compulsory.

Our examinations results were generally good overall, frequently very good with the CSE groups. The A- Level Literature courses progressed predictably and quite successfully, though there was criticism of our liberal entry policies, which were spelled out quite clearly to potential students. It was never a homogenous department, there were several axes of antagonism. Most of my colleagues liked me, which made me a focus of disagreements. Some of them privately questioned my abilities. They may have been right. In general, I got on well with my pupils, as did most of my departmental colleagues.

Using the school minibus I drove two annual parties of fifteen sixth formers to the school's twin town in Germany. It was in what was still the British Sector, not far from the Luneberg Heath, where tanks would practice endlessly. A lady complained to me that she had lived all her life with the sound of gunfire and wished it would stop. Our visits to East Berlin were fascinating.

However, the point of this recollection is to record the experience of tri-partite education that seemed to work as well as it might. British occupation and oversight had imposed the mode and the Germans had enacted what they took it to mean and seemed to have managed a considerable degree of parity of esteem – certainly mutual respect. There was a High School (Grammar), a wonderfully equipped

Technical School, and a Realschule (secondary modern). There was no eleven plus, pupils generally proceeded according to teacher recommendation and parental choice. If a parent insisted against advice the child could enter the high school for the first year but if they failed to prosper would change school thereafter. The Realschule was very well equipped, with well-qualified teachers and a full modern curriculum, many of the pupils spoke very good English. All schools had final and respected examinations which provided access to further training and education, goals that seemed to motivate pupils at all levels. There seemed to be little hierarchical or class preoccupation. The three schools, the town library and museum, the splendid indoor and outdoor swimming pools and the sports field around which there was a high quality 400 metre running track were grouped near one another in the town.

Back at the ranch, we tried some ingenious variations from the norm. Most of the department felt that better work could be done with smaller classes. Once the school roll had settled there were number of huts that were very rarely used. We managed to organise half year groups into classes of fifteen in those huts while I and another teacher ran group sessions in the school hall. It was a worthwhile experiment. However, it was squashed when we were informed that we had no right to use the empty huts. They were subsequently locked.

We also considered the idea of entering every pupil for the mode three CSE examination we ran very successfully. It was interesting and flexible and carried an oral element. We knew such an idea would not be favoured by governors and many parents but welcomed the discussion about how we valued all our pupils. There were significant implications for the grading process that were problematic.

My biggest leadership failure was not to implement mixed-ability classes with my casting vote after a series of bitter and long departmental meetings. I felt that some of the teachers would fail to cope and that this would do more harm than good to our work, which would then have been out of synch with the rest of the so-called academic curriculum. To continue setting would, I imagined, be a broadly equitable approach to our pupils. I am not wedded to the idea of mixed-ability groups as the only way of teaching though I had used it very successfully as had some of my colleagues. There is an awkward symbolic difficulty when grouping pupils in ways that acknowledge their diversity and individual needs; somehow it nearly always seems or becomes discrimination. The point being advocated was to demonstrate to the pupils and the outside world a disdain for the hierarchical tendency of educational provision and a sense of respect for all individuals.

My more progressive colleagues were shocked and lost faith in me. I was also troubled.

After that meeting I sat in my car outside the local supermarket for more than two hours without realising it, until I arrived home much later than expected. I was, I suppose very depressed.

Not long after that I was seconded for a year to undertake a Master's Degree at Exeter University under the tutelage of Mike Golby. It now occurs to me that there was some kind of official gerrymandering. I remain grateful. It was a very good course, demanding and stimulating. Mike was interested in school governors and Kenneth Baker was about to launch the National Curriculum. We set up a Governor Support Centre at St Luke's and undertook Governor training. I was granted another year's secondment to help Lord Young of Dartington try to find alternative meaningful educational uses for the collapsed Dartington Hall School. He was promoting the idea of an 'open school' reflecting the Open University. I also continued to run the fledgling Governor Centre.

It seemed that Joslyn Owen, then CEO Devon, was minded to outsource governor training to a responsible independent educational location in the university. It seemed I might be further seconded. At that time there were messages coming from the school that it was overstaffed, especially with teachers of my seniority. My department was in line to lose staff and they were concerned about who that might be. I was enjoying life at the university and running evening courses and conferences for governors.

Joslyn Owen died suddenly from a heart attack. Sometime later I was called in to the office of the new CEO who explained that policy had changed. The authority would take over governor training and support. I had the choice of resuming my post, thereby making redundant one of my colleagues, or looking for redeployment within the county while retaining my grade. The new option seemed interesting and I took union advice. There were two posts for which I was eminently suited by experience. Sadly, the process was botched and I returned as a supernumerary teacher in my own department. A year later at the age of 50 I volunteered to accept a reasonably tempting offer of premature retirement on the grounds of redundancy. That last word was difficult to bear, and psychologically damaging.

After a short period of retreat, and recovery, I found relatively precarious but professionally rewarding work at the School of Education ultimately leading to EU funded projects in remote and interesting places. I returned from Mongolia to retire from teaching in 2008 at the age of 69.

Afterword

Will offers a graphically rich account of his life in education. He became politically aware in his teens and the values he formed then have been continuously at play in his professional work. Without values a teacher is an empty shell. But there is value pluralism among teachers as the controversy over 'mixed ability' teaching exemplifies. This is surely healthy so long as it is handled collegially, and a school retains stability.

Why did Will so clearly prosper in his first teaching post while as head of an English department elsewhere he met resistance? To address such questions is to probe the relation between school and society in its intricate local context. Teachers need great sensitivity to the cultural contexts in which they work and to the challenge of justifying their own cultural offering. No amount of 'on-the-job' training can be equal to this task for teacher education. It is time to re-vitalise the educational theory that offered Will the resources to argue his case.

Each Way Bets and Individual Needs

Introduction

Here David Atton formerly headteacher of a large urban comprehensive school, describes a set of in-school effects resulting from the phenomenon of official testing of school achievement. The publication of school exam results must rest upon certain criteria and the chosen level of success has been Grade 4 and now rising to Grade 5 or better at GCSE. One consequence of this is that schools may pay particular attention to pupils on the border of that achievement in order to boost the school's rating. As a corollary of that, less attention will inevitably be devoted to pupils comfortably above or nowhere within reach of the watershed Grade.

The following are comments made by teachers.

'With extra help I think she might improve her Maths grade'.

'He'll never get a grade 4 or 5 no matter what we do'.

'There is too much going on in his life for anything we do to make a difference'.

'There is more chance she will make greater progress in her English than he will, so I propose she gets the extra help available and is given a mentor'.

Good teachers work tirelessly to enable each student to realise full individual potential. Respect for them used to go with the job. Now it can be overwhelmed by an intense accountability that has an accepted role to play when part of a balanced and considered approach but can become contorted in ways that become unhelpful and debilitating in the current continuously intensifying climate that too easily overwhelms, giving rise to exhaustion and stress. The risk then becomes to endanger the real imperatives, still seeking to provide good teaching for all children whilst, in the service of school accountability, being obliged to move specific focus away from some in favour of others. This can then heighten the dilemma of the best interests of the institution and its teachers taking precedent over those of individual students. This gap risks widening further to influence curriculum, guidance and examination choices, more influenced by likely data outcomes than clear focus upon what could be most appropriate and advisable, whilst also keeping all doors open to potential future career pathways. The game that can trump all is survival, to get through the next data scrutiny and Ofsted inspection.

We were warned long ago by W. Edwards Deming (1994) that people with targets and jobs dependent upon meeting them will probably meet the targets - even if they have to destroy the enterprise to do it. The enterprise that matters here comes in offering a good education in the broadest and most appropriate sense for every child. Just because the computer enables data processing in a manner not previously possible, it does not follow that we must therefore apply this relentlessly without frontier, setting targets and tracking progress in the quest for maximizing academic outcomes in English and Maths, addressing the competitiveness of global comparison and intensifying teacher accountability. Most families hope for their children to achieve to potential. Many appreciate just how competitive our global world has become. With increased computing power and artificial intelligence developing robots that intensify this race for good jobs and well-paid employment, the demand upon young people in every country is increasing the threat to their mental health and quality of life. Is the only possible way forward to jeopardise this further towards a reckless international race that eventually exhausts human capacity? Does a healthy and fulfilling life not rely upon a sensible set of balances for all of us? Must we all adopt the 'tiger approaches' of the far-east, now being adopted by some academies in this country?

The most insidious effects are intensified by the manner in which schools are held to account via the progress and achievement profile of each year group. With the imperative that a certain and increasing percentage of each cohort is required to secure a pre-determined standard, given their limited budgets and resources, teachers and schools have no sensible option but to focus upon those relatively few underachieving students whose improved outcomes might just tip the balance towards that all-important profile percentage target being achieved. So, armed with their laptops and data crunching programs, groups of teachers gather around tables to review the runners and riders. The challenge focuses relentlessly upon - if given a bit more help and support, which children might just improve most across the target borderline landscape? Which would prove a 'waste' of that precious extra resource? Which would not respond sufficiently and which are sure bets that can be left to the normal classroom provision? Whether it be Pupil Premium, grade borderlines, 'Progress 8' or whatever is devised to improve upon it, the proper focus upon each individual is skewed towards the key 'marginal constituencies' when the crucial outcome measures are in focus. The all-important data becomes pre-eminent as individual students become foot soldiers for the regiment and sacrifices are often self-inflicted in the cause of promoting others to deliver the ultimate GCSE victory, or not, each August. The crucial C/D grade boundary used to focus attention relentlessly upon this particular battleground: Progress 8 makes this less well-defined as it encompasses the potential progress of all students, demanding ever more subtle analysis and judgement upon how to deploy inevitably finite resource in an increasing complexity of progress battleground targeting: where do we most hopefully place our each-way bets now to maximize hoped for GCSE outcomes?

Good teaching and effective support are the keys, whilst careful analysis of the realities for individual students can too often show that underachievement is due to specific circumstances and experiences in their lives beyond the school's control: family trauma or breakdown, bereavement, physical or mental illness, unfortunate life experiences, including homelessness, can all damage the progress predicted 5 years previously by the KS2 SATs. These factors can be disproportionately experienced where school catchment areas become more challenging. There is also a particular challenge when the primary schools have worked hard with borderline pupils and extended them · beyond individual achievement capable of being sustained and built upon at secondary level in anything remotely resembling a supposed and consistent linear progression, leaving hot-housed KS2 outcomes that set an unrealistic baseline too high for the child's genuine ability and potential to be extended significantly through that turbulence of adolescence. Those KS2 predictors have assumed a majesty and pedigree of assumed reliability unmatched by any other assessment regime ever: no margin of error is allowed to cast doubt upon the individual progress over the next five secondary years that they herald and confidently predict. In the real world, learning is a messy business that interweaves in unpredictable ways with ever variable individual development and life stories that we can all reminisce about in our own lives given the benefits of hindsight.

Education is dependent upon value judgements and long experience shows us how whatever is said or proposed will find its critics. To question and criticise is easy, especially in a centrally controlled system and approach of the type developed over the last 30 years, enabling little opportunity for ownership or freedom to innovate. All teachers know how the current accountability model narrows imperative upon just Maths and English and how colleagues in those two subjects are the frontline infantry upon whom they rely to battle Ofsted accountability: whither the troops in those two subject areas? Whatever happened to 'a broad and balanced curriculum' being the optimum recommended for all children? The Arts, even Technology in this STEM era, are left to survive as best they can, with Physical Education running for its life as time is squeezed for the gladiatorial Maths and English campaigns. Whether a student or a teacher, it is all about 'horses for courses', putting your limited money onto likely winners to make the day for the rest of us.

Afterword

David Atton provides just one example of the many ways in which external testing and the resultant publication of results affects in-school policy and practice. In the case he describes 'borderline' pupils benefit while others receive less attention than otherwise they would. The school favours one group of pupils over others for the sake of its external standing.

The school is clearly in breach of social justice in depriving some pupils of the attention that is their desert. There is force in this argument. But as the school management saw it the decision had to be taken for the sake of its future.

However, in some schools a phenomenon called 'off-rolling' has been identified: where schools 'lose' students who would drag down results. This must be, insofar as it is a deliberate policy, grossly unethical.

Test and exams have always held a particular thrall over aspiring parents. There is more than one example in this book of the 11 plus, flying its obsolete flag as 'the scholarship', exercising a distorting force on the primary school. It was the gateway to social mobility in the form of the grammar school. But today's children and parents are subject to a competition at every turn. No longer the 'big bang' of the 11 plus: more the 'continuous creation' of Ofsted inspections and SATs providing a stream of information for choice at every turn.

There is no going back. Let us recognize that testing of children is not per se undesirable nor need it distort the educational process. Indeed, teachers do make assessments of their students' and classes' progress at every turn. Good teaching demands that the teacher knows where the student stands. In the jargon, formative assessment starts the educational process and summative assessment concludes it.

The evil identified by David Atton lies both in the crudity of the measures undertaken, which are not diagnostic and, crucially, in their publication. The publication of results from these crude tests inevitably produces League Tables which have no official standing. In an era of choice, where choice in practice exists, the results are key factors in parental decisions and hence of schools' success in the market.

It is, of course, not only SATs tests and examination results that affect a school's success in the market. Ofsted inspections cast their own bemusement. The figure of the Inspector is a long-standing cultural icon wherever he- historically he- appears. In JB Priestley's play An Inspector Calls he comes wrapped in moral as well as social authority. He is in judgment. Today's Ofsted inspectors no doubt draw on these historical penumbrae. But they are in fact more like MOT vehicle inspectors, working from a check-list and ticking boxes on a form. Their effect, however, is real. Some schools mount 'mock Ofsted' weeks in which the whole school goes on a war footing, preparing for the real thing. And when results are in, if they are favourable, no hint of 'special measures,' the bunting and banners appear outside the school extolling its success. There are companies that specialise in selling such festive material. They too anticipate Ofsted, researching their market and knowing where Ofsted visits next, so as to be on hand with a quick sale. The head and staff have a party.

For those professionals caught up in these circuses it is all surely a diversion from their proper work. It may be survivable and real educational order may reappear. But the energies spent on all this compliance must be at the expense of on-going good practice. There is discussion of school and curriculum development in our Conclusions and Recommendations where genuinely educational methods of school and teacher evaluation are suggested.

For the future there needs to be national policy on testing and educational assessment. Where comparisons between schools' performances are required, for whatever reason, the metrics used and their interpretation should be commissioned from specialist educational researchers.

On Assessment

Introduction

School pupils in England and Wales are said to be the most frequently assessed and tested children in the world. The cost of this policy, in terms of the mental stress placed on teachers and learners, has been well documented. In the previous chapter, David Atton showed also how high stakes, externally-imposed assessment can distort a school's treatment of its pupils. The problem is that when SATs and GCSE test results are turned into school league tables, what is being measured may not be how well schools are providing a rounded education but how well they have learned to 'teach to the test' or 'game the stats'.

Gordon provides a wider perspective on the same problem. Properly conducted educational assessments have always been an essential aspect of effective teaching and learning. But when, in the name of accountability, educational assessment becomes over-politicised, it loses much of its specifically educational value and utility. Gordon illustrates this by looking at two well-known areas: the 11+ exam which is still being used in parts of England, Wales and Northern Ireland for selection purposes, and the Programme for International Student Assessment (PISA) which assesses teenagers worldwide in order to make international comparisons of national education systems.

Gordon provides technical reasons why the mathematics underlying both the 11+ and the PISA tests should be treated with scepticism. Gordon also reminds us that many grammar schools were not that good: his own grammar school failed to 'add value' for many pupils of his era and later. He concludes that the only beneficiaries of educational testing, as it currently operates in Britain, are a small army of statisticians and a large number of profit-making *tutorial organisations which, instead of aiming to 'educate' children, make a virtue of 'teaching to the test'.*

The term assessment is ubiquitous in its application, as can be shown by listing a few synonyms - judgement, evaluation, rating, estimation, appraisal, opinion and analysis. The vocabulary of assessment and judgement is part of the normal discourse of everyday life, and always has been. *'And God said 'let there be light'. And God saw the light, that it was good.'* (What would have happened if it was 'not bad', or merely 'satisfactory'? Heaven knows.)

Without knowing the technicalities in each case, health assessments, tax assessments, psychological assessments and risk assessments are all taken as read by most of us - a necessary part of modern living. So it can be asserted with some confidence that educational assessment has a rightful place within the teaching and learning environment. But are we doing it right? It is my purpose here to comment on the kinds of educational assessment which have been part of my experience as a pupil and as a teacher of children and of adults, and in particular to examine two particular areas of education - the 11+ and the PISA tests. I will also make passing reference to SATs and school rankings.

Let me begin with my own recall of taking the 11+ in the distant past. On that particular day, I was confident that school preparation and my own ability would see me through. Yet during an essay section of the test, unaccountably, I froze, being unable to remember the spelling of a three-letter word. I had been fourth in recent class exams and the school expected the pass rate to be in the teens. The idea of having any kind of anxiety or nerves was outside my comprehension. Yet it happened. That was several decades ago. Although I did pass, that event gave me a lifetime awareness of how quickly and unexpectedly exams can overwhelm. At the grammar school I was placed in Form 1B, one of four streamed groups. The head explained school policy to us: those in 1A had performed well on the verbal elements of the test and would therefore be doing Latin, while we in 1B had done well on the numerical side and would not. It took another six years before a subgroup of 1A and 1B students came together for a crash course in Latin for yet another assessment, this one quite esoteric in purpose.

Where have we reached now with such assessment tests for selection? As a result of comprehensive education being introduced in most parts of the country, the 11+ only applies to a minority of children in England and Wales. But the urge to test and to grade children's capabilities is even more rampant today, to such a degree that Warwick Mansell (2007) could write more than ten years ago that *'Britain's children are now the world's most tested pupils'*. He argued that *'obsession with testing may be good for statisticians but (it is) not good for pupils, for teachers, for parents, for universities, for business'*. One exception to the latter category is of course the billion-pound industry of assessment.

Attempts to measure human intelligence have had a chequered history and are still highly contested by the experts. The 11+ testing procedures and scores present perhaps surprising levels of complexity. One profitable tutoring organisation purporting to 'explain' standardised scores writes: *'standardisation removes variable elements from test scores and allows children to be compared equally. It is fair to say however that very few people understand the process! There are too many factors that are unknown to the general public'* (Technical One Limited). Whether the public could be helped with more transparency is currently (January 2018) being challenged in the courts where a dispute between a parent and Durham University's Centre for Evaluation and Monitoring (CEM) centres on the CEM's methods of standardisation of 11+ data. There is of course a whole stack of reasons why a child may under-perform at 11+. In the press and on the internet parents are frequently encouraged to worry about these possibilities and also to focus on the overall 85% failure rate, presumably so that they will pay for extra tutoring for their own children.

The sophisticated techniques used to establish IQ rely heavily on factor analysis. But Stephen Jay Gould in his book, *The Mismeasure of Man,* said that there was 'a deep conceptual fallacy' in the factor analytic argument. Paul Kline, a leading expert, concluded that factor analysis can be a valuable research tool but '*it must be properly used, having regard to all the problems and difficulties which can render the results misleading and of little scientific value....*(it can) *lead to a numerical psychobabble all too common in the social sciences'.* Interestingly, Kline praised one example of factor analysis done well which he found in the Plowden Report on Primary Education (HMSO, 1967). In looking for factors leading to academic success, '*the highest loading variable... was the intelligence test scores, but crime in the family, the presence or absence of nits in their hair and inadequate cleanliness of the home also loaded highly. This was taken by the authors to indicate... that parental care and parental attitudes were highly influential in academic success at the primary school'.* (Kline, 1994)

In 1960 before going to university, I taught from April to October as a raw unqualified teacher at a tough boys' secondary modern school in Nottingham. The Deputy Head at this school regularly bemoaned the lot of a number of able pupils who had not been picked up early enough to take advantage of sustained serious study. In my time only two boys were being given the challenge and privilege of after-school tuition for O level maths. Three years earlier I had already reflected on the disastrous consequences of using the 11+ test to label boys at such a young age. At my own grammar school the GCSE results showed that from an entry of 113 pupils, only 17 achieved 7 or more passes, while 13 pupils left with just one pass at O level and 9 with 2 passes. (There may have been some with zero passes, but they were not listed). During the three years of my Diploma in Education I concluded that a comprehensive system of secondary education definitely presented the best set of life opportunities to adolescent children.

Later in my career while I was working in three different comprehensive establishments, as Head of Department, Senior Teacher and Deputy Head, various assessment bandwagons hailed their way through the system - some welcomed by teachers, some not. When GCE and CSE gave way to GCSE, norm referencing gave way to criterion referencing and pass/fail disappeared in schools. These were decisions about assessment which had been taken by Examination Boards for sound educational reasons following extensive professional consultation. Politicians, however, demanded the re-instatement of pass/fail; they insisted that anything below grade C be regarded as meaningless junk (despite the fact that Exam Boards had indicated Grade F as the expected grade of the 'average' pupil).

When the National Curriculum hit schools it had the effect of a convulsion. In English, Maths and Science alone, teachers were faced with 33 attainment targets for each child. For every target an average of 3 statements per level was required, leading, according to Caroline Gipps, to 8910 bits of information to be recorded by a teacher of 7-year olds. *(Gipps, 1990)*. This ridiculous number would mushroom as the age range moved to Year 6 and beyond. Although the Secretary of State for Education and Science Kenneth Baker claimed at the time that such assessments were also meant to identify what help a child might need in the future, it soon became clear that *'the prime purpose of tests is to provide information on the performance of schools'* (Mansell, 2007, p 21n). Politicians who talk about external tests today no longer mention the formative purposes of educational assessment. The buzz word in education, as in the other major professions, is accountability. It seems that it has fallen on the shoulders of children to produce the numerical data that is going to determine the integrity and the status of their teachers and even the worth and survival of their schools.

Characteristic of league tables is the vital role played by numbers, incorporating the belief that numbers cannot lie. Yet even in a straightforward sporting context there can be anomalies in crude figures - you can, for example, win more games and more points at tennis and still lose to your opponent. The performance of schools and teachers and the learning of individual children are far more complex matters. Charles Clarke, Secretary of State for Education and Skills, must have been foxed by the maths in 2003 when, on spotting the correlation between pupil success at Key Stage 2 Level 4 and their success at GCSE five years later, he made the absurd claim that: *'It is of fundamental importance to the whole future of your life whether you get the test level 4 or not. That's why most parents are focused on getting their kids to level 4… because if you fail, it's much more difficult to recover later in life'*. His error is the common one of confusing correlation with cause. The problem with such rhetoric is firstly that it might be self-fulfilling - year 6 failures and their parents may simply give up on education altogether, thinking that a good crop of GCSEs is now impossible to attain - and secondly that the person in charge of the education system is apparently endorsing the common practice of teaching to the test.

Numbers and league tables are also used by the Organisation for Economic Co-operation and Development (OECD) for international student assessment. Their programme for international student assessment (PISA) makes comparisons of pupil ability across the globe, which are widely reported by journalists and often believed by readers as valid and reliable. Countries around the world have seen fit to consider radical reform to their education systems in response to low

PISA rankings. However, the OECD approach has been criticised for its lack of transparency and an unstable methodology. The OECD contention that improved PISA ratings can enhance a country's economic performance has always been questionable and now appears even more problematic in the international economic climate. In 2014 84 sceptical academics put their names to an open letter to the director of PISA, calling for a halt to the tests to enable an improved assessment which would *include national and international organisations in the formulation of assessment methods and standards whose mission goes beyond the economic aspect of public education... which are concerned with the health, human development, well-being and happiness of students and teachers.*

I have personally worked through sample questions in the Maths element in the PISA tests. What is immediately evident is the amount of English in the questions. The comparison with Maths sample papers for the new GCSE is revealing. The language of mathematics dominates the GCSE papers, as every 15+ pupil in Britain would expect. By contrast, it appears that OECD decided that the PISA maths questions should be angled towards applicability to 'real life' situations. This gives rise to what are known as mathematical 'word problems'. Some countries actually prepare their primary school pupils for these, as reported by a Singapore parent in the Straits Times, '*Singapore's maths curriculum is intense and full of (those) so-called word problems set far above the cognitive development of an average child in that age group'* (17 Feb. 2017). He suggests that, through repeated drilling, eight year olds who have met this form of word problem many times are enabled to master algebraic problems usually taught to much older pupils in other countries. Significantly he adds, '*without fully understanding the nature of the problem'*.

Mathematics, in my teaching experience from Istanbul to rural North Yemen as well as in Bedfordshire and Devon, is essentially the

143

same everywhere: it is a universal language. To me, **PISA** activity encourages the worst kind of nationalistic bombast as well as being deeply flawed in its testing and data handling. Unfortunately, doctrinaire policies at home are taking the English educational system in the same direction.

Afterword

Gordon's piece suggests that assessment needs to be primarily educational rather than political in purpose. Accountability is important, but there are better ways to ensure teacher professionalism and to improve school effectiveness than by subjecting all the nation's pupils to external tests at regular intervals. The latter distort the curriculum because they have no intrinsic educational or 'formative' purpose.

Gordon also demonstrates that complex human performance in schools, as elsewhere, can never be reduced to quantities and simple numbers. The 'tyranny of testing' described by Warwick Mansell in 2007 has become the 'tyranny of metrics' ten years later (Muller, 2018). Muller shows how unreliable metrics are distorting not just the school curriculum but the entire education process and system. Metrics and algorithms can be beneficial when they serve as a complement to human judgement based on personal experience and a deep understanding of context, but they cannot replace it.

Community College and School: a case study

Introduction

This short case study records Paul's excitement at helping to 'open the door' to community education at a Community College in Devon in the mid-1980s, and also his sadness at having to witness its decline in the decades following the Education Reform Act of 1988.

In the 1920s Henry Morris, when he became Chief Education Officer in Cambridgeshire, seized the opportunity to implement his idealistic vision of 'Village Colleges'. These were local schools that Morris wanted to see operating as a beating heart at the centre of their local community. Morris talked about 'raising the school-leaving age to 90'. The village colleges were to be educative in themselves. Morris ensured that they were designed from scratch by creative architects and that they contained art works which would inspire anyone who entered the premises. They had rooms and facilities for use by youth workers, local clubs and community groups, in the evenings and at weekends as well as during the day. Village colleges might also have the local library or health centre, or even the local post office, located in their grounds.

Morris's vision became known as 'community education' in other parts of the country, including Devon, and the 'village college' became the 'community college' or 'community school'. But the vision and the idealism remained much the same: educational activities should be conceived in a broad and inclusive way.

My experience of community education

At the start of the 1980s, I was a traditional classroom teacher who had no background in community education and was therefore largely unaware of the history or ideas. But when I was given responsibility

145

for primary/secondary liaison at one of the Devon Community Colleges I very soon became a great enthusiast for the community education vision. There were fourteen feeder primary schools, most of them based in small Devon villages, and I needed to explore their culture. I also became a member of the Academic Council and a teacher-governor of the College itself. This enabled me to see just how successful a vibrant community education programme can be, where there is good will and a desire to work together.

In later years, unfortunately, being on these local policy-making committees also enabled me to see how easy it is for outstandingly good educational practices at the county and community level to be undermined by central government reforms and by political decisions taken without full understanding of the nature of education.

The successes of the community education programme in my school were inspirational and much appreciated by both school and town. Within a few short years I was able to list the following educational and educative activities which the community school provided:

- A traditional programme of day and evening classes for adult learners

- Youth clubs for different age groups

- Theatre productions involving school pupils and community members

- The Duke of Edinburgh award scheme

- Overseas visits for pupils

- A school and community jazz band

- Exhibitions of work

- Holiday play-schemes

- Links with Exeter university

- Links with local industry

- Mothers and toddlers group, with adult education for the mothers

- Special needs provision and agencies, including work with mentally handicapped people

- Arts Centre for young adults

- Army cadets

- Air Ambulance support

- Farmers' Markets (before they were well-known)

- Carol services in local churches

- A local museum

- An archery group

- The 'Courier' (a local newspaper)

- Police liaison on a regular basis

- Young farmers' clubs

An Ofsted report in the early 90s asserted that community education at the school was 'excellent'. But the writing was already on the wall for this kind of comprehensive community education, because of the effects of the 1988 Education Reform Act.

The paper that was sent to Devon schools explaining the Act and its implications for Community Education made it clear that there was no intention by the government to kill off community education, but that was indeed the main result. As always, the devil lay in the detail. 'The government believes that all maintained schools should wherever possible play an active role in the community they serve, provided that the prime educational purpose of their premises is safeguarded *and funds provided for educational purposes are not used to subsidise leisure interests*' (my italics). By assuming a definite and a definable boundary between education and leisure and by restricting local freedom to spend money on educative activities, the Thatcher government unintentionally ensured the end of this kind of community education, not just in Devon but eventually all over the country.

Henry Morris and many other enlightened visionary educational leaders of the 20th century recognised that the boundary between leisure and education is not fixed. Learning takes many forms. Informal learning can be just as important to the wellbeing of an individual or a community as more formal kinds of education. Adult learners, or 'returners', will often lack confidence and may have bad memories of schooling. They may need to dip their toe in the water by nervously going to a club or to an undemanding 'leisure' class like cookery or yoga at their local community school, before acquiring the confidence to become a serious student aspiring for a GCSE, or a degree or some other kind of qualification. Reducing education to a narrow focus and making easy assumptions about the motives of adult learners should in my view never have been made the basis of education policy. In many Devon towns, as in many other parts of the country, the local people and the children who attend the local school have undoubtedly been impoverished by the loss of community education as it was understood and practised thirty years ago.

Afterword

In the past thirty years, following the 1988 Education Act, much of the adult part-time learning, youth work and educative provision mentioned by Paul has indeed been lost nationwide. Paul shows how this loss in one small town was an unintended consequence of policy-making by people with no understanding of the detail of good educational practices in local regions. We argue elsewhere in this work that community education with its focus on democratic values should be 're-invented' and reinvigorated for the 21st century (see chapter 13 and Section 5 Conclusions and Recommendations).

13 **Allen Parrott**

Community and School: a lifelong educational vision

Introduction

Allen argues that the visions of community education and lifelong learning, which inspired him and many other adult education practitioners in the 20th century, still have potential in the different social and political contexts of the 21st century. Neither vision was fully realised but both achieved enough to demonstrate that they can enhance democracy and social cohesion. Together, they should become two fundamental building blocks of a just education system. Each of these visions rejects educational elitism and calls for locally-provided educational provision that benefits all citizens, irrespective of their class, social aspirations or academic abilities.

In the 20th century, at least up to the 1980s, there was a lively and pretty constant national conversation about the purposes of the national education system and their relative importance. Character development? Social Justice? Mastering essential skills? Creating a world-class workforce? Bolstering democracy and civic values? Disseminating the 'best that has been thought and said'? Critical thinking? Creativity? Problem-solving? Team work? Child-minding?

Some of this national debate focused on adults and post-school learning. After the First World War - and again after the Second - it was felt that the returning soldiers and their long-suffering families deserved the best that the state could offer them and that this should include opportunities to develop themselves through formal or informal learning. The 1919 Report on Adult Education made the case for 'universal lifelong adult education' on such democratic grounds, with social justice as a high priority purpose. One of its authors, B.A. Yeaxlee, later wrote:

151

'Adult education must provide not only for the people who have had secondary and university education, or who would have profited if it had fallen to their lot, but also for those who, if the highroad had been flung open, neither would nor could have set foot upon it.' (Yeaxlee, 1929)

This startlingly ambitious statement about the provision of education for everyone was not at all unusual among British adult educators for the next fifty years. When I began my career as a full-time adult education organiser in 1973 I was soon made aware that 'adult education' was no straightforward bureaucratic category like 'further education' or 'higher education'. From the 19th century onwards, British adult education had been conceived as a social movement - a cause designed to improve society, with democracy and justice at its heart. In adult education circles, education was quite simply a public good; just like the national health service, it should be available to all. Our task as practitioners and as public servants was to make the benefits of education available and accessible to everyone throughout the course of their life, irrespective of their academic ability, their social class or their life aspirations. I was greatly influenced by this vision of education for all and spent twenty-five years doing my best to implement it in two 'community' schools and one 'tertiary' college. My first job was in a Devon community school similar to the one described by Paul Niklaus in the previous chapter.

At that time the best-known providers of adult education were the WEA (Workers Educational Association), the dozen residential colleges up and down the country providing courses specifically for adult students, the extra-mural departments of many universities and the recently-established Open University. But like Paul I was employed by a Local Education Authority (LEA). Although receiving less media or political recognition than these other major providers, LEA schools, colleges and adult education institutes across the country catered for more adult learners than all of them combined. By the mid-1980s more than two million adults were attending formal day and evening classes each year and those of us working in the field were constantly looking for ways to increase this number, to 'widen participation' in the jargon of the day. In community schools like Paul's and mine, we recognised that the 'education' half of the 'community education' concept would have to be defined very broadly if we were to attract all sectors of the local community, as the Yeaxlee vision of lifelong learning demanded. When a neighbourhood school is seen as a resource for the entire community, it cannot focus solely on traditional adult education courses; it has to cater with equal concern for the many adults and community groups who, for whatever reason, are unlikely ever to contemplate joining a formal day or evening class.

Part of the job was to make contact with local organisations and to consult with local people. Before discussing what they and their community wanted from their local school and whether or not we could provide it, I would sometimes need to overcome an innate suspicion of 'authority' and of schools in general. I would point out that, whatever memories they had of their own schooling, as adult citizens they had an entitlement to benefit from the educational resources situated in their local community, not least because their taxes had helped to pay for all LEA schools and colleges. Paul Niklaus has listed some of the many and diverse initiatives that result from such a broad and democratic approach to educational purpose. Many of the activities he lists, especially those which worked with other agencies to support vulnerable groups in the community, were informal and educative rather than strictly educational, with social and health benefits that were always going to be far more apparent than any measurable 'learning outcomes'. Even at the time this very broad definition of education worried the bean-counters, and community education practitioners had to justify every penny spent and to ensure that income from rent and other sources always covered the costs involved in such provision.

We practitioners certainly felt that the community education we facilitated was 'educational', in the broad sense that everything on offer was imbued with key democratic and human values such as respect for persons and pursuing the common good. Although it has seldom been articulated or supported by policy-makers in the 21st century, the community education vision seems to me still pertinent not just in 2019, when social cohesion and democracy are already clearly under threat from populism, social inequality and technological changes, but also into the foreseeable future when these current threats will undoubtedly be magnified by the impact of climate change (Chapter 6, and Section 5 Conclusions and Recommendations)

The vision which became known as 'community education' in most parts of the country was first articulated in the 1920s by Cambridgeshire chief education officer, Henry Morris, as he sought to introduce his pioneering 'village colleges'. Morris's aspirations for these colleges were even more ambitious than Yeaxlee's vision of a truly universal system of life-long learning. Morris felt passionately that full-time school pupils would benefit from his new schools at least as much as part-time adult students and the local community. One of his insights was that because children will always naturally copy adult behaviour they would benefit while at school simply by having close proximity to adults learning. They would learn by osmosis that education and its values were a normal part of everyday life. He wrote that there was no chance of the country getting education right until *'the duality of education and ordinary life'* had been abolished. *'At the present moment our state system of education is concerned almost wholly with children.*

*We ought to see our way to the organic provision for the whole community. We must do away with the insulated school. We must associate with education **all those activities** which go to make a full life - art, literature, music, festivals, local government, politics'* - his emphasis. (Morris, H. 1925, in Ree, H 1984).

Such a strongly inclusive view of educational purpose, and of the role of schools in shaping an 'educative society', was and remains revolutionary. It contrasts with the conventional, child-dominated and exclusive version of education that is still firmly established in the public mind. From the democratic, 'whole person' perspective of the adult educator, the main function of mainstream education, with its excessive focus on qualifications and examinations rather than on personal development and social participation, has always been to create and sustain an educational elite that will then feed into a social and political elite. Whereas adult educators want everyone to succeed in their own way, and therefore to derive life-long benefit from the education system and from its human, democratic values, the school and university system in Britain has traditionally adopted purely academic criteria of success where only the few are expected or permitted to succeed. This endemic intellectual snobbery and elitism is so entrenched that it is not even recognised as undemocratic or shameful. Today's supporters of grammar schools, for instance, are quite open and unembarrassed about their desire to help a small minority of clever children from poor families, including perhaps their own children, to join an educational and social elite, whatever the cost might be to the majority of their peers who must necessarily be made to feel like educational failures at the age of eleven (see Golby in Chapter 1, Taylor in Chapter 9, Brown in Chapter 11).

The great educator and sociologist, Michael Young, pointed out how elites will always be incompatible with a truly democratic and just society, in his 1954 futuristic satire *The Rise of the Meritocracy*. Young

155

popularised the word 'meritocracy' to describe a 21st century dystopia in which one ruling class based on privilege had been replaced by another equally undeserving one based on 'merit'. However the word soon became used with positive connotations, as it is today. Young himself was not making the case for communism or complete equality in society. He simply insisted that personal merits - including high IQ, exceptional talents and a strong will to succeed - should not be confused with personal virtue or with human worth. Possession of intelligence, talent and drive is a matter of lucky individual genes and of fortunate historical contingency. Societies in the modern world may decide that such merits entitle their fortunate possessors to extra wealth or other kinds of reward, because it is logical to give the most demanding jobs to those who are best able to perform them and because the more talented people may need incentives and inducements to take on these difficult tasks. But the talents and merits in themselves confer no moral superiority nor any entitlement to rule. In particular, today's meritorious elite should not assume that it is entitled to secure advantages for its children, especially if this is done in a way that denies educational opportunity to others as it does through the 11+ exam.

Young pointed out that those repeatedly labelled 'dunce' at school will in later life have to face the same challenge as everyone else: of living morally and of making a meaningful life. As fellow human beings, they still have some capacities and talents that can be boosted by appropriate forms of education. All citizens young and old, however limited their capacities and however un-aspirational their personal goals may appear to others, deserve to be treated with respect and catered for by the state's education system. Since Young was writing in the 1950s and 60s, government priorities and therefore the prevailing educational snobberies have altered greatly. Nevertheless, the way that the education system works today - with an even greater emphasis on tests - still seems designed to reward the minority and to pave their way to joining a successful elite. The consequence is that on leaving compulsory education most people have, at best, mixed memories of their schooling and little or no understanding of how a broader conception of education might benefit their personal and social development into the future. As Henry Morris recognised a century ago, the majority of the population are thereby discouraged from any desire to return to education in adult life. Justice requires that educational values - and the undoubted benefits that education can bring - should be available over a lifetime and throughout society.

Henry Morris, Yeaxlee and the other adult education pioneers over the past century were not opposed to scholarship or to the highest possible academic and educational standards. On the contrary, many of them were scholars themselves, for example R.H. Tawney, E.P. Thompson, Raymond Williams and Richard Hoggart. Nothing was more dear to them than the auto-didactic tradition of the 19th and early 20th century whereby working-class men and women, deprived of secondary education, found ways in later life to become 'proletarian intellectuals' pursuing the 'life of the mind' (Rose, 2001). Scholarship is not under threat from the democratisation of educational opportunity.

What adult educators have always opposed is the automatic equation of education solely with academic and scholarly attainments or with 'high' cultural activity. Poetry may indeed be more life-enhancing than pushpin, but both can give great pleasure. Those who enjoy beer and skittles and who may never discover the joys of poetry should not be made to feel second-rate citizens: they too have an entitlement to the benefits of education.

Adult and community educators are committed, therefore, to the twin, non-patronising beliefs that education has to embrace all aspects of modern living and that, to be effective, educators must start with the real-life experiences of the learners in front of them. These principles apply as much to formal courses as to informal community education activity. An explicit syllabus, detailed lesson plans and a relevant assessment mechanism will always constitute the basic elements of effective and successful adult education courses. But for the best teachers these elements, though necessary, are seldom sufficient. The best adult educators, just like their counterparts in nurseries, schools, colleges and universities incidentally, also manage to create a learning environment where something personally significant or serendipitous might happen for the particular learners attending their courses. Although I have witnessed it many times, this kind of teaching excellence is not easily analysed or described - 'I know it when I see it.' However, Mike Golby's new coinages 'holy ground' and 'educational moments' in chapter 21 do begin to capture this kind of teacher professionalism.

During my adult education career I also heard about individual epiphanies or 'educational moments' from numerous grateful adult learners and I witnessed many examples of how education, broadly conceived, can improve the lives of groups and individuals. There is compelling, if inevitably anecdotal, evidence from the 1980s and 1990s that high-quality adult education provision, whether informal or formal, has health and social benefits for individual learners and, by extension, for their communities. It is no accident that many GPs regularly used to refer patients to local evening classes at a time when such classes were much more widely available and affordable than they are today.

Gail Parfitt describes how year after year she witnessed the profound effect on its students of one particular college's Access Course. But that Access course was full-time and one year long, and all access courses are explicitly designed to be transformative and developmental for the brave adults who make the life-changing decision to obtain a university degree in later life. In my experience even the most humble and much shorter part-time adult education course - maybe dressmaking or English GCSE, or yoga or pottery perhaps - has the potential to shape an individual's life or to influence their personal development in a beneficial and sometimes profound way. Quite often this will be completely unexpected, a consequence of adult education that could not have been planned for, either by the teacher or the learner.

In the 1980s I introduced a very successful category of adult education courses into my college, under the rubric '*Courses for a Better Life*'. There was a fourfold rationale. Through new learning, people can improve their lives at any age; personal problems and even crises can present opportunities for growth and change; our physical, mental and spiritual states are inter-connected and people can learn to take more responsibility for their health in all its aspects; and to learn more about oneself, far from being a self-indulgence, can be the necessary starting point for successful relationship with others. These courses with both familiar and unfamiliar titles, such as Assertiveness Training, Improve Your Confidence, Make Your Experience Count, Meditation and Stress Reduction, Nutrition Workshop, After Divorce - What Next?, Coping with Death and Bereavement, proved just as popular for the next few years as the traditional adult education provision in Crafts, Languages, Physical Education etc. Although I 'introduced' and 'facilitated' this programme, and later wrote it up for professional adult education colleagues, most of the creative ideas came from one or two inspiring teachers or from active members of the local community who brought their ideas or requests to the College's regular User meetings. At these meetings of class and community group representatives, all of whom had been chosen or elected by their peers, the current programme on offer would be critically reviewed and suggestions made for future programmes. In this way adult and community education centres like mine provided a model of democratic practice.

The main lesson I took from my career as an adult educator is one that Henry Morris would have recognised and also one that still seems relevant. Formal education programmes leading to academic examinations or to work-related qualifications represent only one aspect of the enormous kaleidoscope of educational possibilities in a life-long education journey. Given a completely free choice, most adults will opt for informal or leisure or physical education learning courses. Or for personal development courses. Or even for informal educative activities where the learning is largely incidental but no less valuable on that account.

Such a fully inclusive (and fully democratic) approach to education changes the debate about 'standards'. The educational standards that matter the most are moral rather than academic or intellectual. Where personal growth and community development are concerned this must always be the case. From a government or employer perspective, education then becomes a matter of trust in people, and also trust in the professional practitioners whom they employ to do good work with people - and for them. When human contacts with fellow human learners are made in good faith, with good educative intentions, by public servants and skilled teachers, good outcomes will necessarily follow. Such good work can never be directed or managed at a distance. Nor will the same good work ever be done by machines, however advanced and 'user-friendly' the technology becomes.

Educational practitioners must be given the freedom to act flexibly on behalf of the clients (learners) they serve. The dominant belief of recent politicians, shaped by the auditors they employ, is that wherever education is underwritten by the state - even to the relatively tiny extent that adult and community education used to be subsidised - it must consist of formal courses with planned and measurable learning outcomes that can supposedly be accurately audited. From the audit perspective, learning has no reality unless it can be *proven* to have taken place. Such a narrow mechanistic view of human learning greatly reduces the potential of education to do good work. This reductive approach has led to the monetised, de-moralised and in some ways de-humanised version of education outlined in Chapter 2. Whether or not auditors should hold such a one-eyed, value-for-money view of education, politicians should definitely be able to appreciate a bigger and more complex picture. Some of their predecessors certainly did. Winston Churchill - writer, DIY builder, amateur water-colourist, occasional depressive - wrote: *'There is perhaps no branch of our vast educational system which should more attract the aid and encouragement of the State than adult education'.* (Churchill W., 1954)

Henry Morris died in 1961, disillusioned because his ideas about education and neighbourhood schools had not become mainstream. Paul Niklaus showed in Chapter 12 how the central government reforms of 1988, designed to free up schools from LEA control, had the unintended consequence of destroying his and many other community schools freedom to serve their local communities. The Morris vision of community schools was dealt a death blow. Three years later, there was another government white paper which was designed to free up further education colleges from LEA control, and this spelled the end of the Yeaxlee vision of universal life-long adult education as well. Konrad Elsdon, ex-HMI, spoke angrily and despairingly about this white paper:

'If a government wished to destroy the best features of British society and culture - tolerance, respect for others, common culture, political literacy, personal responsibility and community involvement - then the further education White Paper's proposals for dismembering adult education would be the right way to do it and probably fatally undermine the whole democratic system as well.' (Elsdon, K. 1991).

His words seemed extreme at the time, but today they look regrettably prescient. Democracy does appear to be in some danger and the case for linking it with the education system and lifelong learning seems stronger than ever. Elsdon's tolerant, common culture based on mutual respect and social participation required a vibrant public sector in some degree of equilibrium with private enterprise.

Adult education used to be part of a valued public realm, just like parks and libraries and buses and trains, where people of all classes could on occasions rub shoulders and where such contact, however fleeting in itself, contributed to social cohesion. We were all in it together. In the past twenty-five years, government policies, including attacks on the very idea of public service and in the more recent past a deliberate 'shrinking of the state' through austerity, have led to the undisputed dominance of the private sector. One example is that all over the south-east and other wealthy parts of the country, exclusive gated communities and so-called 'villages' have arisen where the entry road is closed at night to all non-residents. When local people are expected to 'know their place' in this very literal sense, social cohesion is indeed under threat.

The pioneers of lifelong learning were concerned above all else with the role of adult education in providing a democratic forum for honest debate about political issues. More than ever such a forum is needed today, in a world that is increasingly dominated by 'fake news', by the abuse of social media and by the black arts of populist leaders with their dishonest and often unchallenged propaganda. The time has come for policy makers to re-establish our understanding of the inter-dependence of education and democracy. A truly just education policy would also need to re-visit the arguments for comprehensive, life-long educational and educative opportunities for all citizens in society.

Afterword

Allen shows why universal lifelong learning, community schools and the notion of an educative society should not be regarded simply as historical episodes. They each have a potentially important part to play in the 21st century world. A new way of thinking is required which embraces a broad definition of education and its benefits to society and to individuals; and which also accepts that much which is educationally important cannot be measured, while a lot that is currently being measured has little or no educational importance. This vision is fundamentally egalitarian. It demands support from all who believe that education can and should confront the injustices evident in our elitist society today.

Re-Visioning the past for our future learners.

Introduction

Gail recounts some experiences as a classroom teacher in a secondary modern school, as head of a humanities department in a comprehensive school, as a community educator and, finally, as a university lecturer. Her stories reveal just how creative teachers were permitted to be in the quite recent past. Gail deplores the centralised control of the school curriculum and the loss of teacher autonomy, because they have made the kinds of classroom creativity that she was able to take for granted much more difficult for teachers to emulate in today's educational climate.

The components of creative teaching that Gail describes and illuminates in the piece below are worth listing:

* *Relating well to children. including those regarded as 'difficult'*

* *Active and collaborative learning on projects and presentations*

* *Finding and using the talents and experiences of all students*

* *Building up social skills and confidence for all students*

* *A focus on oracy as a key skill, alongside literacy, numeracy etc.*

* *Use of drama, role play, improvisation etc. in all the humanities subjects*

* *Developing techniques to motivate hard-to-engage children*

* *Encouraging students to develop empathy with others, including parents*

* *Removing negative labels and proclaiming the virtues of 'mixed ability'*

* *Being a reflective and self-critical teacher*

In the piece below, Gail also identifies the virtues of Access courses designed for adults seeking to return to education and to get a degree qualification. These older learners have frequently had bad experiences of school or have learned to see themselves as academically 'thick' or 'less able', and they can benefit in a very particular way from the human and educational values listed above. The success they often have as high achievers later in life is an implied indictment of a school system where people are tested and labelled too early and too often.

After years of successful teaching in schools and in a community education centre, Gail eventually brought her humanity and inspirational teaching techniques to a university setting where she taught future teachers. Gail writes persuasively about the importance of pastoral care in education and also about the significance of criticality and critical thinking in the curriculum. Gail is convinced that the educational values which she lived by and observed throughout her professional career are needed more than ever, in order both to face the ecological challenges and also to enhance democracy and equity in 21st century society.

This presentation heeds several different but interlocking concerns about educational practices today. Firstly, the current focus on SATs with its restricted forms of learning, its narrowly measured outcomes and its whole school 'league table' version of professional accountability. SATs cannot possibly do justice to the amazingly varied and vital learning potential of our children and teachers. Sadly, the tail of assessment is wagging the dog of education and it's not clear that it's an educated dog.

Secondly, the limitations of the National Curriculum (NC). The 1988 version was severely criticised by teachers and educationalists for its narrow instrumental approach. The Arts curriculum was reduced despite being rooted in aesthetics, creativity and originality. The 1988 NC lacked any influence from the strongly liberal humanist views being expressed at the time by HMI. There was a clear absence of modern subjects and the new curriculum was in fact almost identical to the curriculum in operation in 1904. The '*knowledges*' specified were to be '*delivered*' for testing, thus limiting opportunities for interactive learning. Even when cross-curricular themes like citizenship, which invited democratic debate and reflection on social justice, were introduced to the NC in 1990, the independent sector as well as Academies and Free Schools were allowed to opt out of it. The general population today might prefer a genuinely 'national' curriculum for the whole nation that is ethical at its core and offers chances for active enquiry, creativity and critique.

Thirdly, the closure of the elected local education authorities (LEAs), which used to provide a supportive local advisory service and collaborative professional development opportunities for their surrounding educational communities, has had a negative impact. Free Schools and Academies (often in Multi-Academy Trusts) are now independently linked to central government. Massive, open, on-line courses (or MOOCs) have become the popular form of professional development for teachers because they are cheap to provide. This on-line international form of professional development may encourage a world view, but does not encourage the kind of active, in-depth debates and investigations with colleagues nearby. Yet there is also a need for critical educational networks in the neighbourhood, which can lead to valuable local educational initiatives (e.g. collaboration between schools on green issues).

Fourthly, the reduction in the focus of schools on pastoral care. I remember a staff discussion in Hackney in 1988, when the role of Pastoral Heads of Department was challenged. 'We are not social workers', the teacher said. But pastoral empathic work in the curriculum is not a luxury or an 'add-on'. It builds self-confidence and enables learning development. Sometimes just being heard enables release from negative conditioning and a student's learning block is suddenly removed. A pupil or student becomes open to transformative energetic enquiry and knowing when this happens is also a learning experience. Building - or rebuilding - a local pastoral service that initiates positive school-based practices and understands the link between supportive concern and learning achievement will be essential to a just education system.

I believe that correcting these concerns will be vital for society's economic and cultural survival. Our learners need an education that will enable them to manage change and development in challenging times and also help others to do so too. This in turn requires an informed, discerning, collaborative learning population. As Bauman says:

'Forms of modern life may differ in quite a few respects - but what unites them all is precisely their fragility, temporariness, vulnerability and inclination to constant change. To 'be modern' means to modernise - compulsively, obsessively; not so much just 'to be', let alone to keep its identity intact, but forever 'becoming', avoiding completion, staying underdefined.'

A profound understanding of education and its potential range will become even more important as we, as a nation, embark on dialoguing and building more elaborate connections with other countries. Indeed, we may soon become part of a new era of invention that could become known as a second renaissance. For with the help of wiki technology, 'the world can be in the classroom'. The challenges of climate change and the world of Big Data complexity make the task of education in the next generation even more difficult. We require a visionary new education curriculum for all, and although it will need to be carefully costed this is no time for the serious cutbacks in educational resourcing of recent years.

I hope that the chronological accounts of teacher/student practice shared below will contrast keenly with the required 'delivery' practices currently faced by teachers in our SATs-dominated education climate. The episodes selected involve creative reflective learning processes arising in an era and an ethos of student-centered education dating from the 1960s. These backstories invoke enquiry, empathy and emotional intelligence of the kind that could possibly contribute to democratic development and innovation in individual and socially-orientated learning plans in the next decade or two.

Navigating the back stories

A few points for reflection are flagged up here as you journey through my stories of teaching and learning.

- The shared values of respect, equity and fraternity inform the management and ethos of good educational institutions in every aspect of their work, including an ethics-based curriculum and teacher-led assessment procedures. These values, when fully implemented, have the potential to promote individual excellence and a caring citizenship for the future.

- Children are born curious, but how they learn varies. 'Learning how to learn' is an important and useful learning achievement but it may need teacher guidance.

- There is value in non-streamed classes where, even if the focus remains on the achievement of gaining qualifications, there need be no negative comparisons between students. The avoidance of negative labelling and divisive categorisation can lead to immediate positive changes as the focus shifts to all that every child is actually accomplishing. Individual tutorials to guide each child's personal learning development are recommended too.

- Collaborative discussions on gender class, race and disability build up regard and connection among students in ways that enable an appreciation of difference.

- Family workshops for toddlers and children - involving weekly tutored arts and crafts sessions, music, drama, fun maths, etc. can work particularly well in multi-cultural communities where there is shared parent learning and participation. Practices like this can help build regard across the generations, and between groups that had previously been divided.

- Encouraging positive psychology, self-knowledge and the taking of responsibility for self and others is part of a worthwhile community-based curriculum. Social and media studies curricula offer opportunities to understand how feelings can be targeted for manipulation and to develop critical thinking.

- All students (including those at university) need to fill the gaps in 'on-line talk'. This might entail engaging actively with social issues, use of drama improvisations, film studies, and other cathartic learning practices that enable sociable creative, communication skills and abilities.

- Ethics, empathy, enquiry and critique are essential values underlying my vision of education.

The following accounts of group learning experiences stretch across my work in primary, secondary, further, adult and higher education. They have without doubt led me towards a more respectful, collective, egalitarian approach to education. Perhaps the youngsters involved may yet speak to you between the lines of the stories told. Like Chinese whispers these experiences encouraged me to discern different aspects of learning that may yet shape new forms of curriculum theory in educational community practices in the coming period.

Oxfordshire 1965-68

My first memorable encounter with a community educational group input came when I worked with 4C, a class of 15-year olds at a Secondary Modern school in Oxfordshire. At my first meeting with them, they told me that they had had enough of school and were looking forward to escaping at Easter. I suggested that they might still be interested in a 'Tricks of the Trade' approach to their English timetable, where we would look at work that might have immediate use in their world beyond school. I had come from a council estate myself and was sensitive to feelings of inequality, so able to tune in without patronising them. They did regular comprehension exercises from literary sources and local newspapers, and some letter writing for job applications, which they often made funny for their own amusement although still getting the key principles across. We also covered concrete poetry as food for the soul, and a novel about gang survival in the playground called *'The Dragon in the Garden'*.

This novel probably appealed because the characters Fagso and Nicker had an anti-heroic allure. The main character had to confront a bullying network in the school playground; he went to a secret place, quietly contemplating his problems in sight of a dragon wall engraving. When I asked if they had somewhere quiet and safe to go when they needed to think, you could have heard a pin drop. Gradually these students shared something of their lives and wrote about this too.

I was soon drawn into a county-wide project with fellow teachers - a pre-ROSLA initiative -which provided funds to offer this class something different. We hit upon advertising the school Tuck Shop for a couple of weeks. We looked closely at advertising's persuasive strategies and the students made posters, wrote adverts, sang jingles and produced DJ commentaries. At break time they played records, took requests, displayed and sold tuck shop products, tidied up, and kept financial records and accounts. Despite being regularly ridiculed as '4C thickies' by the rest of the school they remained undaunted. At a special Friday afternoon assembly, two weeks after the start of the project, they were able to stand on the stage and tell the whole school that they had doubled the school Tuck Shop take, while noting (tongue in cheek) what an alarming impact advertising technique can have.

They were well-pleased with themselves. Their thought-provoking intervention and their casual, debonair self-confident style impressed the whole school, especially the staff. Their undoubted achievement had changed the way they were seen and how they saw themselves. Negative labels had been lifted by a collaborative and active learning project.

In the same school in the next school year, senior managers introduced non-streamed teaching for first year groups and my class was known as 1GP (my initials). I had struggled the previous year with a bottom stream first year group (1D) where the children had already internalised negative labels and were hard to motivate and difficult to engage. By contrast, my work with 1GP was an inspiring experience. No-one was withdrawn or uncooperative. In the main the children were motivated, interested, dedicated, hard-working and enthusiastic. They learnt well (at carefully organised but subtle and individually 'learning sensitive' levels), and the school Heads of Department who gave me regular advice throughout the year were pleased with the levels of attainment reached.

I was using dramatic introductions as a stimulus for many of my lessons and when Inspectors (from HMI) had observed my work, they requested that I work with Drama throughout the school. I developed a drama improvisation approach using social/ethical scenarios with a mix of theatrical and literary themes. Students, usually from the lower school, worked individually, then in pairs, and then in larger groups of between 4 and 6. Crucially, they had to be an attentive audience for each other and group listening was a key ground rule. They were learning about social values, about themselves in relationship with others, about deepening their insights and their levels of enquiry, and about putting themselves in other peoples' shoes: in short, they were acquiring the ability to empathise.

One eleven-year-old came into class after being caned by the Head Teacher and asked to present an improvisation. Neither the class nor I knew the back story. Without telling us much about it he enacted the physical impact and shock of the caning. It seemed as if he had been chased along the corridor with the cane. The class - his audience - held the space in silent respect. No one took sides, but there was tangible gravitas and compassion in the room, indicating the depth of relationship and support generated among the student participants. They showed themselves to be a fraternal community and their insights anticipated themes of rights and responsibilities that would later be addressed in citizenship courses.

Drama was also an extra-curricular activity. Some students in a youth club play improvised a 'light take' on Romeo and Juliet. Here my intent was to bring Shakespeare within reach. I don't believe their interpretation was disrespectful, but one twelve- year old C stream boy amused the audience when, drawing on his father's experience as a builder, he replied to Juliet's famous question, 'Romeo, Romeo, Wherefore art thou Romeo?':

'I'm down 'ere holdin' up the balcony!'

Kentish Town (1976-80) - an Educational Priority Area Primary School

While doing a part-time Honours degree in the Sociology of Education in the 70s, I also worked in a Kentish Town Primary School. Although I had responded to a request for Social Science teaching, the Head looked at my record and asked me to offer Drama Improvisation to each of the mixed ability junior classes.

As previously, I invited the youngsters to enact personal and social situations, first singly, then in pairs and finally in larger groups. The themes were usually provided by me and sometimes included the use of mime. We also used different types of fiction, for example books like 'Not now Bernard' (about a parent trying to read his newspaper), 'Alice in Wonderland' and 'Just William'. Children might take the part of parent or child and these improvisations, involving typical childhood challenges, offered moments from humour through to anguish, all of which enhanced emotional intelligence, empathy and critical enquiry. The pupils also gained self-understanding and maybe some insight into the different pressures involved when school rules were contrasted with consumerism and the world outside school.

Ethical issues often arose. Social and emotional learning has to be safe as well as adventurous and enabling, and this required careful organisation and a constant willingness on both sides to allow improvisations to be punctuated or interrupted if the need arose. To my joy, some youngsters spontaneously spoke in patois the better to illustrate their home life and this was accepted and lived as something normal and was well-received. There was never any sign of racism or negative criticism, just a lot of applause. A lot of the parents - from all faiths - would come at Christmas time to watch the children's plays and to enjoy a range of multi-cultural foods, together with lively chatting between staff parents and pupils.

As Bruce Weinstein (2009) says, if schools have a code of conduct, they are teaching Ethics. He identifies five basic principles that are common to all faiths

1. Do no harm

2. Make things better

3. Respect others (I would add, respect your own self too)

4. Be fair

5. Be loving

The pupils also engaged in play-writing, which gained whole school acclaim. One third year girl won a national competition run by the Royal Court Theatre and the Observer newspaper, and the next year a group of six children produced a play from their improvisations which, amazingly, won the same prize. In both cases these plays were produced by the Royal Court in their Theatre Upstairs (Still available to audiences as the 'Jerwood Theatre Upstairs').

The children were closely involved with the actors in their productions which were well-received by West End audiences. These were mixed ability classes displaying creativity and academic excellence in their play-writing, working collaboratively and respectfully with each other and enhancing both their school and their local London community.

A Secondary School in Camden. (1983-85)

In 1983 I became Head of Humanities at this accomplished, prestigious and well-known comprehensive secondary school in Camden Town. There was no streaming in this department and my colleagues and I worked with all students using a range of teaching methods. I'm pleased to say that there were never any disparaging comments about inferiority of race or class, or disability, and all students remained committed.

In Year 7 (age 11/12), the curriculum content that I had inherited included an egalitarian anthropological study of the Kalahari Bush people, which might have increased pupil aspirations, alongside the Trojan War, which was full of power issues. Together they provoked lively debate and written analysis and provided a foundation for later engagement with world religions, democracy and the nature of social life. In Year 9 (age 13/14), as part of a critical Sociological/Citizenship course, we examined questions on Race, Class, Gender and Disability. Sustainability would now be included too.

Covering social class, I used a section from the television series 'Seven Up' to stimulate debate and discussion. Could reading the Financial Times every day make a seven year old more intelligent, as the programme seemed to suggest? The girls thought not, but they did notice a kind of knowing, authoritative confidence in the seven-year-old. They were not necessarily impressed but it made them think. Non-streamed teaching which aimed at creating critical thinkers was always challenging work, but I found it very gratifying and broadly successful, as proved to be the case a few days later. For a small group of students suddenly stopped me in the corridor to ask me what I meant by critical thinking and how people did it! I responded by giving illustrations of logical and ethical thinking (deep questioning, the weighing up of evidence, checking out the quality of particular arguments and asking whether they express a sufficient depth of fairness and effectiveness).

In my Department we worked towards anti-racism and one Year 9 girl challenged us by expressing serious concern about the study of the slave trade. 'It's got nothing to do with us', she said. (Back then we didn't know about the continuing presence of trafficking and slavery in this country.) I thought about it and saw what she meant. Nobody in the class had disagreed with her. While it seemed important to try to connect with the suffering of the slaves, the factual approach was not providing any connection: the girls had not been directly involved. I told them that the fault was with my presentation and uninspiring teaching materials. When I began using the film of Billie Holliday's life 'Lady Sings the Blues' the girls became involved. In one scene Billie is on tour in the Southern States and her transit van is brought to a halt by the Ku Klux Klan and all the students started to lean forward in deep concern for her safety.

We moved back to the slave trade with that concern and this was a real lesson for me. Not just about the need to involve students when trying to increase their critical understandings and their empathy for others, but also that in discussions about politics and human rights educational interventions have the potential to rouse very deep emotions and heartfelt concerns: even to be cathartic. This makes it important for teachers to be sensitive and even-handed in preparing material for controversial issues regarding forms of power, media manipulation and the like. The students at Camden began to see the value of debate and the nature of critique. Thankfully, there were no complaints about bias from students or parents and I believe this experience contributed to the lived equity and lively fraternity within the school.

A Community Education Centre in Kentish Town 1885 – 90

In 1985 I became Deputy Director of one of six Education Centres set up by ILEA. Set up in 1974 the community education ethos and practices were well-established when I arrived, but there was also flexibility and openness to new developments. I found the institution relaxed and dynamic, friendly and creative, collective and democratic, responsive to local needs yet still committed to a broad, balanced curriculum. The cross-cultural learning strategies included the recognition that students varied as to which strategies suited them best; so, for instance, phonics was not regarded as the only effective method for teaching reading. This view resonated with my own experience and was particularly firmly held by teachers of English as a second language, if not by recent governments. The sense of a community was enhanced by the openness of the buildings from ten in the morning to ten o'clock at night with youngsters and oldsters from many cultures and ways of life coming through the door. We even had an allotment.

The outreach activities included work with the local schools and charities and the nearby hospital. The mixed age theatre, arts and music projects were really successful as were family workshops and jazz groups. The organisation was managed in a democratic fashion with all affiliated groups having a voice. But one practice at Fleet stood out for me: the popular and friendly Thursday afternoon family workshop attracting over 80 parents, carers and toddlers a week. The warm multi-cultural quality of each gathering was taken for granted, with a heartening level of participation and involvement. A large hall and separate rooms for special interest groups were used to provide arts and crafts, pottery, music, drama, fun maths and a supported reading corner. Parents were invited to intervene or add to what was on offer. At first they tended to watch their toddlers learning, but later they were encouraged to join in the learning activities. So, unlike the average nursery, there was a considerable amount of shared learning and it was enquiry-based fun!

When a large anti-racist conference was held at the community education centre, some tentative contributions were made to the politics of democracy too. This kind of community education showed in a small way how local people could be consulted and involved in their own communities to their great benefit, and I retain a belief that community education learning processes have the potential to enable all students to flourish both socially and educationally. Unfortunately, funding was always minimal and after the 1988 education reforms, including the newly imposed National Curriculum, community education of this kind was not permitted to have a place in the new system.

I was seconded for three years from this Education Centre in 1988 to become an 'Evaluation Consultant' for several London boroughs. Although schools were cautious about my work at first, seeing me as part of the new Inspectorate, I tried to work with them to support their shared concerns about educational development. I aimed to encourage the independent reflective enquiry of parents, students, teachers and other school employees within and across schools. My job was to encourage everyone to share and evaluate their educational experiences, make new connections and to increase sensitivity and understanding within and across the school communities, so that all the stakeholders could learn to see school life from the perspectives of others; and so that, together, they could plan for the future of their school. I found that children, parents, cleaners and school keepers were enthused at the chance of interviewing and being interviewed. This was a novel and successful experience, which aimed to support whole school development, while also strengthening the build towards community within the school.

Exeter University 1990 onwards

In 1990 I became a Lecturer in Development and Evaluation at the university of Exeter. My two courses for third year undergraduates included a popular curriculum innovation and development module. We focussed on the cross-curricular theme of Citizenship and on how issues under this heading might be introduced relevantly in subject areas across the primary and secondary curriculum. The students and I enjoyed working reflectively and creatively with highly charged ethical issues, that on occasion were actually being lived in their own lives. Following a morning seminar where a mix of drama improvisation and reflective analysis was involved, the students would stay well into their lunch hour because the discussion had moved closer to their collective everyday conduct and communication, and they were fascinated.

As part of this course we played a card game called 'The Men's Game' (developed in Tower Hamlets), which involved issues that engaged with gender education as well as the citizenship issues of power, respect, rights, attitudes, commitments and responsibilities. All the young men and women became very involved. This was also enjoyed and led to thoughtful discussions. Most of the students were physical education specialists and suspicious of 'theory' for its own sake, but this largely 'academic' course with its focus on reflective enquiry, critique and empathic understandings captured their imagination because its active learning methods had relevance to several aspects of their teaching practice in local schools as well as to their own lives and the rest of their degree studies. Such approaches could be usefully adapted to the world of dialogic internet development and evaluation too.

Access Courses for Adult Learners

I was asked to take on mentorship evaluation work in a further education college in Somerset. For the next ten years I researched and witnessed three parallel Access Course tutors supporting their student year groups to achieve an almost 100% pass rate to university entry year on year.

These students came from all walks of life, usually from the less privileged sections of the community and often with no school qualifications at all. The full-time course, developed by a team of adult education specialist tutors, had a core curriculum of English, Maths, Psychology and Sociology, which was offered in a cross-curricular way that would prepare them for access to a university degree in one academic year. Students had the possibility of entering either humanities or social science academic degrees, but most chose to go for one of the three vocational options which this Access programme also offered: social work, nursing and teaching.

At the beginning of the academic year I would meet a new intake of students from each course. Invariably, most were uncertain of their abilities and doubted that they would ever achieve university entry. But there was very effective pastoral support on this course, led by the Dean and his Access team all of whom were profoundly insightful, wise, empathic and very supportive of the students and each other. Some tutors had attended introductory counselling courses which enhanced their ability to listen, to advise, to build up their students' self-confidence and develop their learning skills. The students were also encouraged to support each other, and each group soon developed a collaborative working style that they really valued.

In my role as a moderator I would meet students once more half way through the course and again at the end of the year. I would interview them individually and in seminar groups, and also read a substantial cross-section of student assignments. By mid-year they had definitely formed an education community and every student had a greater sense of their potential abilities. Their educational attainment had been turned around. They would explain to me that, unlike at

181

school, they now found tutor assessments affirming of what had been accomplished while also carefully alerting them to what they might do to improve. They would tell me, 'we're not talked down to' and 'the tutors really care'. They had new insights into their own learning as well as new confidence in their future. Nearly all these students were able to move on to higher education and there were often tears of disbelief and joy at this transformation in their lives.

Final ponderings

One lesson from the Access Course and from the other areas of learning accomplishment that I have described is that there is much more achievement and nuanced grace to be found among learners than most people realise, including the learners themselves. A different approach to teaching and a different form of educational development is needed so that the learning potential of all learners is no longer limited or discouraged. The ethos of educational institutions should be that every learner has a contribution to be recognised and welcomed. For more on the subject of the import of equity for all, see Wilkinson and Kate Pickett (2008, 2018).

Children develop in unique ways and at different rates. Negative labels discourage many from achieving their potential and this labelling starts early. Even four-year olds are currently being 'classified' in terms of ability in today's nurseries. Labels like 'C stream thickies' or even the 'less able' may be intended to inform teaching strategies, but they can end up becoming a self-fulfilling prophecy that affects people for the whole of their lives. Principles of equity and justice demand that all such hierarchical assessment rankings are reduced; society cannot afford to waste the potential abilities of any learners. Both Grayling (2017) and Olssen (2010) argue, from somewhat different perspectives, that a well-conceived education system supporting the achievement of all would strengthen and deepen our democracy. Experiences of poverty and hardship, together with well-established threats like climate change and the finite limits of the earth's resources, and more recent problems like IT data theft and the strategies of Cambridge Analytica, make an intelligently-designed, ethical national curriculum essential now.

Every citizen needs to be discerning and critically-informed, while also possessing a fraternal and kindly supportive heart. In 1996 the Delors Report for UNESCO spoke of education as vital for the survival of the global village of community education. Within the democratic educational communities of our schools we need to help add enlightened insight, wisdom love and support creatively across our world.

Some personal insights from the career briefly described above, are as follows:

- When youngsters or adult learners sense that the light is seen in them, their negative labels drop away. I delighted in watching their transformations as they began to teach me more about themselves and our life in this world.

- Group learning, which involves the emotions as well as rational enquiry, can sometimes lead to shared empathy and a deeper understanding of injustice locally and across the world.

- If children get involved in drama improvisation, they can learn how to interact with and understand others, at creative, kinaesthetic, dialogic and collaborative levels. They may also begin to develop ethical commitments too.

- Experiencing large weekly Family workshops, like the ones at The Community Education Centre in Kentish Town, led me to consider the contribution that education could make towards harmonious mixed age social developments in the future.

- The Access Tutors in Somerset working with and for their students gave me a glimpse of how learning success in the sciences and the arts flow from in-depth listening, encouragement, and respect.

- The cool, easy-going university students created a collective buzz of insight as they got heavily into interactions about relationships and began to appreciate universal connections.

- Learners need to access information, as well as engaging in active enquiry, but as indicated above, they don't like to be talked down to, and flourish when information is shared rather than dictated. It's yet another way of living equity and respect in practice.

Afterword

Most of us use terms like 'more able' and 'less able' unthinkingly. Gail suggests that although such labels appear to be neutral or merely administrative categories, they can scar individual learners for life. All learners have potential. Her exceptionally wide experience of teaching in many different circumstances demonstrates how an intelligent and committed teacher adapts to all contingencies by drawing upon underlying educational values. Gail argues that the education system itself has the potential to improve social justice, reduce racism and increase social harmony, provided only that teachers are afforded the freedom to act out of their autonomous judgment.

15 Maurice George

'Geniuses were also welcome: Oxford in the Fifties'

Introduction

The following three papers reflect historic and current debates about higher education. Our authors' experience is located in very different areas and institutions and at very different junctures over the past fifty years. Over that time, of course, there have been enormous changes in scale and kind, responding to a diversity of ideas and pressures as to the purposes of university education. As a result, we now face important decisions on its future.

Maurice George is a product of a time when higher education was the preserve of an elite attending Oxbridge, a few ancient establishments and the city universities of the nineteenth century. In 1945 less than 2% of the relevant age group went to university. Maurice joined what he even then recognised as an elite, which he has for ever since sought proudly to undermine. This is a paradoxical position not unknown to the elven-plus successes among us who, enlightened, seeks it abolition.

I was an undergraduate at University College, Oxford, from 1951 to 1954 and nothing much seems to have changed since then. My story may intrigue you. My parents both left school at the age of 14 and worked in a local factory. I was a bookish lad and much to our amazement I won a free place at our fee-paying grammar school where I stayed until I was 18. Then came National Service. My best friend in the army was called Tony Moon, a dedicated communist. At his suggestion, we both decided to apply for places at Oxford. He convinced me that this was the perfect way to subvert the class oligarchy of privilege and power. So we started together an intensive programme of study based on the internal Entry Examination papers.

This stood us in good stead; we then passed the interview stage (I wore my army uniform) and we both won places. This was a minor miracle. Perhaps we had been chosen as token working class entrants.

We soon saw the class system from the inside. It was clear that most of our fellow students were from public schools or had been officers in upper-crust regiments or were skilled rowers or athletes or had fathers who had been to Oxbridge or who came from extremely wealthy families or who were peers of the realm or were otherwise members of the establishment. Geniuses were also welcome. Tony and I were fish out of water. Although Oxbridge often claims to have reformed its selection criteria, nothing radical has been done. For these and other reasons, I am ashamed to be a product of this disgusting medieval institution although I must admit that the education I received at Oxford was unsurpassable.

My main inspiration at Oxford was an eminent nineteenth century academic called F.D. Maurice (no relation). He came from a poor background. His father was a Unitarian preacher. His son followed in his footsteps and, in order to gain a degree at Cambridge University, became a Church of England minister. His photograph shows an impressive long-bearded man of serious demeanour. In 1854 he founded the 'Working Men's College' in London following his profound belief in equal opportunity for all.

My experience of Oxford has never left me. The unfairness of the system, its exclusiveness and its patriarchal base mean that I never miss an opportunity to attack the political foundations which support it. This is not inspired by bitterness or anger but by my belief in true democracy.

So what could be done to reform it? The word 'reform' is inadequate. Oxbridge should be shaken to its financial and political roots. It should lose its status as a charitable entity; there is nothing charitable about prejudice or elitism. It should lose its donations from the state. Its fee-paying system should be ended. It might be necessary to privatise it. The trouble is that these changes would need the approval of the very M.P.s who are often the products of the system which itself needs to be overturned. The chances are zero. And a new British Revolution is rather unlikely. End of story?

Afterword

Maurice's views on his Oxford education appeared originally in a letter to the editor of the Guardian *generating interest at a time when Oxbridge was under increasing criticism, largely on account of its recruitment policies. Eight of the UK's top schools get as many students into Oxford and Cambridge universities as three-quarters of all the other schools and colleges put together. Analysis by the social mobility charity The Sutton Trust showed that in 2017 eight schools sent 1,310 pupils to Oxbridge over three years, while over the same period, 2,894 other schools sent just 1,220 students between them. (Montacute, Sutton Trust 2018).*

Though Maurice's is an historic recollection its potency lives on. A more recent graduate, Tina Marinos writing in a letter to the Times Literary Supplement *on 30 November 2018 recalls a gruelling and belittling interview experience. Later, teaching in an inner-city comprehensive school she found she was 'often again an outsider, because having been to Oxford I was 'posh'. The chasm is deep.*

Another TLS correspondent Catherine Constable writes that the interview experience reflects a larger theme: 'an indictment of the way in which the British ruling class favours a confident demeanour and a glib answer over someone who is thoughtful and a bit 'queer'. This is the theme of Bluffocracry *(Ball and Greenway 2018).*

Whatever the truth of the matter, we are bound to conclude that the thrall of Oxbridge is pervasive, if only because whatever the reality stereotypes are amazingly resilient.

The Inner Role of the University and the Academic in the
Knowledge Market: Inner and Outer Roles

Introduction

*By the nineteen-sixties following rapid expansion of the sector with the 'red brick'
and 'plate glass' universities, the participation figure was around 10% and by
1990 it was 25%. In 1999 Tony Blair set a target figure of 50% and this has
now been more or less reached.*

*This 'success story' was founded upon a general belief that higher education
was a good in itself and ought to be accessible to all who could benefit from it. The
foundation myth of higher education-that it was a gateway to 'the best that has been
thought and said' - is owed to Cardinal John Henry Newman whose book, The
Idea of a University, followed his advocacy for a Catholic University in Dublin in
the 1850s. This concept of a liberal education survives in the popular mind as
justification for sending young people away from home in order to study subjects of
no obvious relevance to any potential employment they may later undertake. 'Away
from home' is a prevailing assumption, one which Willetts (2018) says originates
from the fact that Oxbridge virtually monopolised university education and the
privileged 'went up' to the university!*

*Academics in this traditional state of affair were privileged (with salaries,
pensions and unbounded professional autonomy), as guardians of untrammelled
enquiry.*

*There were and there remain disquiets concerning fair access to the university.
Also, and increasingly as time went by, the role of the university in relation to the
economy came into serious question. There is now real tension between these two
ideas: education as an intrinsic personal or private good on the one hand; and
education supplying knowledgeable, skilled and motivated staff for the economy on
the other hand. Can the square be rounded in terms of vocational degrees? After all,*

the vocational subjects of law, theology and medicine are historic mainstays of traditional higher education.

Britain's economic competitors persevered with vocational or technical institutions while Britain instead decided to declare its polytechnics universities overnight in 1992. Would it have been wiser to declare the universities polytechnics? For the gravitational pull of the ancient university tradition led the former polytechnics into a masquerade of equivalence. One famously adopted a corporate logo amounting to a capital letter. Ted Wragg quipped 'They should have come to me. I've got twenty-five more of them!'

All the institutions adopted forms of governance based on business. Vice-Chancellors became also Chief Executives. Echelons of managers were created where previously in the old universities autonomous self-government had been the rule. Salaries became highly differentiated until in 2017 a number of revelations around Vice-Chancellors' pay and expenses began to call a halt. The Office for Students was created on the back of these scandals, but its real power has yet to manifest itself.

The introduction of student loans in 2010 cast the student as customer. No longer the postulant, the student was now a consumer. But competition extended only marginally to the price of a degree. A naïve government had set a maximum level of fees. It became an admission of inferiority not to charge the maximum. Earlier, a group of vice-chancellors from well-established universities declared themselves 'The Russell Group' after meeting at the Russell Square Hotel in London in 1994. These establishments adopted the description 'research intensive' thereby laying claim to be 'leading', 'elite', 'world-class' or even 'real' universities. In this new market, competition drove universities to expensive capital projects on buildings and facilities; to strenuous publicity campaigns at home and overseas (where premium fees applied) and to intensified efforts to boost research rankings, student satisfaction, completion rates etc via the various League Tables.

Paul Ernest illustrates the effect of all this on the work of the academic.

This chapter is about the roles of the university and the academic in the past few decades, looking mostly at the UK experience through my insider's vantage point as lecturer through to professor in four universities. I have also served as external examiner and visiting professor in scores more, both in the UK and abroad.

The inner role of the university

By the 'inner role' of the university I mean the goals, aims and practices of a university as a largely autonomous and self-regulating institution. The traditional university is based on the values of the pursuit of knowledge and objective truth. Discovering and sharing knowledge and truth are its goals and purpose. Power and money are not allowed to distort this truth or access to it. The critical examination of truth claims is part of the business of the university and speaking truth to power is an accepted role of the academic. However, the inner role of the university is not merely to seek knowledge and truth. It is also to pass it on to students, together with the methods for both extending and testing it. In the modern post-war era, UK students from any background were allowed free and supported access to university and the truth it safeguards, admittedly for the benefit of the knowledge fields, for society, as well as for the students themselves. This is regarded as a great social good.

Chris Brink, the former Vice-Chancellor of University of Newcastle, points out that the university is one of the oldest institutions in the world, over 2,500 years old. He draws on Boethius for his idea of the traditional purpose of the university. He takes Boethius' thirteenth century dictum as the motto of his book '*The supreme good open to humankind is to know the true, to do the good, and to delight in both.*' (Brink 2018: vi). Building on this Brink argues that the university is as much about the good as the true, the ethical as much as the epistemological.

In contrast to the traditional aims of the quest for knowledge and truth for their own sake, in the universities of the post-modern Third Millennium knowledge is bought and sold as a commodity. Students pay for access to knowledge. Academics are workers whose outputs in terms of knowledge production and dissemination are regulated and measured. Knowledge workers have measures of output to meet to keep their jobs or gain promotion. Intellectual rights for academic workers' products are owned by the university.

In the knowledge business, the traditional values of truth and freedom of access to it are not only superseded but also abnegated. Knowledge is monetized both directly and indirectly. The direct sale of knowledge is to grant providers, marketable patent rights and other buyers in the knowledge market. The indirect value of knowledge output is to increase the capital of the university − attracting more students, especially overseas students, bigger grants, and the overall market value and capitalization of the university. In the University Rankings criteria improved proportions of international students mean improved grades. As Brink (2018) points out, one of the major goals of the postmodern university is to maximise its ranking. Like a share-price, or some other numerical measure of merit, this reduces the value of a university to a single score on a linear scale. But as he says, it might be distorting to measure either research excellence or public service to a single figure. But to combine the two, with many other arbitrary measures, to give a single score is educationally unsupportable unless one makes the assumption that all universities are cast in exactly the same mould and pursuing the same goals.

In the new knowledge market, the values are no longer truth versus falsity but monetized knowledge versus free knowledge. The biggest sins might now be said to be (1) giving away/sharing marketable knowledge media such as films, books, software, music, etc, including academic books and papers; (2) the free sharing of powerful knowledge by WikiLeaks, Edward Norton, the Panama Papers, etc. But universities are no longer the dominant players in the knowledge economy. Most of the biggest multinational corporations are part of it too, e.g., Microsoft, Apple, FaceBook, Google, Amazon, Uber, and so on. Is Academia.Edu, the fast-growing academic knowledge corporation going to join them, on the backs of unpaid knowledge workers (including myself)? The answer is yes, because now some of the detailed data available through this site requires a subscription.

What is the role of the academic in the new postmodern knowledge market? Universities tolerate some free sharing of academics' knowledge product (freely available papers) because it adds marginally to the capital of the university. However, employed academics must produce a minimum number of peer reviewed papers in high impact journals as part of their conditions of service, as well as obtaining research grants (not to mention teaching and managerial duties). Virtually all high impact journals are expensively priced, and only allow papers to be openly accessible (free to all) for an up-front payment usually in excess of £1000. Publishing in high impact journals incurs high labour costs. In addition to the initial 1-2 months minimum time to write a publishable paper, there is usually a revision process that takes a minimum of one-week full time. Thus a 'countable' academic paper takes at least 10% of an academic's total annual full-time work, and it can easily be 20-30%. Thus, the independent researcher, unless in receipt of research grants, has to invest a significant part of their unpaid labour for just one 'countable' publication. Small wonder that many are turning to other outlets such as blogs, free online journals and other unpaid dissemination sites.

Another central role of academics is to obtain grants. In the UK there is a 7% success rate in high value grant applications in social sciences. If it takes an academic one-month full time to write a grant application that is 9% of their annual work. Thus, simple arithmetic shows that an academic must work on average 125% of their time to obtain grants, and there is in addition the time taken to conduct the funded research and other normal duties of writing/publishing, teaching and managerial duties. How can this be possible? Mathematically it appears impossible. It is only possible because of a number of distorting factors. Academics work many hours of unpaid overtime. Some apply for a few grants and give up without success. Many academics have part time university jobs and subsidise their work with their own time. Some move to teaching only contracts to ease the demands of the job and accept lower pay and status. Successful academics at high prestige (highly capitalized) universities have a greater grant success rate and employ junior researchers (junior in terms of prestige and pay, but not necessarily in terms of experience and expertise) to perform the paid for research work.

Another outcome of the knowledge market is the knowledge commissioners own the rights to the truth of the knowledge they buy. Government commissioned research is embargoed, and only favourable results are permitted to be published. Another example is provided by the Big Pharma companies that buy the knowledge that warrants the efficacy and safety of their products both directly and indirectly (Goldacre, 2012). The direct warranting is by constructing studies with multiple outcomes and cherry-picking good outcomes and suppressing negative outcomes; commissioning in house papers for prestige journals and paying academics to lend their names to them, and so on. Indirect warranting is conducted by constructing conflict of interest scenarios with editors and researchers who must provide the desired outcomes in order to continue to receive financial support (colloquially know as bribery and corruption). If the Transatlantic Trade and Investment Partnership or some similar treaty was made law in Europe and the UK, corporations will be able to sue not only governments who enact legislation that impacts on market share or profits, but also any academics who publish findings critical of their products or practices as well as the universities that employ them.

However, despite these negative developments, we should not be too nostalgic for the passing of the traditional university. It was tainted with elitism and was primarily a white male bastion. Outreach, informing the public, and the role of the public intellectual were looked down upon as low activities that are beneath a 'proper' don's dedication to pure truth. Popular culture was regarded as unworthy of intellectual attention until the likes of Raymond Williams challenged such presuppositions. Although preeminent in British cultural studies Williams was grudgingly promoted to full professor (in drama) only during his last years. However, the role of the academic as independent critical intellectual has almost been lost and the modern or rather post-modern academic has been proletarianised and is now just another worker, engaged in intellectual rather than manual or semi-skilled work.

Thus, what Brink (2018) takes as the soul of the university: to know the true and to do the good, has vanished. Pursuing knowledge, largely for its direct or indirect marketable value, remains a goal. But doing good, in the sense of benefitting society and all of humankind, for its own sake, no longer counts.

Ironically, just as the cutting-edge intellectuals in sociology, post-structuralism and post-modernism were announcing the death of objectivity and truth (or rather exposing it as a myth) the knowledge economy emerged in which truth, knowledge and objectivity are bought and sold. Knowledge and truth are not pure, floating above human affairs and interests, for 'knowledge is power', as Bacon wrote, and it can never be separated from money (as Foucault wrote). We now see this in the monetized modern university and the proletarianised modern academic / knowledge worker. If knowledge and truth are no longer seen as intrinsically valuable and adding to human flourishing and the public good no longer count among the university's aims, then we can announce the death of the soul of the university.

The outer role of the university

Just as the values and organisation of the university as seen from within have changed, so too has the social role of the university and the academic changed. The university is no longer seen from the outside as a bastion of expertise, disinterested objectivity and truth.

In the 1980s two major changes affected universities. First, there is the change in its role from only serving an intellectual elite. Universities went from providing higher education for 6% of the population (1963), academically selected as the most able, to serving 40% of the population (2001). One may, in passing, note the inequity in that the 6% were almost exclusively grammar and private school educated students, and thus did not represent the full range of raw talent. With its expansion, the mission of the university changed from preparing an intellectual elite to providing extended education for the academically average and above. Broadening educational opportunities is intrinsically a good thing, although one must also look at the broader social costs of doing so.

Second, universities and higher education institutions were no longer trusted to self-monitor and self-regulate for quality of provision and outcomes. During the Thatcher years (1980s) it was said that professionals in academia (and law, medicine, education generally) were driven by self-interest and not the public good. (Rather – the good of their clients – as according to Margaret Thatcher 'there is no such thing as society'). It was also claimed, on no systematic or evidenced basis, that academics as critics of public reforms were Marxist or at least left-wingers, ideologically opposed to free-market reforms. At the same time the objectivity of the BBC was questioned by leading right-wingers including Norman Tebbit. Various measures put in to monitor, regulate and control universities were instituted. Teaching, research, student application numbers, student satisfaction, student employment, etc were 'measured' as indicators of performance.

But note Campbell's law: *'The more any quantitative social indicator is used for social decision making, the more subject it will be to corruption pressures and the more apt it will be to distort and corrupt the social processes it is intended to monitor.'* (Campbell 1979). Many institutions, including universities, schools, hospitals, prisons, police forces, given targets ('quantitative social indicators') to achieve quickly switched their attentions away from the old, consensual and professionally agreed 'goods' to focus on these new targets. The result is almost inevitably a decline in values and services. Boxes are ticked but the unspecified goods of professional practice are missed out.

With the growing distrust in professionals, the notions of truth and objectivity, as standards characterizing the outputs of the university, are rejected. Instead the knowledge of experts became seen as either (1) self-interested opinion, especially if critical of government policy, and (2) useful (technical) knowledge if of economic value. Reports of 'political correctness' as restricting free speech were circulated sometimes based on false or fabricated claims (e.g., 'Baa baa black sheep was banned' is untrue) to show the 'politically correct' bias of untrustworthy left-wingers' in challenging the epistemological status quo. (This is not to deny that there have been abuses due to 'political correctness'. However, such few documented abuses are small compared to legitimate complaints of injustice due to race, gender, sexuality, etc., which political correctness aims to reveal and counter.)

In postmodernity, universities are characterized by governments and most of the print media as follows, organized into 3 dimensions (Newfield 2008).

1. **Economics.** University education is an expensive 'good' that adds value to professional and knowledge workers but needs to be accountable to its clients (students and research funders) and should not be a burden on the state.
2. **Politics.** Universities are politically unreliable, either out of touch (ivory tower), self-interested (academics as entrepreneurs), or hotbeds of left-wing thought.
3. **Culture.** Universities carry frivolous studies (media studies, pop music specialisms, Media Studies and Queer Studies). They are ideologically unsound and silence dissent. Any criticism of left-wing shibboleths is 'unplatformed', that is, silenced. Universities are hotbeds of Islamism, pro-Hezbollah, anti-Semitism, anti-government, anti-American, etc.

These are tragic distortions of the best and even the commonplace university practices.

An active agent against university autonomy and freedom has been Michael Gove, a former Secretary of State for Education. He voiced a populist meme in claiming in the Brexit campaign that experts offer us nothing of value and cannot be trusted anyway. People Have Had Enough of Experts. He argues that challenging conventional wisdom is necessary for future prosperity but that universities now stifle this by silencing dissent. (The Times, March 3 2017).

The lack of trust in universities by politicians and government is made clear by the strong system of surveillance, regulation and control of universities and academics, now internalized by university .

administrations who strictly police themselves. Reduced funding for teaching per full time student (FTE) forces serious constraints on personal contact and lecture group sizes in teaching. Reduced research funding has been masked by an intensive system of competition for research funds.

The public that is exposed to the corrosive effects of the biased media has less and less trust of the universities and academics. For example, this was manifested in the Brexit campaign. Leave voters' scepticism means '54 per cent do not trust academics, while just one in four do trust academics. 70% of Remainers trust academics.' Overall, to quote a *Twitter feed*: 'Remainers trust academics, business, economists & distrust politicians, journalists. Brexiteers trust NO-ONE.' Nearly half of Leave voters 'think that is likely the referendum will be rigged', meaning they no longer trust our democratic system. (The same is true of Trump).

There are, of course, sound and principled reasons for both *remain* and *Brexit* positions. The problem is that the Brexit campaign tapped into and exaggerated both anger and distrust of experts and based much of the public case on irrational rhetoric (including racism and xenophobia) as opposed to reason. Reason and argument are now broadly in decline, involving as they do a respect for your opponents' position. Such respect has been declining in politics since the Thatcher era. In too much of modern politics the goal is victory (defeating one's opponents) rather than compromise (finding a solution that carries everybody's assent).

In the post-truth era fascination with celebrity gossip – valued for its sensationalism, whether true or not – has been conflated with serious political, economic and social claims. Sensationalism, impact and confirmation of pre-existing views have become the yardstick for how any 'knowledge' (information) is evaluated. The *Daily Mail* runs one of the most popular websites online, purveying a mixture of information, gossip, sensationalism, whimsy and right-wing slanted news and stories. The testing / warranting of knowledge, the long-term business of universities and scientists, has fallen away as a gold standard for much of the media and public. Academics and experts are now widely distrusted. Of course, the distortion of research findings by Big Pharma companies and other mega corporations in favour of their own economic interests has also served to undermine traditional respect for scientific knowledge. This has resulted in many citizens no longer trusting scientific findings. Many still avoid the MMR vaccine even though claims that it caused autism were scientifically refuted decades ago.

Behind all this lies the big picture of neoliberalism and the privatisation of public goods for private profit, (Molnar 2017). Health, schools, universities, justice, even government, etc are all being increasing privatised for corporate profit. The neoliberal perspective regards the market as the sole arbiter of value. From this perspective the University Rankings provide the true measure of value of a university. The higher up the rankings, the more desirable it is, irrespective of the specific discipline or course of study and its traditions and history.

However, this is not an analysis of despair. We are becoming increasingly reliant on experts and specialists in all aspects of public life. We have both trust and distrust in the expert society. If we institutionalise distrust (understood as lack of *automatic* belief and trust) as accountability conducted in a fair and impartial way, the social institutions involved make professionals more trustworthy. No more rogue academics who, though a small minority, abused the system in the past.

The democratisation of information is also a boon. Anyone (above the divide that separates the digital haves from the digital have nots) can research anything and tap into masses of expert knowledge and opinion for free. After an initial distrust, academics have come to respect Wikipedia, for example, as a source of knowledge, and indeed write many of its entries themselves. However, not everything it says can be taken at face value, especially in controversial areas. Across society the necessary spread of criticality needed to evaluate the plausibility or truth value of claims has not yet taken place. Inculcation of a healthy scepticism (not cynicism) and a critical mindset must now be a central goal for education at all levels, for the preservation of democracy.

Finally, let me return to Brink (2018) who argues that the university should not only be for truth, but also for good. Are universities serving the public good and the flourishing of humanity as a whole? The good is no longer the explicit goal of the university as it was once. Nevertheless, some of what universities do is good and for the good of society. Almost all of the data that demonstrates global warming and human causality in climate change stems from the universities. University academics who serve as public intellectuals, alongside the best journalists, reveal and offer principled critiques of harmful policies and practices nationally and worldwide. Thus, universities together with the best of the media serve as pricks to our consciences, and guides to action. Through their creativity as well as providing technical innovations that improve day to day living, they also offer visions of new ways to organise society, new ways to understand human relationships. However, their most important contribution to the public good should be the inculcation of a healthy scepticism and the critical mindset mentioned above.

Afterword

Paul's is a stout and informed defence of the academic role in a social and political climate that that no longer grants its autonomy and privileges unconditionally. There is no going back to an Oxbridge elitism. The door to a university education of some description for all is now wide open. However, there is as yet anecdotal evidence that increasing numbers of would-be students are declining the offer. The cost is undoubtedly a factor but there may be other motivations among the young, for example the desire to get an early foot on the career ladder.

Universities would do well to consider their answer to Chris Brink's question 'what are you good for?' as well as the easier 'what are you good at?' In one Russell Group university city it is popularly believed that the potential of the local music scene has been diminished by the closure a generation ago of the university Music Department.

Finally, a range of other initiatives has further complicated the idea of a modern university. A variety of franchising and out-sourcing initiatives together with a range of 'alternative providers' are proliferating, all engaged in a struggle for market share.

17 **Gordon Brown**

Keele Experienced

Introduction

In this account of his time as an undergraduate at Keele University in the early 1960s Gordon pays tribute to the pioneering ideas of its founders AD Lindsay and RH Tawney. In those days universities benefited from institutional autonomy and curriculum freedom. Keele made more use of them than most universities by creating a distinctive undergraduate curriculum which emphasised breadth - all students had to study both arts and science subjects-and depth: 'the heritage of western civilisation' was a compulsory foundation module. Teaching, or the dissemination of knowledge, was regarded as a more important function of the university than research or the creation of new knowledge. Equally importantly, Keele University's founders brought from the world of adult education their profound belief in the link between education and democracy(see also Chapter 13).

Collini's book What *Are Universities For?* (2012) is presented on the cover as a *'spirited, compelling argument for rethinking the way we see these institutions, and why we need them'*. However, he gives only a passing reference to important innovations at Keele (p 54) and leaves A D Lindsay without even a footnote in educational history. From my perspective as a Keele graduate, I think his estimate lacks insight.

Here is Sir James Mountford's comment, for Keele's 21st anniversary,

> *'In the world of universities there are many mansions. There is no conceivable curriculum which is universally valid...But there is no mistaking the fact that Keele, a pioneer, has carved out for itself a distinctive and enduring niche... Keele is more than a page in a textbook of educational history. It is a living*

thing and its duty now to itself and to university education as a whole is to do all it can to ensure that its own distinctive quality is not lost amid a tide of uniformity.'

The chief architect of Keele was A D Lindsay (Lord Lindsay of Birker, Master of Balliol College, Oxford), aided by historian, R H Tawney, and a small yet dedicated group of educators and politicians, who with experience in the Workers Educational Association (WEA) found themselves wedded to a common cause.

Lindsay had been concerned with overspecialisation and argued, in *The Modern Democratic State (1943)* that, 'since a democratic community depends on mutual understanding, there can be no effective democracy without an educated people.' The universities, in response to demands of a technology revolution were increasingly narrowing the curriculum and thus failing the key purpose of university education.

Other commentators agreed including the Spanish writer, Ortega Y Gasset who claimed that students were becoming specialists instead of being educated and feared that many universities were developing training and research at the expense of the culture which had formerly bound Europe together.

Lindsay was a strong advocate of adult education, which he promoted through Oxford University Extra Mural Studies and, with Tawney taking tutorial classes for the WEA in North Staffordshire, they agreed this was the suitable area to consider setting up a new university, post-World War 2. The founding of a College at Keele with Lord Lindsay as Principal was granted its Charter in 1949 and became the University of Keele in 1962. The tragic blow of Lindsay's sudden death in 1952 left the newly appointed staff and committed students the responsibility of bringing about the realisation of the funder's ambitions.

When I arrived in 1960, I had already experienced a broad General Studies course alongside my 'A' and 'S' levels. At Keele, the Compulsory Foundation Year, based on the Heritage of Western Civilisation, the Experimental Sciences and Modern Democratic Institutions, for first year students extended the range to all departments with senior staff providing leading introductions to their disciplines through lectures that ran from Monday to Friday, 9am to 11am. Weekly mixed tutorials considered matters arising as well as dealing with the particular expertise of each tutor. In addition, in-depth study for that first year demanded of students two sessional subjects in areas not studied at A level. Concurrent with these, expected joint honours subjects were 'kept warm' through coverage on a termly basis.

Over the next three years two subsidiary subjects running for one year each were picked up, to be taken alongside the joint honours, the proviso being scientists take at least one non-science, and arts/social scientists to take at least one science (for artists).

My choices were:

Year 1 – History, Political Institutions, alongside 1 per term of Maths, Physics then Chemistry, and

Years 2, 3, 4 – Maths and Physics with Subsdiary History (Year 3) and Diploma in Education (Years 2, 3, 4, giving exemption from a second subsidiary subject).

These choices I made were, on reflection, too conservatively 'safe' and I wish I had had the courage to risk further study away from my A level background. A popular joint honours was Physics and Philosophy. The opportunity to pick up degree subjects not studied at school did lead to a drift away from the sciences, which may have led to trouble for expansion plans at Keele later.

What did Keele do for me? 'What did the Romans do for us?' I am not of that kind of persuasion that enables another to claim, for example that 'the army was the making of me'. I do believe that infusions of experience stimulated me to realise that academic disciplines can be looked into later, as an autodidact, without fear of being out of my depth. Moreover, I did reckon that the 'Keele Experience' was commendable. The complete on-site residence for all students and the high number of staff accommodated on campus, coupled with the remoteness of the nearest town, engendered more in-depth intellectual and social interaction than I suspect has been yet achieved through the likes of today's technological networks.

Collini quotes two flippant definitions from American university leaders, that, 'a university (is) a series of schools and departments held together by a central heating system', and a generation later as, 'a series of individual faculty entrepreneurs held together by a common grievance over parking.' Yet, seriously, Keele was 'held together' by a set of common purposes.

One of the most dynamic dons, Professor D J E Ingram (Physics), a strong advocate of the Keele idea, explained at conferences to heads of schools why it was important that all students should study arts and sciences. Quoted in The Times (April, 1972) he commented,

'No student can be considered as properly educated today unless he has some knowledge, both of the approach of the humanities and their methods of assessment, and also the meaning and reasoning of the scientific method in action.'

Mike Mansfield QC, in the same year as me, who represented those wrongly convicted of IRA Guilford and Birmingham pub bombings argued (at a lecture at Dillington, Somerset a few years ago) that his

Keele education, which in his case included Maths for artists, gave him the breadth of knowledge to tackle the technical elements involved in forensic science evidence. He is reported as maintaining, *'forensic science is not immutable... the biggest miscarriages of justice in the United Kingdom (arose) from cases in which forensic science has been shown to be wrong.'*

In the Keele Society Newsletter, Autumn, 1991, he went further

'Without fully realising it, Keele has endowed me with precisely what was needed – intellectual curiosity, a desire to question established order, pursuit of logic and a commitment to equality of opportunity.'

Today the university scene is very different. Funding has dominated development and research ratings through Research Assessments Exercises, and the Research Excellence Framework have determined the rise and fall of departments. In the UK expansion of places for universities now yield about 130 establishments. Hierarchies predominate based upon sometimes dubious league table systems. Where once ex-students may have payed debts of appreciation for the experience they had, they now face a lifetime process of monetary debt repayment.

Keele has changed too, of course. Diversification has enabled expansion into widely different areas from conventional disciplines. Health and Forensic Science for example, provide new pathways into higher education.

Yet Keele still has been able to sell itself on some, at least, of the founding principles. Full residency on site has gone, though the claim of the largest UK campus remains. The Foundation Year was abandoned but later reinstated as a first year for those without the usual school exam roots, in a similar way to the Open University. Three year degrees are standard fare but a four year option is available, with joint honours and diverse subject groupings encouraged. For financial reasons the three year education diploma has been replaced by a one year post grad. course.

Though the raising of the University research profile would have had Lindsay loudly protesting, he would have been proud to know that excellence in the teaching at Keele still ranks as high, as does student satisfaction.

Rumblings of discontent at the direction universities have taken, may be heard as voices crying in the wilderness – the 'there's no economic alternative' response - yet surely Collini's appeal to the two principles of the University of Bologna, Europe's oldest university, deserves space. They are firstly,

'The university is an autonomous institution at the heart of societies differently organised because of geography and historical heritage.' and, second,

'Freedom in research and training is the fundamental principle of university life and governments and universities… must ensure respect for this fundamental requirement.'

(The *Guardian*, 24 April 2018). Autonomy and Freedom are not now evident features of UK universities.

Afterword

Gordon has pointed out how in universities today, as in other public services, discussion of moral purpose and consequently appropriate conduct has been largely replaced by discussion of economic purpose and funding arrangements.

As we have noted above Chris Brink (2018) has recently made the case for all universities to ask once again the question 'what are universities for?' The history of Keele could help them find a new civic purpose for the very different challenges of the twenty-first century. Justice demands that universities and indeed all educational institutions should look closely at what contribution they are making to society. Survival of democracy and of the good aspects of western civilisation may come to depend on visionary educators finding the right ways ahead.

18 **Mike Golby**

International Comparisons 1 Finland

Introduction

Our knowledge of education beyond our shores is anecdotal. Stories reach us of phenomenally 'successful' education systems in places such as Singapore or China where apparently highly drilled children perform computational feats. In Germany, a legendary vocational sector apparently delivers a substantial part of that country's now faltering economic well-being.

Now, the lens through which we perceive these features is of course specialised. We are alert to magic potions: more times-tables by rote in the primary school; more cash for universities that bend towards the vocational. We tend to overlook other features in the situation overseas that might be less attractive or less transmissible: in China a deplored authoritarianism; in Germany an enviable and long-standing intimacy between education and industry. The obvious danger of these narratives is that appearances are taken for reality.

On the other hand, it would also be characteristically English of us to dismiss out of hand all possible lessons from abroad. Indeed, to recognise that Scotland has things to offer the rest of Britain (in, say, science teaching and support for university students) might be a beginning to a more discerning open-mindedness to the foreign. Travellers' tales will continue. We best learn from practical examples. There follow brief discussions of two cases. The first is an account of a seminar presented in the University of Exeter Graduate School of Education on Finland. The second is a discussion of Chinese schooling.

This report of the Exeter Seminar is included merely to illustrate one of the channels through which international comparisons are made. The academic route to international understanding is poorly charted. There are international research projects many of which are European-funded and with an uncertain future.

Itinerant speakers are always welcome at universities and this was to be one of the more successful of such events.

This was a most stimulating presentation. I don't think it delivered what was advertised, an account of research on play and learning. But it certainly described the, or perhaps a, Finnish view of 'play' as central to learning. Finland ranks high in international league tables, well above England and Wales and somewhat below the usual Asians. Is this due to the saunas, the high consumption of coffee and fish; or to teacher education and 'play'?

Who knows? If we did in fact know why, which we are a long way from knowing, we might consider importing some features of the situation to our own practice. Is 'play' such a feature? Would, say, an English interpretation of play inserted into an English context improve our PISA standings? Acres of doubt occupy the space between these questions.

No researched insight was offered but a strong suggestion that a 'playful' education explains success underlay the talk. The Finnish education system was characterised, as offering:

* Equal opportunities for all
* High status of teachers
* Local autonomy and de-centralisation
* An 'holistic' approach with emphasis on well-being
* No private schools
* Creativity valued
* An 'entrepreneurial' mind-set encouraged
* Secondary schools often 'traditional'
* Education seen as a life-long engagement

- 'Play' appropriate at all ages and stages

- Assessment seen as an authentic process aimed at understanding learning

- A National Curriculum (introduced 2004, renewed 2014)

Lists such as this demand interrogation. To parcel out features like these in the hope of finding some relationship between them (exactly how important overall is a National Curriculum? or teachers' status? or 'play' etc) would require a massive empirical project: to establish their collective effect in comparison with other education systems would be, I suggest, next to impossible. And the reason for this inter-cultural impossibility is that every education system comes as a package deal wrapped in its host culture. There can be no super-ordinate, judgemental, 'objective' statements because any such thing will be necessarily rooted in its own values and estimations. There is no God's eye view.

The presentation moved on to elaborate a conception of play with signposting quotations from GB Shaw ('you *don't stop playing because you grow old: you grow old because you stop playing*)' and Plato *('more is discovered about a person from how they play than in a year of conversation'*). There were bibliographic references to Sutton-Smith (2001) and Miguel Sicart (2014) both demanding further pursuit. A more familiar name was Vygotsky though no firm definitions of play or 'playful learning' emerged. Candidate ideas were offered including progress, fate, power, identity, imagination, humour and frivolity. However, no formal definition was arrived at. We were on firmer ground with 'creating meaning' in a 'rule-based activity'.

With practical illustrations the approach became a little clearer. Play requires 'expanding learning environments'; physical space that offers supportive social and emotional contexts; and time. There were pictures of the Learning Lab in Helsinki, a set of spaces so fertile for creativity that senior members of staff elect to hold meetings there. The university's website offers some pictures.

The merit of this presentation lay in the many questions it aroused in discussion. These naturally concerned what may be transferable to England and Wales where after the false dawn of Plowden (1968) matters have regressed, and dramatically so. My conclusion, pending further investigation is that Finland, while no Arcadia, offers a working model of what is possible *under certain economic and political conditions*. Those conditions seem to me unlikely to present themselves in Britain any time soon. I discern in the above list of Finnish education's characteristics only at best four that one could consider to be apparent in Britain today. To cherry-pick desired elements, such as 'play' or an 'entrepreneurial mindset' without the cultural background that gives rise to them would be futile.

All generalisations contain falsehoods. An aside from the professor that sticks in the memory is that there is an epidemic of obesity among the Finnish young. All cannot be entirely well. In a macabre way, that is strangely reassuring.

Afterword

This brief account is a simple instance of one route through which we learn of education overseas. International research is very scant and ad hoc. One could hope that liberal educators across the westernised world would come together to consolidate the case for free, secular and democratic education across the board. It is a developing theme of this book that the classical humanist project is endangered by a range of forces of unreason including populism, nationalism and racism. However, at the time of writing the omens do not look good for genuine international work on the educational principles of democracy.

International Comparisons 2 China

Introduction

Rosemary starts by recounting the experiences of two Chinese girls, Monica and Christina, who wanted to go to university in America and explains how and why both girls found their schooling stultifying and illiberal. Because China achieves good ratings in the international comparative ratings, some people think that the Chinese school system in general - and the teaching of mathematics in particular - should be emulated in the UK. Rosemary asks whether opinion-formers in Britain should allow themselves to be so influenced by the crude, context-free quantitative assessments which lead to these international 'league tables'. The Chinese political and cultural context has led to a school system that 'is built to suppress intellectual curiosity, creativity and individuality', which in turn makes it absolutely inappropriate for British politicians even to consider copying Chinese educational policies and practices.

Rosemary's further account of her own experience as a health educator shows up the dangers of seeing education narrowly as 'delivery' of content that is already known and easily testable. Quite separately from the impact of international league tables, this 'Chinese' version of education has been infiltrating mainstream political opinion in Britain for many years. But it will not help pupils and students to learn how to think critically, solve problems creatively or become active citizens in a flourishing democracy.

However much we may dislike quantitative assessment of pupil learning, school and teacher performance it is a fact of current political life. The challenge for professionals is to illustrate to policy makers that what appears effective elsewhere may not be always be possible or appropriate to the educational situation at home.

China is currently regarded by certain politicians as the country whose educational system the UK should emulate. Larmer, writing in the Economist, cites the experiences of two particular Chinese pupils. The first, Monica, had an affluent upbringing, growing up as the daughter of a China's People's Liberation Army (PLA) Colonel, living in a gated compound, effectively a self-contained isolated island with its own shops and other facilities. At school, pupils spent their time memorising information for the next exam and any independent thought was suppressed in order, as Monica was reported as saying, 'to make everybody the same'. Larmer commented, *'Chinese students are products of an educational system that, for all its high achievers, is built to suppress intellectual curiosity, creativity and individuality...' (p.85).*

Monica was unable to face a further three years of 'preparing for tests like a machine'. This is known as the 'gaokao' system of preparation to attend a Chinese university. She told her horrified parents, who had previously dismissed her remarks about a liberal arts education as 'idle chatter', that she wished to go to university in America. This would mean Monica leaving the gaokao system to prepare for a completely different system of standardised tests and a complicated application process. Moreover there could be no going back to the gaukao system in China, if she was unsuccessful. To cut a long story short, she subsequently won a place at the University of Chicago – with the very hard-won agreement and, ultimately, the support of her parents.

Christina, the second girl, had a less affluent upbringing. Her educational aspirations had been stimulated by the gift of her grandfather's western novels, at the age of seven. He had hidden them in his attic during the Cultural Revolution. Because the finance was not available for Christina to attend an international or boarding school preparation for an American university, she continued in the gaokao system whilst simultaneously working to earn money. Eventually, she was asked to leave school to focus on her American applications, a process known as 'tuochan' a dubious Mao-era word for being relieved of 'productive duty'. Again, there would be no way back into the Chinese system for Christina. Sadly, both Christina's and Monica's stories unearthed many expensive and corrupt methods of achieving a place at an American university such as untrustworthy school documentation, paying for essays to be written and many more unsavoury examples.

Christina's parents, despite the political climate, made considerable sacrifices to enable Christina to be guided by a consultancy called the Elite Scholars of China (ESC). The ESC also helped Monica, but with less parental sacrifice. The ESC students had to write their own essays and push beyond the 'gaokao mentality'. Christina found this approach very disorientating but did not give up, while Monica found it liberating. Christina was ultimately accepted by Smith College in Massachusetts.

Clearly, American processes and approaches could also come under scrutiny but for the present our concern is whether we really do want our pupils to follow a domestic version of the Chinese, illiberal, experience. Do we really understand the social and cultural contexts and the historical and political influences from which the Chinese approach stems?

Clearly, American processes and approaches could also come under scrutiny but for the present our concern is whether we or (more relevantly) our educational policy makers really do want our pupils to follow a domestic version of the Chinese, illiberal, experience. Do they really understand the social and cultural contexts and the historical and political influences from which the Chinese approach stems?

One of my own experiences echoed Stella Darke's comments in Chapter 8 about being encouraged to *develop a project based approach...*

and investigative approaches to Maths and Science...' during her teacher training and, in the early stages of her career, being able to *'engage pupils and develop their understanding of the world around them'* and to help children develop their confidence and self-esteem – this was in the late 1960s and onwards – until the *'cumbersome and unwieldy'* National Curriculum descended onto teachers' desks.

It was during the early 1980s, whilst working for a District Health Authority as a Health Promotion Officer, that I became involved in partnership with an LEA teacher, in encouraging the (voluntary) use of a particular health education project in primary and middle schools. It had been designed as a cross curricular project and used the same words that Stella used in terms of assisting pupils to develop their confidence and self-esteem. The excitement of the children was almost palpable, in terms of their learning experiences, and the teacher's enthusiasm increased markedly as the children began to use the ideas in their maths, science, creative writing and art work and exhibited their work at parents' evenings. My role with the project came to an abrupt end when a new manager (with a medical science orientated training) decided that the NHS should not be working with schools in such a way! The experience gained through our work in schools had a marked influence on the way I attempted to develop my own teaching when I became involved with the teaching of health care professionals. Later, likewise, higher education policy makers and managers began to constrain such approaches to facilitating learning in favour of a return to more didactic and instrumental approaches and their notion that filling a lecture theatre would enable more measurable 'learning'. Evaluations of students' classroom experiences, which included questioning what they had found most helpful for their learning and why this was, were dominated by comments about learning from each other through discussing practical experiences and being able to critically discuss relevant theories. Clearly, the values and assumptions underpinning the different approaches are far apart in terms of encouraging or, indeed discouraging, meaningful learning. The significance of knowledge without understanding seemed irrelevant to the policy makers, whether politicians or managers, as education became more and more of a business.

A further insight into the tension between the professionals and policy makers came in an Exeter Society for Curriculum Studies seminar in 2016. Mary Bousted from a teachers' professional organisation had been in discussion with a government minister who was insistent that children should learn 'the facts' and only then go on to apply them in 'real life'. This is very much what the Chinese story illustrates while Mary was trying to argue the need for children to combine theory with its application, through play in the early years and, as time progresses, to learn through making and doing, and experimentation.

Mary Bousted indicated that her arguments did nothing to persuade the government minister with whom she was dealing. And yet, elsewhere, she found Andreas Schleicher, director of Education for the OECD, an organisation not infrequently regarded with some scepticism, suggesting that education has to do more than 'transmit educational content' (back to the Chinese story) and that students need to be able to think critically, solve problems, make decisions and develop their ability to communicate and collaborate in order to prepare them for jobs that have not yet been created, to use technologies that have not yet been invented and to solve problems that have not arisen before. This, clearly, would be anathema to the government minister with whom Mary was trying to argue constructively, and to her political colleagues whose values and assumptions are evidently totally driven by the need for children to learn facts and who are currently trying to make schools emulate the very Chinese approaches which drove Monica and Christina to search elsewhere.

How is it possible to counteract these obsessions and to educate the politicians and policy makers? There is still something of a stand-off between the politicians and the professionals. Teachers threaten to boycott tests, as do some parents, but there appears to be little dialogue around the basic educational issues at stake. A standard Department of Education response is then to accuse the professionals of disrupting children's education. By this is meant, of course, the education so carefully mapped out by the bureaucrats, not the rather messier, potentially disruptive processes of learning known to teachers and children on the classroom floor. How far are we from a dystopia where the teachers are fully co-opted into the state as operators of a mechanistic system aimed at total compliance? In Auden's poem The *Unknown Citizen* teachers are already co-opted into the state:

He was married and added five children to the population,
Which our Eugenicist says was the right number for a parent of his generation,
And our teachers report that he never interfered with their education
Was he free? Was he happy? The question is absurd:
Had anything been wrong we should certainly have heard.

Yet all may not be lost! Mary Bousted did report some scope for optimism. For example, the new chair of the House of Commons Select Committee on Education was keen, apparently 'to do the deep thinking' and the CBI who would like to see the curriculum include the development of 'resilience, determination and creativity'.

There is then the general public and specially parents to consider. How can the general public become more engaged in educational issues? This takes us too far from China but the struggle for hearts and minds can be observed in the daily press, in school governing bodies, and at the school gates.

All of this seems to bring us back to the beginning of Monica and Christina's story and to the reported Chinese approach to education. Measure everything and everybody and effectively depersonalise all.

Afterword

There is no international or universal discourse in which we can make meaningful statements or comparisons about the quality or 'effectiveness' of different education systems. The idea of reducing comparisons to numbers is a naïve chimera. This is because education is a cultural phenomenon springing from the very different traditions existing in very different social and political practices. To understand an educational system is also to understand a culture. For this reason PISA tests and the like are a kind of Esperanto incapable of significant communication when comparison between complexly different cultures is concerned.

Travellers' tales need to be validated by serious research. There is little of this available and we suggest public money would be better spent on comparative studies by reputable academics than on political 'fact-finding' trips overseas. We will add a proviso: that government undertake to act on research findings and to make public any reasons for not doing so.

How can politicians be persuaded that it is positively anti-educational to focus solely on what is definable and measurable when considering the school curriculum? Or teacher performance? Or what constitutes good educational practice?

III

Teaching as a Profession

20 Allen Parrott

'GB Shaw was wrong!'

Allen raises a number of issues about the role of teachers and their professionalism. G.B. Shaw famously and wittily suggested that teaching was the easy career option for those who couldn't do anything else. ('Those who can, do; those who can't, teach'). Allen uses the work of Lee Shulman and others to show that Shaw could not have been more wrong. Teaching well is the hardest and most complex of all jobs. But it is also the most important. He suggests that the teaching profession should now be given a lot more support and respect by educational policy makers than it has received in recent decades, because the country is going to need half a million well-educated and dedicated teachers in order to meet future challenges in society (some of which are identified by Bassey in Chapter 6). He argues that in this respect at least Britain could definitely learn a lesson from Finland where teaching has in recent years been made a difficult profession to enter. Aspiring teachers in Finland need to show excellence both in their intellectual and in their human qualities. The professional practitioners teaching in nurseries, schools and colleges are then given much more autonomy than their counterparts in Britain, in return for which they have to work in a transparent manner and to demonstrate accountability to all the stake-holders in the education system, including government, taxpayers and parents.

In 2016 I wrote a piece for the Exeter Society for Curriculum Studies (ESCS) which argued that modern politicians have 'got education wrong for forty years', this being the period during which national politicians at Westminster had gained full centralised control over educational policy and much of educational practice. I observed that during this period at least one Prime Minister and several Ministers of Education had been unnecessarily hostile to the teaching profession and rudely dismissive of teachers' expertise. James Callaghan, by contrast, had started his 1976 Ruskin College speech by praising the enthusiasm and dedication he had found on his visits to schools. His criticisms of the educational status quo may have been the first ever made by a serving Prime Minister, but they were designed to provoke a national conversation on the education system not to revolutionise it. I wrote, 'he (Callaghan) could not have envisaged, nor would he have endorsed, today's politicised education system (2016) in which every last educational policy detail (of curriculum content, teaching method and learner assessment) is decided upon in Whitehall, ratified in Westminster and imposed on the nation's schools and teachers by *'here today, gone tomorrow'* Ministers of Education.' I also suggested that the politicians who had been re-shaping the education system in England and Wales since the 1980s were 'know-nothing' amateurs with little understanding of the complexities of educational purpose, organisation, pedagogy or curriculum.

I am now forced to recognise that such polemical language, whether or not it was justified, was counter-productive to my intentions in writing the paper. In 2016 the ESCS first had its vision of politicians and educators coming together to formulate and agree a new set of educational goals and policies for the 2020s and future generations. I had wanted my paper to help end the decades-long hostilities between politicians and the teaching profession, not to make a further contribution to them. This contradiction between intention and tone was pointed out in a written response from Baroness Estelle Morris. As the only education minister in recent times who had also been a professional teacher, she was exempt from the charge of educational amateurism. Her letter closed by saying: *'If you criticise politicians as a group - and I was grateful for the exception you made of me - then we don't move forward'*. (Private correspondence, 2016).

Consequently, I have revised the article below to focus entirely on the positive attributes found in the best teachers and on the enormous benefits that professional teachers - and only professional teachers (not their teaching assistants, not unqualified ex-servicemen, and certainly not some future ultra-smart robots or holographic technologies) - can offer the nation in the next few decades. Since our current political leaders are unlikely to re-discover the democratic and educational benefits of a decentralised system, it is even more important to persuade them to appreciate what it is that good teachers can do for the country and why it matters greatly. There are over 400,000 school teachers in Britain, most of whom entered the profession in order to do good work on behalf of other people's children. What the profession now needs, in order to become an even more potent force for good than in the past, is political recognition of its potential. The best thing that politicians could do for the education system is to promote teaching as a higher-status, better-supported profession.

Finland offers a precedent for how politicians and teachers can achieve great things by working together in harmony and with mutual respect. In 1990 the government and leading educators in Finland came together to look at solutions to their failing education system. For over a decade now there has been a general consensus that the Finnish education system is one of the best in the world. According to Pasi Sahlberg, two of the key factors in this turn-around were:

* *making teaching a prestigious profession with probably the most competitive teacher education system in the world* (i.e. difficult to enter)

* *giving Finnish teachers a great deal of professional autonomy and access to purposeful professional development throughout their careers* (Sahlberg, 2010).

Of course, Britain in 2018 is a very different country from Finland in 1990, with a larger population, a less homogeneous culture and more complex educational problems. But the chief lesson from the Finnish experience is one of universal, world-wide relevance: national governments, if they want to improve educational performance in their countries, have first and foremost to enhance the professionalism of the teachers.

Shaw's calumny and why it is completely wrong

In 1903, in an appendix to his play 'Man and Superman', George Bernard Shaw coined the well-known aphorism: *'He who can, does. He who cannot, teaches'*. This gibe was unjustified then and is even more of a lie now. Shaw's low opinion of teaching had in fact been contradicted two thousand years earlier by a greater and deeper thinker than him. Aristotle was perhaps the first person to express the modern truism, that there is nothing like having to teach a subject to ensure that one really knows it, when he wrote in his Metaphysics, *'Broadly speaking, what distinguishes the man who knows from the ignorant man is an ability to teach'*, (cited in Wheelwright, 1951). Three years after *'Man and Superman'*, Shaw extended his cynical net more widely when he had a character in his play, 'A Doctor's Dilemma', say that all *'professions are a conspiracy against the laity'*.

As the twentieth century progressed, both these Shavian witticisms seemed to strike a deep chord in British society. By the 1980s and 90s they had apparently become the basis for government policy. In Grantham during the 1930s and 40s the young Margaret Roberts absorbed from her father, a hard-working grocer, a disrespect for the professional classes which she retained as Prime Minister for the 12 years she was in power after 1979. In the class-dominated, deferential society of pre-war Britain it is easy to see how Mr Roberts and other taxpayers running small businesses might have resented the high fees, the sense of superiority or the cushy lifestyles of many doctors, lawyers and other professionals, and also how they might have begrudged teachers their long summer holidays or their pensions. No doubt too there were examples of sub-standard or self-serving practitioners in all the traditional professions who deserved his and Shaw's opprobrium. But there were many more practitioners who did not. Then as now, most professionals were committed to serving their 'clients' as best they could.

The vast majority of teachers in mainstream schools through the 20th century had made their choice of profession not for the money, the holidays or the pension, but with the strong desire and intention to do good work on behalf of society. It is true that, by modern standards, many were unimaginative in their teaching methods and over-harsh in their disciplinary strategies. Some of them, especially in boarding schools, had warped, non-educational values and behaved appallingly. But in the main the teaching profession in the 20th century was rightly seen as a force for good in society and, according to opinion polls, teachers as a whole have always been well-respected by most parents and by the general population.

Since the Thatcherite era with its well-known mantra, 'there is no such thing as society', it has not been fashionable to talk positively about serving the public or having a 'calling'. The vocabulary may have gone, but I know from my own children and their friends that the idea of a personal vocation is still resonant. Public service motivation may even be as widespread among young people today as it was a century ago. And not just among young people. In 2016, after 30 years as a successful journalist, Lucy Kellaway left her job on the Financial Times in order to become a Maths teacher in a tough London secondary school. At the time she said to an incredulous interviewer: '*I craved one thing above all: the luxury of being useful*'. A year into the job Kellaway wrote a short article describing both her positive experiences and her feelings of failure, in a way that many experienced teachers will recognise or remember. Her vivid account undermines Shaw's view that teachers are inept or incapable of 'doing' and it also confirms that teaching is a lot more difficult and complex than most non-teachers realise:

'Instead of feeling useful, for large chunks of the day I feel useless...There is only one thing I am not useless at, and that is standing at the front of the class and talking. I had thought this would be the bulk of the job but it turns out to be a small part...Teaching is hard in so many ways. There are at least a dozen roles you need to master - including performer, marshal, counsellor, clerical worker, mathematician, role model and nag - and you need to know exactly when and how to be which.'

'Teaching is brutal. Yet even in my most painful moments there are joys of teaching that I never lose sight of. The first is the students. For the first time in my working life I'm doing something that is not about me. Teaching is about them. When, at the end of the first half term, I watched the heads of my pupils bent in silence over their test papers I felt a passionate involvement in their progress. So much so that when I was marking papers at home later, I found myself whooping out loud, 'X' has got the hard negative number question right!' (Kellaway, 2017).

The variety of demands placed on teachers has always presented them with intellectual and personal challenges. Today's teachers also face extra and sometimes crippling external pressures. The reformed education system envisaged in these papers must start by reducing the amount of time that teachers have to spend on non-educational requirements which have no relevance to good teaching or effective learning. It would then seek to ensure that all teachers entering the profession have both the intellectual capacity and the personal attributes to cope with the inherent difficulties and complexities of the job. As Finland recognised a long time ago, teachers have to be chosen from among the 'brightest and the best' in society.

The need for the 'brightest': the intellectual demands placed on teachers

In his comparative study of the medical and teaching professions, the American educator Lee S Shulman looked closely at the complexities of skilled performers in both. His conclusion was that *'the practice of teachers involves a far more complex task environment than does that of medicine.'* The regular classroom teacher, he went on,

> *'is confronted not with a single patient, but with 25-35 youngsters. The teacher's goals are multiple; the school's obligations far from unitary. Even in the ubiquitous primary reading group, the teacher must simultaneously be concerned with the learning of decoding skills as well as comprehension, with motivation and love of reading as well as word attack, and must both monitor the performance of the six to eight students in front of her while not losing touch with the other two dozen in the room...The only time a physician could possibly encounter a situation of comparable complexity would be in the emergency room of a hospital during or after a natural disaster.'* (Shulman, 2004).

Learning to be a confident, competent teacher presents a crucially different kind of intellectual challenge from that faced by medical students and junior doctors. Teacher education courses can only partially prepare new teachers for the fact that good practice in teaching is a contested concept. Junior doctors can be confident that the texts, the protocols and the authoritative instruction from their senior colleagues, which together shape their years of medical education, are based either on accepted medical science or on a current consensus in the medical profession about what constitutes good medical practice. In medicine newcomers can be pointed to and actually shown 'evidence-based best practice', however provisional it might be and however open to revision in the light of ongoing medical research. While acknowledging that there can be some significant mystery surrounding the 'therapeutic relationship' between doctors and their patients (consider the placebo effect), and that diagnosis and treatment in all medical cases will frequently require the complex exercise of professional judgement rather than the simple application of rules or protocols, it remains the case that the objective notions of 'best practice' and 'scientific' medicine have considerable traction in that profession. This means that for junior doctors the road to becoming a competent professional is well trodden and well understood.

By contrast, teachers have to find and make their own road to becoming a competent professional. Aspiring teachers have no Grey's Anatomy and no text books offering them up-to-date accounts of universal good practice. There are generic books on 'how to teach' which provide technical tips, tricks, 'tools of the trade' or 'survival kits'. Also, most schools will support their new teachers with some form of personal mentorship. But neither generalised texts nor support from more experienced colleagues, however helpful, have the authority of a medical text book providing 'right answers'. The processes and interactions inside every classroom are complex, uncertain and ambiguous, requiring the constant exercise of judgement. In classroom teaching the stakes may be far lower than in medicine - no-one is in danger of dying if mistakes are made - but objective 'best practice' simply does not exist. Teachers spend every working day having to make countless decisions in situations of uncertainty; all they can hope to achieve is their own best possible practice in that situation and with those learners. Purely as an ethical concept, 'best practice' remains professionally meaningful: all experienced teachers understand that they have signed up to a set of ethical behaviours higher than those expected of most others in society and there is widespread professional agreement about how teachers should behave towards learners in the course of doing their work. But there is no such professional consensus about the actual work itself. Despite many claims, there has never been an accepted scientific evidence base about 'what works'. There is not even agreement about whether teaching practice ever could have such a scientific basis. While every rational person supports the idea of 'evidence-based' practice as a principle, in education plausible 'evidence' can always be found to support different and competing beliefs about what constitutes good teaching.

A particular intellectual challenge facing British teachers is to understand and negotiate the fifty-year conflict within the profession and the wider society between 'traditional' and 'progressive' views on educational purposes and practices. Even if they have come to regard this split as unhelpful and unnecessary, as they develop their own 'pick and mix' personal repertoire of practitioner skills, teachers can never entirely ignore the debate. Media discussion of education is dominated by the stereotyped pairings of authority versus freedom, knowledge versus skills, facts versus understanding, subject-centred versus learner-centred, etc. Unfortunately, some influential people inside and outside the profession remain convinced that only one of these ideological approaches can lead to good practice in school classrooms.

David Didau's recent book with the provocative title, *'What if everything you knew about education was wrong?'* challenges many 'progressive' notions about good practice. Didau describes how he himself has altered his teaching practice, and changed his views, as a result of the great faith he now places in the scientific findings of cognitive psychology. These have convinced him that there definitely could, should, and eventually will, be a science of teaching with its own incontestable evidence base. In the meantime, he questions nearly all the current mainstream orthodoxies about teaching and learning, including *'formative assessment, lesson observation, differentiation, character, praise, motivation and creativity'*. His chief argument is that because learning is invisible at the time it is happening, it is easy for teachers and observers to make assumptions about good teaching practices without knowing if what has been done or what has been observed in the classroom has actually been effective, i.e. has actually led to successful learning. Teachers and observers may be deluding themselves by confusing good teacher performance with good student learning. His book demonstrates that as of 2018 the professional debate about good teaching is nowhere near being settled. 'Best practice' remains elusive and perhaps illusory. One of Didau's best chapters asks critical questions about the relationship between teaching practice and educational research and he titles it *'You can prove anything with evidence!'*. But in several other chapters he ignores his own sceptical exclamation mark and makes large claims for the usefulness to teachers of recent academic research in psychology (Didau, 2015). Historical names like Thorndike, Watson, Binet, Skinner and Eysenck should remind us that the history of education since 1900 is full of optimistic false dawns, periods of time when policy-makers and practitioners had convinced themselves that the latest theory from scientific psychology could provide authoritative answers to the complexities of education and of teaching practice.

The traditional-progressive conflict may be a largely British or Anglo-Saxon phenomenon, but the intellectual challenge of becoming an effective teacher is universal. Lee Shulman spent his career as researcher and teacher-educator studying teaching as a form of intellectual work that goes much deeper than applying a set of techniques or 'delivering' content. He called this the 'scholarship of teaching'. Good classroom teachers learn from experience that they have to adapt pre-specified course designs, including their own lesson plans, in order to respond effectively to the learners in front of them. Course design and individual lesson plans remain essential as starting points, but *'design is less than half the story...teaching begins in design, but unfolds through chance...teachers learn quickly that the heart of teaching is developing the capacity to respond to the unpredictable'* (Shulman, 2004). In England Lawrence Stenhouse did similar studies in the 1970s and came to similar conclusions. Generic approaches to teaching are simply not sophisticated enough for truly effective teaching and learning. Every teacher needs much more than content knowledge plus basic all-purpose teaching skills. Ideally, every teacher should have the opportunity and the time to go more deeply into the scholarship of teaching, to become a practitioner-researcher. (Stenhouse, 1975).

Shulman and colleagues demonstrated that just as there are specialist pedagogical requirements for the different age groups in the primary sector, so too different subjects in the secondary curriculum need their own individual ways of being taught. It is not enough for a single subject teacher to know the content of their subject inside out, they also need to acquire a different, highly specialised kind of teacher knowledge involving the detailed reformulation of all that content in order to make it comprehensible to learners. Each subject has its own 'pedagogical subject knowledge' (PSK), which can be derived from detailed case studies of how the most successful teachers have made the subject 'teachable' for all abilities of learner. According to Shulman, good teacher-education programmes should introduce aspiring teachers to this long-standing tradition of enquiry with its own canons of scholarship. PSK is a specialist epistemology that can only be generated by participants, i.e. by teachers themselves. With such intellectual challenges and expectations placed on modern teachers, the Finns have understandably made it a requirement for all their teachers to obtain a Masters degree. Shulman himself came to the conclusion that classroom teaching is *'perhaps the most demanding, subtle, nuanced and frightening activity that our species has ever invented'* (Shulman, 2004). Shaw was not just wrong, he could hardly have been more wrong.

The need for the 'best': personal demands placed on teachers

Possession of a Masters degree, while necessary, is rightly regarded as insufficient for new teachers in Finland: even more important than intellectual credentials is the right kind of personality. The transmission of knowledge may be the central feature of most teaching, but such transmission involves a lot more than sending content directly from the teacher's brain to the learners' brains. Good teachers need to have broader personal attributes and skills which enable them to create a positive learning climate, to communicate effectively with groups of learners and to offer individual learners emotional support or personal challenge as appropriate. Much of the complexity of teaching comes from the fact that learners as well as teachers bring a distinctive personality to the classroom. Good teachers are concerned with the 'whole person', partly because this is an ethical imperative for educators (as opposed to 'trainers' or 'instructors') and partly because the rational, cognitive business of learning a subject will often bring up non-rational reactions or emotions in learners. The good teacher will often need to address such feelings because they can get in the way of effective learning. Good classroom teaching is tied up, therefore, with the teacher's ability to respond appropriately to personalities in all their variety. As Eisner pointed out many years ago, this involves the bodies and the feelings of learners as well as their minds and intellects. Teachers have to respond to real life pupils with *'enigmatic messages on their faces, in their posture, in their comportment.'* (Eisner, 1983).

In a book reflecting on his teaching career, English teacher Jonathan Smith expanded on this insight. Smith tells us that as the pupils came into the classroom for his lesson he would consciously try to catch their eye, to make human contact with each individual. He soon realised that this unspoken communication was two-way. *'Children see much more of us and in us and about us than we would like to imagine...They read us. They see our body language and see through it...they work out our values and smile at our evasions; they perceive our natures and assess our flashpoints'* (Smith, 2001). The educational engagement between a good teacher and a group of learners is therefore between human beings in their full complexity, not just between minds or intellects. Like doctors, good teachers have to care deeply about what they are doing. But many hospital doctors and even many General Practitioners can often do their job well enough by focusing on their patients' symptoms; teachers, however, are routinely expected to care for the 'whole person'. Pasi Sahlberg quotes a teacher-education student Veera Salonen:

'Teaching is a profession that you can successfully do only if you put your heart and personality into play...I want to do good for other people, care and love them. I do love them and thus I will be a teacher'. (Sahlberg, 2010).

'Love' may be a problematic word in this context for some readers, but most teachers will understand her words in the right way. There may never be a 'science' of teaching, precisely because the teacher-learner engagement is a human relationship involving the entire body-mind and not just the rational brain. Several of the most significant human activities - romantic love, play, humour, friendship, religious faith, creativity and spirituality - have also resisted meaningful scientific analysis, for much the same reason.

One Finnish educator, Matti Koskenniemi (1982), wrote of 'pedagogical love' and this is a concept that is likely to be required more and more as the 21st century unfolds. Some enthusiastic technophiles, perhaps with a Shavian contempt for teachers, see teaching as one of the many traditional jobs that are likely to be 'robotised' in the next few decades. But if the proposition is accepted that there is something necessarily human about what good teachers do with and for their pupils, this should not be allowed to happen. Even if algorithms could be devised to cover the purely intellectual aspects of effective teaching, which seems very unlikely, artificial intelligence machines could not conceivably mimic - or improve on - all the personal and emotional qualities which good teachers bring to their work.

Lucy Kellaway wrote that one of her unexpected tasks in the first year of teaching was having to be a 'role model'. Is it too far-fetched to suggest that, in some near-future world when economic activities and much of daily life have become dominated by super-intelligent machines or 'cyborgs', young people may need reminders and role models about the nature of humanness itself? If or when electronics are routinely implanted in people's heads or bodies in order to speed up the brain's information-processing and speed of communication, an important goal for education systems may be the fostering of those different types of knowledge and human wisdom which offer richer life experiences than mere information or speedy data-sharing. Half a million teachers in Britain might be required, as an important part of their job, to be exemplars of what it means to be a thinking, feeling, embodied, well-educated human being.

To sum up, good teaching has everything to do with a teacher's knowledge, their professional skills, and their ability to make relationships with learners. Good teaching also requires the teacher to have the autonomy to deploy their intellectual and personal skills in the most appropriate way that will be of most benefit to their pupils and students. Good teaching is an embodied, quintessentially human activity situated in a particular time and place and it cannot be dictated, managed or controlled from elsewhere. Good teaching has nothing to do with the heavy external burdens that are now placed on education institutions and teachers alike - the over-testing of children, the excessive amount of record-keeping, the targets, the league tables, the performance indicators and the unforgiving school inspections.

Lucy Crehan is a young teacher-researcher who has confirmed the absolute importance of good teaching with up-to-date evidence from across the world. After three years as a teacher in a London comprehensive school, she became disillusioned by the excessive workload: *'The hard work I was putting in wasn't making much difference to the children in my care. Much of it - lengthy lesson plans, extensive marking and regular data entry - was required by the school management to help them meet external targets and pass high-stakes school inspections. What time I had left didn't seem enough to overcome the systemic disadvantages that many of my students faced...'* (Crehan, 2016).

She therefore set out to find out whether education systems could be run better than the system in England. She researched and visited five of the top-performing countries in the world, as measured and listed by the Programme for International Student Assessment (PISA) organisation. As well as Finland, she looked at the education systems of Japan, Canada, Shanghai and Singapore. In her detailed report on her enquiry, Lucy Crehan concluded a fascinating discussion by proposing five key principles for 'high-performing, equitable, education systems'. All five principles implicitly assume a body of high quality, professional teachers and three of them are quite explicit about it.

The first principle stresses the value of play-based, high quality pre-school education.

The second makes the case for greater autonomy for teachers.

The third is about high expectations for all children.

The fourth is 'Treat Teachers as Professionals'

The fifth is 'Combine School Accountability with School Support (rather than Sanctions)'.

Reviewing this book, Melissa Benn wrote, '*With 'Cleverlands', Lucy Crehan gently nudges the nation towards a saner future*'. (Benn, 2018). Let us hope so.

Conclusion - a personal statement

There is no doubt in my mind (other ageing ex-practitioners may disagree) that classroom teaching in general has improved greatly since I was a bored pupil in the 1950s and 60s. Most of the time, the only two teaching methods deployed were reading (a text book) or listening (to the teacher). At my secondary school all the teachers had a degree, but none had a specific or separate teaching qualification. I can remember no imaginative approaches to the transmission of knowledge, to classroom organisation, or to pupil support. Away from the classroom, in other areas of the curriculum - in music, drama and, above all, sport - there was sometimes a more fully human engagement between teachers and learners. The reason I enjoyed my schooldays overall, far more than many of my peers, was because I enjoyed sport, did a lot of it, and was coached by a few enthusiastic teachers who enjoyed this part of their work much more than they enjoyed their mainstream 'chalk and talk' duties.

The improvement in classroom teaching today is in my view entirely attributable to the profession itself and to the way in which a wider range of methods has been spread, both by initial teacher education programmes and continuing professional development activities. Since the 1970s the level of 'chalk and talk' in modern classrooms has declined and there is a greater sensitivity among most teachers to the ways in which learners are responding to their teaching. Active learning, group-work, discovery methods have reduced the boredom, stimulated the learning and increased the fun. Talk and chalk (or the use of the white board) is all the more effective today, because it is used more strategically and more sparingly. This general improvement in classroom teaching may be coincident in time with the advent of central government's external and strictly-imposed teacher accountability measures, e.g. via Ofsted; but this is correlation and not causation. Ofsted has actually done less to spread good teaching practices than its much-vilified predecessor body, Her Majesty's Inspectorate.

David Didau tells readers that he was a very poor teacher when he first started. Lucy Kellaway and Lucy Crehan describe the downs as well as the ups of their first years as practitioners. In the same spirit of honesty, I should admit that as a young man I would almost certainly not have got through today's rigorous selection process for entering teaching in Finland. I could probably have met the intellectual hurdles, but I definitely lacked the personal skills and the level of emotional literacy which is the other, even more essential requirement. Perhaps because my schooling had offered me no good role models for classroom teaching, or perhaps for more deep-seated reasons, I never felt entirely comfortable in a class full of young learners. Fortunately,

I was able to make a career as a full-time adult educator where over time I became more confident and competent; but even with adult learners I never became more than an averagely good classroom teacher.

Any expertise I possess about the nature of good or excellent teaching practice comes from working alongside some brilliant teachers at various times in my career. Also, from several decades of conducting frequent teacher observations, first as an adult education organiser responsible for a large programme, then as a university lecturer on B.Ed and M.Ed programmes, and finally as an education consultant employed to observe and support senior doctors teaching their junior colleagues in hospitals. I have almost certainly seen more teaching - good, bad and indifferent - than even the busiest of Ofsted Inspectors, and unlike them I have always tried to have at least one supportive 'professional conversation' with the individual teachers whom I have observed. Excellence is rare, but I can assert with great confidence (though without the aid of any metrics or scientific proof) that it does exist. The overall professional standard could certainly be improved by making teaching a better-paid, better-supported and more autonomous profession. The world needs good, very good and excellent teachers, in vast numbers, because education itself is a force for good: the development of individuals and the flourishing of democratic society will depend on the quality of the education system, which means the quality of teachers.

Afterword

Our proposed National Education Council must explore ways whereby the teaching profession in Britain can be enhanced. New requirements and expectations on those wishing to enter the profession will be necessary. Why not pay scales commensurate with the medical profession? The political commentator Robert Peston has gone so far as to suggest tripling teachers' pay. This in consequence of his observations as a parent at a comprehensive school. (WTF? p 244) (WTF? is the book title!). There must be new mechanisms to provide ongoing support for teachers, like the local Teachers' Centres of the sixties and seventies. Regular sabbaticals for continuing professional development are essential.

As a matter of urgency, many of the current, extraneous and non-educational demands placed on teachers should certainly be removed for example the excessive paperwork associated with testing and inspections. They are raising the levels of stress for no good reason and causing good teachers to leave the profession

Teaching as a Profession

Introduction

The claim that teaching is a profession and as such merits and requires certain privileges is here examined from a philosophical point of view. Are teachers just 'knowledge workers' to use Paul Ernest's phrase above? Paul was referring to the pressure on academics to produce research marketable in terms of income or status in the competition between universities. Is the work of school teachers likewise to be valued in terms of marketability: to provide what consumers require? 'Consumers' in this context might include parents, employers, citizens, government and pupils and students themselves. Credible answers may begin with 'all of the above'. That could be a valuable beginning.

Yet there is another and vital claim on teachers. And that is the idea of education itself. The argument here is that because teachers owe fundamental allegiance to the cause of education itself, the job of teaching is necessarily one of some independence from authority, whether political or of the market.

I want to approach the question of teachers as professionals unconventionally. The standard approach is sociological. It locates professions (of various kinds) in some sort of social, hierarchical setting. Professions, it is noted, enjoy high status. They are in an important degree self-governing. They set their own standards for entry to-and exit from - their ranks. They deploy considerable technical knowledge and special skills. They uphold a strict ethical code.

All of this is empirically interesting and correct. The classic professions, law, medicine, the church, all in their own way exhibit these characteristics *par excellence*. Viewed from outside there is much amusement to be had in comparing and contrasting, celebrating and deploring the many ways in which these elite clubs comport themselves, their ceremonials, their gravitas. They take themselves very seriously, these people. And very well they might for they embody are our best hopes of health, justice and salvation.

What I want to consider however is not the fascinating grain of their social embodiment, their rituals and traditions. Instead I want to notice what they have in common, these highly diverse social phenomena. And what they have in common is that they serve fundamental aspects of human welfare. Law serves justice: Medicine serves health; the Church serves God.

Now, before the spluttering begins at the mere mention of the latter, let me say straightaway disavow any religious pretension on my own part. The church is only noted empirically as one of the three classic professions and 'the love of God' a plausible overall aim.

The essential point is that there are overarching ideas or set of values towards whose fulfilment the respective professions are dedicated.

What is the good of teaching?

It is respectable, it is enjoyable, it is what the government requires, it pays the mortgage.

These are all answers-and many more are possible. However, I want to say that 'education' is the overall aim of teaching. Moreover, and to be to be a little more precise, I want to say the promotion of 'wisdom' is the overarching point of it all. For wisdom is a virtue, being knowledge deployed in practical situations. We want to produce wise people, not just clever, competitive, aspirational or otherwise admirable people.

Teachers are then, I submit, front-rank professionals because their work addresses fundamental questions of human welfare just as much as do the doctors, the lawyers and the clergy.

Teachers' guiding principles derive ultimately from their conceptions of education as a practice just as doctors, lawyers and clergy are guided ultimately by their conceptions of their practices and the good that they serve. The fundamental reasons for change at the level of daily practice consist in the conclusion that a particular practice is not conducive to the overall good pursued by the profession: health; justice, the love of God-and education.

Recognising the 'holy ground'

No, I am still not about to become pious here. It is simply that if teaching is fundamentally about the promotion of wisdom, it will require certain very specific conditions under which to work.

First, there will be authority. Teachers will be, relative to their students, authorities in their subjects. And their classroom authority or power is granted partly on the basis that they possess matters of value to pass on. Until the early sixties all graduates were deemed of 'qualified teacher status'. For originally in the great universities a degree was precisely that, a licence to teach.

This gulf in standing between teacher and taught is justifiable only if the teacher is capable of communicating. It was an act of brazen courage on the part of several undergraduates in Exeter in 1960 to stage a demonstrative walk-out protesting a lecturer's obvious and gross inability to communicate, accomplished scholar though he was.

We had trampled the sacred space where innocence can talk to experience. This special relationship between teachers and taught creates what DH Lawrence called the 'holy ground' between teacher and taught. (Peters, 1966)

Rather than trying to expound this area of thought further, I want to offer two examples of practical teaching. They illustrate contrasting traditions in pedagogy. They show in the first case how a faulty conception of teaching disrupts and corrupts; and how in the second case an enlightened conception of teaching serves and sustains education. How in the first case, shouting across a chasm cannot be effective, the chasm between teacher and taught an area of desolation: how in the second case communicating in the specialised and highly complex ground of a modern classroom can.

The standard case of teaching: teaching as transmission

It is in all the films and novels from *Goodbye Mr Chips* to *To Sir, With Love*, in the pedagogic folk memory. The teacher in front of the class.

Let us consider first the 'standard case' of teaching as something one lone adult conducts with a class of learners. We know of course that not all teaching is so organised. There is group work, one-to-one teaching, demonstration, pupils learning from one another and much else in today's busy schools. Yet 'class teaching' persists, and it is not in principle to be decried. 'Full-frontal' teaching can be done well or badly. Much can be learned that way. Clear exposition and charisma can go a long way.

But it's dangerous because it can all too easily become routinised and a poor substitute for effective communication.

So let us take the teacher in front of a class as a simple example of a situation in which education in schools is typically (still) often pursued.

In this apparently simple situation we may say that learning is what is happening to individuals as a result of what is transmitted one way or another by the teacher. It may be 'teaching by telling', often and a little more subtly consisting also in asking questions and getting answers that lead along the path to 'knowing something'.

The model is of a central message distributed by a transmitter (a teacher) to localities (students). It is like a radio broadcast.

But the metaphor will not do. Metaphors are of most use at the precise points where they break down and fail to be applicable. Metaphors highlight some features of a phenomenon by likening it to another. So, where does the idea of teaching as transmission cease to apply? At what point does teaching cease to be like 'transmission'?

What can be transmitted is linguistic or numerical information, data. The times-tables, dates of the Kings and Queens of England, the Periodic Table are random examples. Pupils are to learn these 'facts'. But what do they know when they do rehearse these propositions correctly? I have a mnemonic for the planets in the solar system. But what do I know of the solar system when I recall it? Something for the pub quiz perhaps. At best, a knowledge of sentences which may or may not usefully connect with other experiences I have had. At worst, a number of utterances that are no more than chants.

Now, what can be transmitted verbally as fact is already highly abstract. The 'times-tables' are related to the idea of multiplication and it is not at all certain that all youngsters who can recite the times-tables fully and well really do understand what they are doing. Ask such a pupil what thirteen times twelve is and there may well be bemusement: and all because there were twelve pence in every shilling!

In the above case the propositional knowledge transmitted to them has been detached from its origins in practical enquiry and offered as pre-digested information. What are pupils to do with this inert transmitted knowledge? Unless they already possess the means of integrating the transmitted knowledge to other understandings of theirs, they are at a loss.

We have here a fundamental issue with transmission. Transmission depends upon learners having the equipment to receive and decode the message. It is a core part of the teacher's task to understand what pupils bring to the situation and then to connect them to the greater understanding at hand. Understanding students as more or less efficient receivers of messages is essential to teaching. Effective teaching has to connect with students' understanding of the world as a whole. Not as the possessors of strings of discrete linguistic formulae.

Similar considerations apply with mnemonics of all sorts. What help is Every Good Boy Deserves Feeding when approaching a keyboard? Or 'Richard of York Gained Battles in Vain' when trying to understand a rainbow?

Ideally, we like to think that all the learners will learn the same things from the lesson, that reception will be perfect. In cases better described as 'training', where total mastery is an important goal, say in First Aid, all the learners will learn the same things and there will be tests and practicals to ensure that is the case. But in the majority of classroom situations it is seldom like that. Some learners will half-understand, others will be in the dark. Some will want to understand, some will be unmotivated. There will be varying degrees of attentiveness, interest and readiness to learn. In this standard case of teaching as transmission, 'cleverness' will be attributed to successful learners and 'dullness' to the unsuccessful. Sometimes IQ, sometimes home background and other factors such as fatigue (too many late nights) and nutrition (no breakfast and junk food) or poor concentration (too many on-line games), are all candidates in explanation of differentiation among learners. Think of these factors as 'interference'.

So complex is such a situation that teachers-and others, such as their managers and inspectors, can make only approximate judgements on the 'success' of lessons of this sort. They will generally be judgments about the social order, discipline and behaviour rather than the quality of learning in the classroom. There is some 'science' from observational educational research available here. (Flanders 1967, Wragg ,1999, Bennett,1976) But, significantly, most of the available research assumes a simplicity in the situation, which is belied in practice. It is relatively easy to count how many questions, 'open' and 'closed' perhaps, a teacher might ask; to see how many questions are directed at individual pupils, by gender perhaps. In its own terms research like this can produce helpful insights into classroom practice.

But of course, empirical research by definition excludes what is unobservable!

What cannot be accounted for in this 'standard model' of teaching is the 'black box' inside the students' heads. And for that matter the 'black box' inside the teachers' heads. Observational science cannot reach these parts at all. It cannot access experience, only visible behaviour.

So long as teaching is conceived as transmission from one brain to others, difficulties like this will arise. Teaching will equate to theatre; learning will be reduced to performance.

This standard model of teaching as transmission thankfully applies less these days than a generation ago. Elements remain however. There are charismatic teachers who can cast spells all day long. But that is no basis for the medium and longer term. Unless what the students bring to the situation is connected to the lesson, the teacher's work will be all uphill. This is why the characteristics of a conversation must be imported into the situation.

Teaching as conversation

This alternative model of teaching, not as transmission but as conversation, has ancient origins. Socrates was a peripatetic conversationalist. In our times Michael Oakeshott (1989) popularised the idea of education as a many-sided conversation between generations and cultures. And every syllabus, lesson plan, test and examination, every interaction in school is a contribution to that conversation.

Does this mean that classrooms are to be hubbubs of talk, talk, talk? No. that is a far too literal interpretation of the classical idea. It is rather that the teacher is, so to speak, 'the adult in the room'. But the teacher's task is not in any crude sense *to lay down* what is to be said and known. She, being senior, is responsible for good order and to propose an agenda. She, having traversed some of the ground between herself and her learners is to accompany them forward. This is called learning and she, the teacher while guide is also a learner, the senior learner. As I have said above, It is well known to thoughtful teachers that one can often learn from students, whose insights challenge their own.

Some may find this more generous model of teaching fanciful. They may think it applicable perhaps at sixth form level or much further beyond. But consider the primary teacher who sees along with the children new significance in the old stories, who is struck by the beauty of symmetry or number theory, who experiences the anxiety in a child's eyes when struggling with something new. I have been that teacher.

Learning on this account of things is a matter of entering into conversation and working with someone more experienced, a teacher. Teaching is not something done to recipients of messages; it is a set of activities offered to participants.

It is difficult to express this second concept of teaching. This is because the transmission model has held sway for so long. It is also because, frankly, the teaching moment is not well understood even by the very best of teachers. It can be seen to work in practice. But does it work in theory?

It is one of those phenomena that are recognised when

experienced but which are otherwise ineffable -like good and evil.

Teaching as conversation: a snapshot

It's a busy primary school classroom. Some children are sitting in groups working together, some in pairs in discussion and a few are working alone. They are all addressing the poem Andrew the teacher has introduced to them before allocating the tasks they are to work on. They all have copies of the poem and worksheets to consult. Andrew has already put in a lot of routine but highly intelligent work on all this organisation. Now he monitors the class seeking out where his intervention will be productive. He notices Bobby, working alone and perhaps a little sad.

'Don't you like this poem?' asks Andrew

'No, I don't' says Bobby.

'Why's that, Bobby?' asks the teacher.

'It's all about fighting and killing, sir'

'You not keen on fighting and killing, Bobby?'

'No, and dying too'

'Does that worry you then, Bobby?'

'No, sir but the boys on the bus keep talking about it. And I don't want to wake up as a skeleton'

'O, Bobby, I don't know much either, but I do know you won't wake up as a skeleton'

'Right, sir, shall I finish the poem now?

Yes, please, Bobby. Well done'

The teacher turns to another group of pupils who seem to be having an argument, whose gist Andrew has captured even as he conversed with Bobby.

Commentary

In this example you have only the words, not the situation and not the history. But, having observed this event I can say with some confidence that certain inferences are correct.

First, Andrew asks a question about Bobby's experience. Does he like the poem? He is not asking for a precis or for correct answers about the poem's vocabulary, rhyme scheme or whatever. Andrew elicits Bobby's 'reader's response' to the poem. Bobby touches upon his feelings about death which are clearly genuinely felt. Andrew gently pursues this fear. 'Does that worry you then, Bobby?' Bobby connects to the boys on the bus and his worry about being a skeleton. Andrew shares his own ignorance of the after-life. But offers firm reassurance in the matter of skeletons. Bobby closes the episode 'Right, sir, shall I finish the poem now?' There is a sense of closure. Andrew moves to speak with another pupil.

All of this happened. And in probably less than two or three minutes. But time stood still. How was this possible? No teaching machine, motivational coach or digital hologram coach could do it. It was a teacher's feat, demonstrating levels of perception and insight rare outside in the ordinary run of life. Remember too that this cameo was no random event but part of the educational fabric of the class and school. That teacher was quite capable of running a 'whole class' conversation in which diverse views could be expressed. Conversation is not necessarily a one-to-one event.

Afterword

Mike's argument for teaching as a profession rests upon a view of education as fundamental to human welfare in the generous sense that it is 'of the whole person'.

To date we have tended to educate only the left side of the brain, the rational, linguistic hemisphere. But all of a person's potentialities must be present and engaged for a situation to be fully educational, carrying the possibility of real growth. And this applies, we must infer, both to students and to their teachers.

How often is it the case in schools and colleges that pupils and teachers are fully, honestly present to one another? Time-serving and short-term compliance - the 'mechanical obedience' so deplored by our predecessor and forerunner Edmond Holmes in 1911- are the safe and sterile options here.

It is in moments of revelation, such as that involving Bobby, that we realise the fuller possibilities of education. Such moments are, Mike believes, deeply latent in all social situations. But it is schools 'unique job to maximise their occurrence. Coercive power, rule-following and blind routine, whether prescribed internally or externally are enemies of education, necessary only as minimum requirements of basic social order. Only in an educational situation where there is a genuine conversation, linguistic and non-linguistic, can 'the whole person' be engaged in learning.

What does all this mean for the education of teachers themselves? Michael Bassey in Chapter 6 above has made interesting suggestions for widening teachers' experience in their training. Current school-based teacher training regimes have gone some way towards rooting theory in classroom practice. What is vital now is to ensure a critical and reflective edge to this practical work. No doubt it is here today, to the extent that it is possible, in the work some trainees do with their in-school mentors and college tutors. But it should be a key task for our proposed Enquiry and the subsequent National Education Council thoroughly to investigate teacher education and the values it conveys.

School Inspection Re-visited and Re-envisaged

Introduction

Probably no other aspect among the many educational reforms of the past generation has proven more controversial than school inspection. The replacement of the elite body of Her Majesty's Inspectorate of Schools by teams of 'lay' inspectors trained in empirical methodologies of dubious validity was necessitated by the idea of a market for education. The much-valued independence of HMI from the government of the day was replaced by an Office for Standards in Education (Ofsted) which has a definitely much closer, relationship with the Minister for Education and his government department. Colin offers here his understanding of the calamitous turn this new regime took. Very broadly, it is a rejection of truly qualitative judgements made by experienced and respected professionals in favour of a mechanised process operable by anybody with a checklist. He re-states very clearly the educational principles and approaches that would be needed to transform Ofsted into a more professional inspection body: in turning inspectors into cameras there is forsaken the one essential, the insight that knows where to shine the light.

Misconceptions

Ofsted inspection has been the subject of many misconceptions. Its advocates see it as providing an objective, incontestable and authoritative assessment of the quality of an educational institution. Many insiders in Ofsted have tacitly accepted such an accolade. Its critics see it as an example of flawed social science and have castigated it for its unreliability and unreliability. The current chief inspector appears to be emphasising its social science research credentials but does not, as yet, recognise major problems relating to reliability and validity. Both conceptions are misconceived and fail to recognise the peculiar features of inspection as a form of educational appreciation/connoisseurship, more akin to aesthetic criticism than to natural or social science. The implications of such a view need spelling out and clarifying and would do much to dispel the mystique, the problems and fears currently associated with the inspection process. This is my attempt to do so.

The centrality of judgment

The essence of inspection is not the so-called but misnamed 'measurement' of quality but the exercise of professional judgment – easy to say but very difficult to characterise; easier to recognise than to define. It's certainly not a matter of ticking off a hundred and one vaguely expressed and contestable criteria. Vickers gets close to it in his book *The Art of Judgment (1983)*. He usefully distinguishes two aspects of that kind of overall appreciative judgment which school inspectors have to make:- reality judgments involving facts about the state of any system such as the school being inspected, and value judgments 'making judgments about the significance of these facts'. Vickers terms it an 'art'; it is not an application of social science or evaluation theory.

The contestability of judgment

In an inspection reality judgments are derived from observations and discussions in class and around school but crucially these are mediated through past experience and involve 'mental processes often complex and prolonged, resulting in inferences, forecasts... and conclusions'. Such judgments cannot be characterised as objective or regarded as unproblematic. Nor can the value judgments that have to be made: they 'cannot be *proved* correct or incorrect; they can only be *approved* as right or *condemned* as wrong by the exercise of another value judgment'.

The notion of objectivity, claimed by some of Ofsted's supporters, is replaced by the notion of 'trained judgment' in order to make an aspect of the world – in this case a school-intelligible. All this implies that inspection cannot and should not claim to be more than the professional subjective judgment of a group of experienced, expert observers. As such the findings of any inspection are contestable and never definitive. This needs recognising in any future re-evaluation of inspection.

The collective nature of judgment

Crucially inspection relies on the collective, not the individual, judgment and experience of the inspectors. As Vickers stresses, 'judgment and decision, though mental activities of individuals are…part of a social process. They are taken within and depend on a net of communication, which is meaningful only through a vast, partly organised accumulation of largely shared assumptions and expectations, a structure constantly being developed and changed by the activities it mediates'. This collective judgment-making is based on wide experience of a variety of institutions in different educational contexts nationwide. It is 'forged' or metaphorically 'hammered out' through lengthy discussion and deliberation with other similarly experienced colleagues. The result is a collective but unique set of judgments, not a set of off-the shelf ones. The notion of collective 'hammered out' judgment is crucial; no published report should be the work of one individual alone. Individual views need to be moderated with those of others to arrive at as defensible and reliable a judgment as possible.

Inspection as a form of educational connoisseurship

Though it may appear pretentious, inspection is a form of joint educational connoisseurship, not bound by clear-cut, straightforward criteria, as Ofsted handbooks of inspection imply. In considering how an 'expert connoisseur' makes aesthetic judgments the philosopher Wittgenstein gets close to helping us understand the nature of inspection judgements and how they are justified. He comments:

'We learn certain things only through long experience and not from a course in school. How, for instance, does one develop the eye of a connoisseur? Someone says, for example, 'This picture was not painted by such-and-such a master'. He may not be able to give any good reasons for his verdict. How did he learn it? Could someone have taught him? Yes – not in the same way as one learns to calculate. A great deal of experience was necessary. That is, the learner probably had to look at and compare a large number of pictures by various masters again and again. In doing this he could have been given hints. Well, that was the process of learning. But then he looked at a picture and made a judgment about it. In most cases he was able to list his reasons for his judgment, but generally it wasn't they that were convincing. The value of the evidence varies with the experience and the knowledge of the person providing it, and this is more or less the only way of weighing such evidence since it cannot be evaluated by appeal to any system of general principles or universal laws.'

Applying these insights to inspection implies that professional expertise cannot be acquired from 'a course' or, at least, not just from a course or series of courses run by Ofsted. It involves learning from a wide range of teaching and inspection experience in a variety of relevant contexts, preferably not confined to a single geographical area. It involves looking at and comparing a large number of lessons by 'various masters again and again'. It is not like 'learning to calculate' or its equivalent - learning from an inspection rule book or tick list. It involves learning from others more experienced in making judgments of teaching quality who can 'hint' at what is required and who can discuss the complexities and intangibles of classroom observation-hopefully as a result in part of joint observations. Like connoisseurs inspectors should ideally be able to 'list reasons' for their judgments but these can never be absolutely 'convincing' given the difficulties involved in interpreting learning. The value of the judgments and the evidence they use to back them up depends on the experience and knowledge of the person making them. Quoting Wittgenstein 'this is more or less the *only* way of weighing such evidence since it cannot be evaluated by appeal to any system of general principles or universal laws' enshrined in any inspection handbook or subsidiary guidance.

Inspection as sui generis and time-bound

Because of the mix of reality and value judgments involved in the act of educational connoisseurship an inspection team can never claim that their interpretation of a school is the only correct one. Nor should inspectors ever claim a monopoly of objective, authoritative, judgment. Equally importantly, that unique set of judgments cannot be directly or robustly compared with the equally unique set of judgments of a school in a different context or even with the judgments of the same school (which never remains 'the same school') inspected at a different time. Each set of inspection judgments is in a sense *sui generis*. Despite Ofsted's policy and practice since its inception in 1992 direct comparison of inspection judgements over time or from school to school is at best highly problematic and at worst invalid.

With their focus on observation and discussion inspectors can only report and interpret activities seen at a particular point in time – a 'snap shot'. They cannot comment with any plausibility on what has happened in the past or predict what will happen in the future. Unlike in the current Ofsted inspection regime, inspectors cannot comment with any authority or conviction on progress over time, whether by groups of pupils or the school itself, since they do not have first-hand access to the past. Admittedly they may have a past inspection report to refer to; but they do not have full access to their predecessors' assumptions, expectations or deliberations for comparison nor can they know with any certainty what has transpired in the interval between inspections. Data from the past may be available but data are fallible, contestable, variously interpretable and very partial as indicators. They cannot be interpreted except in the light of close knowledge of the context in which they were generated and this is denied the inspectors visiting and reporting later. The judgments inspectors make can only be as 'they seemed to them at the time'. Every inspection report is inevitably to some extent out-of-date immediately after the inspection but that does not mean it is not useful in the short-to-medium term as a basis for professional reflection and development. The time-specific 'instant' nature of inspection judgments and their inability to comment meaningfully on progress, whether by the school or by its students, need to be more fully recognised in any re-valuation of inspection.

Inspection and the quality of teaching

Despite the bias of Ofsted reports emphasising data the heart of inspection is a professional judgment about the quality of teaching experienced by pupils in a school. Arriving at that judgment does not involve looking for particular teaching methods and then gauging their effectiveness in terms of promoting learning. Rather the reverse. Inspectors look for evidence of pupils' learning in terms of their observable responses to teaching and then work back to those factors that have promoted, or hindered, their learning. Ofsted has been right for once to point out that there should be no automatically approved teaching methodology. 'The unanticipated success of the wrong method' needs to be recognised and celebrated. Judgments about the quality of teaching in lessons and in the school as a whole are properly tentative and consequently have to be offered as such in any feedback to those who have been observed. There is inevitably a considerable degree of inference involved in the judgments, especially those relating to the extent to which learning has taken place; there is inevitably too an element of professional judgment as to which features of the lesson have contributed to, or inhibited, whatever learning is inferred as having taken place. That tentativeness is crucial to the context in which any feedback is being given. It offers the opportunity in dialogue for other tentative, evidence-based, interpretations to be offered by the person being observed. Abandoning the making of judgments about the quality of teaching in a school would deal a death-blow to professional inspection and leave data as almost the sole determinant of quality. It should be fiercely resisted.

Qualitative judgment, not numerical grading

The evaluation of teaching and other aspects of the school is inevitably qualitative; nothing speaks for itself; everything needs interpreting and that interpretation inevitably involves value judgments and the use of qualitative descriptors such as 'good', 'very', 'excellent', 'satisfactory', 'reasonable', 'fair', 'poor' etc. There can be no stipulation as to which qualitative terms are to be used; they must 'fit' the perceptions of the activity or activities being evaluated. They cannot be reduced to just four numerical grades as under the current Ofsted regime; reality is much more complex than that four-fold categorisation. That over-simplification may be useful for the purposes of educational accounting but fails to take into account the many-varied facets of educational reality which can only be captured (and then only in part) in well-crafted prose. Inspection teams need the freedom to dispense with artificial, misleading constructs such as overall inspection gradings and to present schools in their idiosyncratic variety with idiosyncratic descriptors to match. Each inspection report has to be bespoke – not a formulaic account with minimal variation from school to school. Misleading over-simplistic grades should make way for prose which gives a vivid sense of what a particular school is really like – as seen by a group of experienced, expert observers. That's the way schools are. That's the way they should be reported. That qualitative richness needs to be built into any new inspection model.

Recommendation, not prescription

At least one other feature of old-style HMI inspection needs incorporating. No school, however notionally 'outstanding', is perfect. There is always more to learn from the experience of other schools and inspectors can help bring that experience to bear when making their recommendations. Inspections should result in recommendations, not as at present diktats as to 'what the school needs to do to improve'. Inspectors should raise issues a school needs to consider, not necessarily to act on; that's a crucial distinction. However, there is a professional obligation on the part of schools to respond publicly on how and why they have considered those recommendations, even if it is to reject them in part. This both reflects and reinforces a view of inspection as providing a set of provisional, tentative, time-specific judgments which inform, rather than necessarily override, the similarly provisional, tentative and time-specific judgments of staff and governors. Providing recommendations to consider, not slavishly and fearfully to act on, serves to respect rather than undermine the professional judgment of staff but also needs to be complemented by the need for a considered, public response to be given to a school's stake-holders, be they parents, governors , local authority officials or schools commissioners. Unlike the current situation inspection reports should never of themselves determine an institution's future but should inform it- another crucial distinction. Such reports can be powerful in their advocacy of the need to consider changing policy and practice on the part of those for whom they are written. That change in tone and substance would need to be part of a re-professionalised inspection system.

Curiously, even paradoxically, there will no more timely an opportunity to re-instate the key principles of an educational approach to school inspection than currently with a relatively new chief inspector and of a new Ofsted chair. Both will need to foster a change in the teaching profession's mind-set towards inspection so that it comes to be seen a developmental, educational enterprise, not a fault-finding, accounting process. Revisiting HMI's original principles could be a valuable way of reviewing the inspection process as well as renewing a two-way educational conversation with schools and teachers.

Afterword

Colin Richards has pierced through to the core point. There can be no naïve, primitive, untutored light shining on educational events that can possibly reveal the truth about them. Only those with experience and wisdom know where the light needs to be shined. Inspectors of education must have their credibility as 'experts' or 'connoisseurs' on teaching and learning restored.

Schools and colleges deserve quality, validity and reliability when they receive detailed reports or feedback on their work, just as individual pupils and students do. This is the most effective way in which people learn, develop and improve. It is the educational way. School inspection needs, therefore, to be a very early subject of root and branch review and reform. See Conclusions and Recommendations.

23 Mike Golby

Maurice Holt: educational leadership

Introduction

Maurice was a long-standing supporter and friend of the Exeter Society for Curriculum Studies. His clarity of thinking on comprehensive schooling and the curriculum necessary to it; his trenchant views on passing phases of educational reform such as TVEI (the Technical and Vocational Educational Initiative) and of course on mechanistic forms of assessment and evaluation spoke eloquently to our professional experience. Maurice demonstrated a consistent commitment to the idea of professional deliberation which, egalitarian and exploratory as it is, he would maintain is the key ingredient in leadership. The obituary below appeared in the Guardian 16 July 2016.

Maurice Holt has died in France aged 84. Maurice was a leading figure in a generation of progressive, school and university-based educationists who have left a rich legacy of educational thought and theory awaiting discovery when the present dark ages have passed.

A Cambridge educated engineer, after a spell in industry Maurice soon found his vocation becoming the first head of Sheredes School, Hertfordshire, a post he occupied for eight years up to 1969. There, in an admittedly favourable social and political climate, he went a long way towards implementing the kind of broad and balanced curriculum based on deep educational principles that he later came to illuminate in his renowned early books, *The Common Curriculum (1978)* and *Regenerating the Curriculum (1979)*. These were fully argued ripostes to the already discernible crudity of official thinking about education following the so called 'Great Debate' of 1976-1977.

Now that the 'secret garden of the curriculum' was open to all a crass instrumentalism had set in. Education, rather than an end in itself was now conceived in the public discourse as means to an end; and that end was to be material and measurable. Designing the curriculum meant stating desirable outcomes, usually in terms of skills, employability and conformity; and then designing 'learning experiences' which would produce these results. In turn evaluation meant measuring the desired 'behaviours'.

All of this was anathema to Maurice and other pioneers like Denis Lawton, Eric Midwinter, Caroline Benn and Malcolm Skilbeck who were following up the practical implications of comprehensive schooling. Among our own authors here Paul Niklaus was active alongside Maurice and local authority advisers in promoting successful comprehensive reorganisation. The Open University course *Curriculum Design and Development*, taken by tens of thousands of teachers, had also popularised new critical approaches to theory and practice.

But Maurice and Paul carried the credibility of having fully 'walked the talk'. A common school with a common curriculum accessible to pupils of all abilities and backgrounds was possible. It would be a conversation between the generations and represent to the young a 'selection from the culture'. You might say 'the best that has been thought and said', the highest forms of human achievement. But this was no high-minded restatement of mid-Victorian values with their elitist intent. It was a demand for a re-thinking of the curriculum based on quality and equality for all, a curriculum balancing the arts and sciences and equipping all students for lives informed by a critical spirit.

As it turned out we knew by the early eighties that we had experienced a late and false dawn. For government action on education was swift, brutal and philistine. Ted Wragg prophesied in

1980 'ten steps down the slippery slope to state controlled knowledge'. This was 20/20 vision. In these circumstances, the flame had to be kept alive and Maurice moved to the College of St. Mark and St. John, Plymouth where with Con Murphy he ran the inspirational '*Ten Schools Project*'. Since Ofsted and HMI were rampantly engaged in 'inspecting' schools in a naïve empiricist fashion, Maurice turned much of his attention to evaluation, publishing *Evaluating the Evaluators* in 1981. For Maurice, following Eisner in America and Stenhouse at home, educational evaluation was more a matter of connoisseurship than measurement; and teaching more a matter of artistry than working on a production line.

This perspective was given close definition in Maurice's doctoral thesis at the University of Exeter whose title says it all: *Practical and Moral Aspects of Curriculum Change* (1985).This work, which I had the privilege of supervising, celebrated in detail the pragmatic notion of 'deliberation' as the key feature of educational as opposed to technicist thinking. Deliberation fuses means and ends in a continuous process of situated judgement. For Maurice the exercise of such judgment was definitional of professionalism in education. Maurice and Bill Reid of Birmingham University made many new American connections, successors of John Dewey, in the development of these insights. Maurice brought them to our Exeter Society for Curriculum Studies at several Conferences and supported the Society throughout the years. Here Della Fish carried the torch into medical education. Ideas spread through convivial social connections and Maurice understood and relished the fact.

The American connections came to a fruition with Maurice's appointment to a Chair at the University of Colorado at Denver. There he made a huge number of connections with American educationists who, while also trammelled by political imperatives, nevertheless found more 'wriggle-room' and continued to develop generous philosophies of education. Michael Fullan and W Edwards Deming made regular appearances in the regular bulletins that came to Maurice's large number of correspondents in this country.

Returning to Britain Maurice opened another front in his war on ignorance. No doubt inspired by Geraldene's artistry in cuisine and in neat contrast to the malignancy of 'fast food', he embraced the 'slow school' movement. And in an era when 'mindfulness' is a respectable NHS therapy the 'slow school' is surely a piece of the wreckage we should cling to.

To explain Maurice's indefatigable energies is to recognise an outstanding intellect, a deep interest in the matter of being human-including its trivia and gossip-and a practically polymathic range of abilities. A final cameo illustrates this.

When I first met him Maurice he was establishing an educational consultancy in Devon. One afternoon I found him installing a central heating system at home while after a cup of tea getting back to composing a musical for Tiverton High School. I have the original cast sound recording and I can tell you it's West End material.

A great life, a great educator and a great human being.

Afterword

Leadership is always a moral matter. People will follow principles where they are conveyed by the example of personal commitment. This applies, it must be said, whatever the principles, good or bad. It is fortunate for education that leaders like Maurice Holt have appeared to inspire us. It is to be hoped that such figures will continue to emerge to sustain us in the face of ignorance and the abuse of power. To provide for this we must nurture a critical scholarly culture around teacher education in both its pre-service and in-service phases.

IV

Awakenings:
for Justice in Education

Awakenings: for Justice in Education

Introduction

In this section we address a defining issue of our time, the part that education has to play in the struggle for social justice. It is safe to say that all those writing in this book will have had an acute sense of the many inequalities that afflict our population. Some have actively worked with pupils with special educational needs. Others have woken early to gender differentials of various kinds, the bias towards boys in science and technology for example. Familial and community factors have loomed large, particularly for those working with younger children, for example in the early Educational Priority Areas suggested in the Plowden Report of 1967 and in the Sure Start Centres of Tessa Jowell and the Blair government. It cannot be said therefore that we have been entirely blind subscribers to an education system that seems to perpetuate historic inequalities.

All the same, the recent events mentioned in our Preamble -the election of Donald Trump, the Brexit referendum, the Grenfell Tower disaster and the Windrush scandal-have taken our awareness to a new level. At one of our many discussions as we contemplated a new political ethos in the making-one in which the disadvantaged have come to make their presence known among us - Mary Wilkinson exclaimed 'What do the people want?' This was a telling moment. It was as if we had not seriously considered the full import of the question before.

Now we do so. At the beginning of this work we rehearsed our understanding of recent educational history. Ted Wragg's 'ten steps to state control' came into reality, to be sure. The National Curriculum with its apparatus for the measurement of outcomes came into place in 1988. Ofsted, SATs and the regime for school inspection, similarly innocent of any doubt concerning the perception of

271

human behaviour, came into full spate following the Education (Schools) Act of 1992. But who in 1976, when Ted was writing or even in 1988 when Kenneth Baker's Education Reform Act was passed, could have predicted what was to come?

State control, it seemed, was here to stay. But all the while a new sentiment in favour of the market was developing-and fast. The centre-left politicians who followed Ronald Reagan and Margaret Thatcher, notably Bill Clinton and Tony Blair did not challenge the central premise of the Reagan-Thatcher era that market mechanisms are the primary instruments for achieving the public good. They welcomed globalisation and embraced the expanding world of the financiers. In this world to be 'competitive' and 'aspirational' was to be virtuous. On top of state control, which might conceivably have worked from alternative principles for the public welfare, the market was to be freed and diversity celebrated. Ever widening Income inequality saw a Labour minister of the day saying he was 'intensely relaxed' about the super-rich.

Hence today's predicament. Inequality is built into a social order based on competition. So as inequality grows, we now see the less successful deeply alienated. Let it be said also that large numbers of the comfortably off are also deeply troubled by the divided land we live in.

There are standard governmental responses to inequality. None of them addresses the issue squarely. In education there is the ludicrous belief that equality of opportunity will suffice. Create more Grammar school places! Surely just a greater opportunity to become unequal? George Osborne, promoting regional equality via his Northern Powerhouse, proposes running 'Dragon's Den' types of events in academies across the region in order to identify and celebrate 'entrepreneurship' and so to re-vitalise the regional economy.

These breath-takingly absurd ideas are signs of political desperation and, most seriously, of a loss of moral compass.

For a moral crisis is upon us. It is a crisis because it is not only income inequality that is at issue. That is severe enough with foodbanks across the land.

272

It is a crisis because meritocracy has imposed a hierarchy of esteem in which the work done by financiers and business people is privileged and more highly esteemed than that of others. In education the commercialisation of schools into academies and then into conglomerate chains is a permanent loss of public assets and a celebration of the business person as an heroic figure of our day. It is all reflected in the obscene salaries academy managements award themselves.

And so equality is not only about income, wage stagnation and the loss of jobs. It is also about the loss of social esteem. It is not only about unfairness; it is also about humiliation. Among the very many types of inequality along with income inequality we confront essentially the same problem. Ethnic minorities' access to Oxbridge? Working class people, especially boys in the north east? Rural deprivation? LGBTQ+ people? Wherever we find inequality we must deal with the root cause: contempt for the aspirations of those 'not like us'. (Sandel, 2018)

The first draft of Mary Wilkinson's paper below was produced in the aftermath of the events mentioned above: Trump; Brexit; Grenfell and Windrush. Subsequent work on the paper has not reduced its fervour.

Education for Justice

Consider the following quotations:

When my country in which I have just set foot was set on fire about my ears, it was time to stir. It was time for every man to stir. Thomas Paine (1776)

The downside of capitalism and its perversions have no spokesman. A gap in the political market opens up. Segments of the electorate await it. There is space for forceful attack, rooted in ideas, not gestures. (Hugo Young, 2003)

Who are we? Scarred, scared and divided; ...our divisions are rising from a deep malaise ... values vanish under the debris of fear...'You heard it in the cries in the air, howling for justice.' (Ben Okri)

We have a politically divided country in a way that I have never seen before. I have never seen a situation where the correlation between political alienation, social dislocation and economically being left behind is as absolute as it is. That is what is going on. Look at how people voted in the EU referendum. There are a lot of reasons why people voted the way they did, but it is not a coincidence that of the 65 areas that we say they are the worst parts of the country for education, employment and housing prospects going forward, only five voted to remain. (Alan Milburn in Evidence to Parliamentary Select Committee on Education March 2018)

Social division is not new. The roots of today's injustices lie deep in history and they are embedded in the social structure. Today it seems that a stunning maelstrom of events has come together to create a renewed sense of crisis. Trump. Brexit. Grenfell Tower. Windrush.

These events accentuate and define an era. For many of us it is a crisis of values, a moral crisis.

And it's not going to go away by thinking great thoughts. Nor by one-off initiatives on limited fronts. Education in its present institutionalised form is a part of the problem and not the solution. In its visionary aspect, however, it is our only hope.

Consider the confusion.

We are confused over a plethora of matters due to a mixture of concerns regarding climate change, wealth polarisation, the failure of capitalism and the accompanying asset-stripping, corruption and poverty; movement of populations including movement across continents as well as from countryside into cities; the threat of nuclear destruction; the rise of the political right and the shaking of confidence in democracy. Also, the collapse of confidence in established bastions such as the police and the judiciary. All this accompanied by exaggeration and denial so people find difficulty in distinguishing what is real and what is important, what can be ignored and what is fake.

Artificial Intelligence and the rise of robots is taking jobs as Brexit leaves people elated or depressed or simply confused, Productivity is low and Parliament, indeed the whole of society, is thrashing about with sexual accusations. Binary conceptions of gender have become problematic.

Around the country people in deprived communities feel misunderstood and unheard. Housing conditions are a clear indicator. High rise flats where lifts don't work and landings smell and there are no sprinklers to protect against the spread of fire; and there's fear of the gangs engaging with drug-dealing enforced with knife and acid crime. All this induces a sense of insecurity within a neighbourhood, which can all be heightened for females who are frequently overlooked, often abused, often living in desperate fear.

Among the scared are some ethnic groups, the homeless, stressed families, the abused, immigrants, prisoners and ex-prisoners, some people of colour, some religious sects, those living in overcrowded conditions, families damaged by debt and addiction. Newly high numbers largely of young men who, traumatised, are turning to suicide.

Suffocating poverty is a ground cause of these miseries. But the social exclusion that goes with it is still harder to combat. The tidal wave of social problems is racing towards all of us because of this unsustainable inequality has the potential to overwhelm society. It's not just economic hardship, but poverty of the sort that fertilises cultures of abuse. This problem transcends left/right politics and will eventually overwhelm any society that refuses to deal with it.

Our lower working-class families have been identified among the deprived and depressed - socially, intellectually, economically depressed. But an equal malaise affects the affluent: the obsessive pursuit of status and wealth, materialist values bringing their own stress-related disorders. There is a new phenomenon haunting the suburbs: the private tutor is abroad hawking expensive help with homework and crashing to the scene when GCSE and A level panic afflicts the aspiring parent. Universities are on suicide watch and there is a many weeks wait in the student counselling services.

The most worrying and concerning aspect of these deprivations is the dispiritedness of it all. If the underclasses cannot ascend upon the gravy train, the actual passengers are anxious for their destiny.

What's education got to do with it?

Can we achieve equality?

How can we ensure that many more of the dispossessed, of society's rejects, the ones we under-value, enjoy a new vibrant, purposeful life contributing to the general good? What would equality look like and feel like for this large minority of British people?

Britain is still largely class-driven with the privileged living in a degree of luxury and comfort and expecting to be honoured. This system of entitlement has been challenged down the years with a Conservative Prime Minister paying lip service to the welfare of the 'just about managing' and vowing to create 'a Britain that works for everyone'. Then we learn of the vast amounts of wealth stored away for purposes of tax avoidance offshore. As one system crumbles a new group of 'exceptionals' arises - the newly rich who are separate and distant. They flaunt and squander and waste. Meanwhile politicians seem to view power as an end in itself; and politics comes across as a cartoon soap opera, a sideshow.

Those who live with a vestige of education understand that we live in a magnificent universe whose wonders we are exploring and harnessing. Education in its true sense means understanding that fact and becoming part of the human project to explore our predicament. It is a project that will encompass the major areas of enquiry and expression available to us. We need a curriculum that incorporates these understandings and activities-and engages all who can benefit in them. The past forty years have not progressed the idea of a common heritage to be safeguarded and passed on in schools. Instead schooling has been the scapegoat and servant of materialistic values, most crudely in the equation of schooling with employability.

A philosophy of generosity would find an equilibrium between the haves and the have-nots. It would articulate a common consensus, a democracy of relationships expressing human values of solidarity, 'we're all in this together'.

Finally, some facts about inequality as food for thought and action:

- Average private primary school spend per pupil £12,200 p.a.

- Average state school primary spend per pupil £4,800

Children on free school meals are:

- 50% of intake in one fifth of schools

- under-represented in academies and free schools, which receive favourable funding over state schools

- over-represented in under-achieving schools

- are less likely to achieve five or more GCSE grades at A*to C including English and Maths

Reay (2017)

Pursuing Education

Introduction

Mike reflects on his career in schools and as an academic in universities. He has always regarded himself primarily as a teacher rather than as an academic. He traces his understandings of educational purposes as they have unfolded for him in the light of experience. There are chance elements, and a sense much of the time of 'muddling through'. Yet there is progress too. Lately he has re-visited his assumptions about social inequality. As a result, new vistas have opened up for him. If we take respect and honour as key virtues in any social system, we need to take a fresh look at the cultural values we bring to the people. In doing so, it is also necessary to review our own values. Is our curriculum offer authentically our own? Or are we unwitting purveyors of goods we do not fully believe in?

Mike's career, like any other, can serve and be understood as a kind of tracer through some of the broad educational scenes and dramas of our days. His work as a jobbing teacher and academic was underlain by a search for personal meaning, which continues.

In the first place, I was born of aspiring working-class parents at the outset of World War Two and the London blitz. My primary schooling was dominated by the eleven plus, the gateway to the grammar school. I 'passed for grammar' while most of my mates either 'passed for technical' or they 'passed for secondary modern'. That was the phraseology used in the school hall when our names were read out and each category ritually applauded.

I was no more deceived by my 'success' than were my mates by their 'failure'. We saw it coming and we knew the score. We parted in

July 1951 and after Test matches played all summer long in the school playground went our separate ways. My parents though were thrilled.

Of course, I now realise that my parents' aspiration was predicated upon a view of society as hierarchical, each exam pass a cleared hurdle to something better. What that 'better' was lay undefined. Certainly financial security was uppermost-they had lived through the hungry thirties. Yet I now believe it went further and deeper than that. Educational success meant respectability alongside income. What I have until very recently viewed as the snobbery of my mother and the cynicism of my father I now see as their struggle to be valued, for honour in the eyes of the world. This latter factor, the need for respect, I now - and very belatedly - see as a predominant motivation throughout society.

Arriving in the grammar school, it became clear that the primary school race had to be re-run. I was in the B stream and needed to be promoted. I was and so my 'O' levels would include Latin and, as everyone knew, that would open extra doors. Later, a malcontent in the second year Sixth, I was told a third year there would be necessary, and I would need to do 'S' levels and take the Cambridge entrance exam. This was a breaking point and I applied independently to a provincial university, as you could in those days, and was accepted sight unseen. I left school under a cloud.

Today I see this independence as an unarticulated protest against the value-system of the school and to a degree of my parents. I didn't want to be a success in their terms. But I couldn't verbalise this and I didn't know what else to do.

There I was, then, a survivor of the school system, albeit a lonely one. What had these years of primary and secondary education taught me?

Principally that life was a contest. As grit in the oyster, there was joy and meaning in some parts of Eng. Lit (Yeats with Mr Dingle was a revelation), some satisfaction in learning French and German, and exhilaration in competitive sports.

There were, I now see, three types of boy. There were the uncritical conformists, identifiable from the outset as keen to please, punctual with homework, strict adherents of the uniform policy, seated front and centre of every class. They would go on through GCE 'O' levels smoothly to house captaincy, the prefecture and the university. (I think I despised these boys as tedious creatures of the machine)

Then there were the outright refuseniks. Homework was done, but reluctantly. Uniform was worn but ties were knotted in unusual ways and shirt buttons casually undone. In the fifth form they developed a romance around shoplifting expeditions in the High Street. These boys were destined to leave after 'O' levels and, as I recall, went to destinations like the police, the army or clerical work. Today they would be good middle range students getting safe GCSEs.

I think I stood in some awe of these boys. They dared to be who they were. To hell with it. But I wasn't brave enough to join them.

The third category, probably the majority, were the compliers. Probably not clever enough to be in category one nor brave enough to be in category two, we went along with things and took satisfaction where we could. When a terrible bout of antisemitic bullying broke out we either avoided the scene or patronised the victim with our custom for his pornographic photographs. My own lifeline was football and athletics, where you could earn respect for achievement and some toleration of your doing quite well academically.

I applied for philosophy at university, I think, because I thought it might make things more meaningful than the school subjects I had taken. I was a serious fellow underneath, quite the Adrian Mole, a sampler of various churches and a regular visitor to the Friends Bookshop on the Euston Road.

However, philosophy was to disappoint my infantile intellectual ambitions. It was taught through its history. Fair enough: but that teaching amounted, more or less, to 'reading round the class'. We dealt with Locke, Berkeley and Hume that way. Of course, that was valuable. It was an initiation to the English empiricism that had reached a cul-de-sac in the shape of the logical positivism and linguistic analysis that prevailed in Oxford before and after the war. Our professor had studied in Chicago with Rudolf Carnap of the Vienna Circle, gone on to be a scientific adviser to the UK government and professor at the University of the Witwatersrand. His special field was philosophy of science and mathematical logic. The former meant looking at Popper, all to the good. The latter was torture.

Prof's standard question when we could be induced to make any kind of assertion at all was 'And what would be evidence for that view, Mr Golby?' Unless that evidence were empirical it could not be accepted. In the library I daily observed the golden words around the ceiling *'Wisdom is the principal thing. Therefore get wisdom and with all Thy getting get understanding'*. I did wonder what contribution my desultory studies were making to that end. In thrall to the bleak dictum that no proposition is meaningful that does not carry a method of empirical verification, too many channels of experience, all but scientific ones, were written off the philosophical agenda.

What escape from this myopia? It happened that the girlfriend I eventually found was working in the British Council and considering teacher training. When she joined a London teacher training college I was able to follow quite closely the ideas she was being presented with. These were broadly of the progressive type. Child-centred education was the word. Rousseau, Froebel, Pestalozzi, Piaget: these were the pantheon.

This was 1961. Thinking about schooling, like much else, was changing. A Primary PGCE seemed a reasonable move. It bought time and I would have the benefit of Pat's support and practical advice. In my London PGCE I met a second inspirational teacher in PS Wilson who was later to publish *Interest and Discipline in Education*, to my mind still the best available philosophical account of education. I took to heart his dictum: however trivial and inconsequential a child's interests may be, there is nothing else in terms of which he can become educated. This spoke to my condition.

(Anybody who has experienced depression will know what a salvation it is to find oneself interested in something, in anything. It is a salvation because an interest entails activity in its pursuit, beyond oneself. It is a recognition of value-in-itself, beyond what it will buy, what doors it may open, beyond even respectability).

Energised, I passed the PGCE and Pat and I married. My induction into primary teaching opens this collection of papers, a glimpse of the licence enjoyed and endured by teachers in the sixties.

I did not mention in Chapter 1 what occasioned our departure for overseas, but it has since become relevant. We were renting a third-floor flat and when Pat became pregnant with our firstborn we applied to the new town Development Corporation for ground floor accommodation. This request was not granted so we moved with the British Army Education Service to Malaysia. Returning, we had accumulated enough savings to put down a deposit on a home-of-our-own. Teachers were always mobile and always paid just enough to run a mortgage.

We had escaped the Tower Block.

Later I read Stuart Hall who notices the middle ground occupied by teachers - between the elite and the masses. They have 'horizontal' relationships with the communities local to their schools and 'vertical' relationships to the sources of power in the wider society. They mediate between the two and their currency is the curriculum. All too often they are mediators with no real position of their own. In an OU seminar Stuart cited English teachers commuting daily from respectable suburbs across hostile territory to inner-city schools, there to teach Shakespeare-only to return home in the evening to watch Coronation Street.

After a number of years teaching at home and abroad the opportunity arose to move into teacher education. The new B.Ed degree called for educational theory in the shape of the 'four ugly sisters', the philosophy, psychology, sociology and history of education. Someone somewhere, I suspect on the train between London and Bristol, had invented this canon, the 'Disciplines of Education (Tibble, 1966)'. This replaced 'the great educators' (Rusk 1957), as the staple of educational theory. Some said it would replace 'mush' with 'mesh'. However, the great thinkers and practitioners of education from Socrates onwards to Dewey (1916), Russell (1926) and Whitehead (1929) did deal in the round with the practice of education and the values it promotes. The new curriculum recreated the schism between the 'is' and the 'ought' of education in the interests of the academic rigour required by the B.Ed degree.

Thus it happened that my degree in philosophy and my teaching experience gained me a post in a new teacher training college in Lancashire.

Now I was to pursue education by teaching its theory to students. I found two big problems in this situation. In what ways could the philosophy I had learned as an undergraduate be of use to newcomers to the profession? How could the 'disciplines of education' relate to one another?

That philosophy could present answers to the ultimate question 'why?' had been my initial delusion in applying to study it as an undergraduate. Philosophy now could only be clarification of meanings. Yet, there was something, in fact a lot, to be said for this activity. We spent time analysing 'education', comparing and contrasting it to 'indoctrination', 'training', 'brainwashing' and the like. We contrasted 'teaching' and 'training;' 'explaining' and 'expounding;' 'needs' and 'wants'; 'theory' and 'practice'.

While setting about all this with some zest, I began to suspect that we philosophers of education were engaged programmatically in promoting a particular view: the idea that 'education' is a superior kind of activity to its rivals, for example 'training' or 'socialisation'. We were shoring up an elite by pretending we were custodian-practitioners of 'education', defining its rarefied characteristics with our linguistic acrobatics. We deemed education to be of 'intrinsic value' bestowing 'cognitive perspective' upon its initiates. I have not entirely shed this view. But it was an early intimation that our answer to Mary's Question - what do the people want? - is not the 'liberal education' we envisaged for them.

(We had a facile way of dealing with the Mary Question. We said what they want is not to be equated with what they need. They may want burgers and fries; they need halloumi and green salad; wanting pushpin, they need poetry).

If there were limitations to philosophy, a second problem lay in the integration of the disciplines of education into students' thinking and of course into their practice. This came home to me one afternoon around 1970 when an eager student taking the psychology course- they specialised in just one of the disciplines in the fourth year- came to see me with a question. Dr West had been discussing Pavlovian theory and she had asked whether it was alright to punish children in school since it worked well with rats. His reply was 'Well, that's a moral question. Ask Mike Golby'. I don't remember my reply. I certainly didn't pose as a moral authority. And I don't think I gave her a potted account of intuitionism and act-and rule-utilitarianism and I hope not. But it's possible.

Years later, and in view of political developments since, it struck me that if academic disciplines had to be picked out for would-be teachers, then Economics and Politics were probably stronger candidates. But they too would have had to face the issue of how they were to relate to educational practice. Academia faces one way, professional practice another. As it was, the academic divisions among the disciplines of Education were putting down roots; books and journals, learned societies, conferences national and international, careers burgeoned. Many a distinguished philosopher of education wanted nothing to do with schools.

As it happened, I was rescued from the career cul-de-sac that philosophy of education was to be by the Open University where I was appointed to a lectureship in 1976. We were to produce a massive course on Curriculum Design and Development. I was a receptive but unsystematic reader of the emergent literature of protest: Ernst Schumacher, Ivan Illich, John Holt, Michael Young, MFD Young, Richard Hoggart, Raymond Williams. I responded to the popular culture: Pink Floyd's Another Brick in the Wall ('we don't need no educayshun/we don't need no thought control/hey teacher, leave those kids alone'), Sam Cooke's' (What a) Wonderful World ('don't know much about history/don't know much biology/don't know much about a science book/don't know much about the French I took).

Moving into Education as an academic at the Open University, I was detained by issues of educational research. It had to be done if one wanted a career. Initially, curriculum questions defined the agenda. How to research the curriculum, defined in the most general way in terms such as 'all the learning for which the school is responsible'. I fell in behind Denis Lawton, Lawrence Stenhouse, John Elliot et al as a proponent of the 'teacher as researcher' movement: It was, we said, integral to teachers' professionalism that they should research their own practice.

We also perceived that positivistic methodologies could offer only superficial knowledge of educational practice. The classic example of this is to be found in the furore over Neville Bennett's book *'Teaching Styles and Pupil Progress'* in 1976.

I had crossed paths with Neville Bennett at Lancaster. In 1974 or thereabouts he had rung the college in which I was working to seek help with his doctoral research. He was investigating the relationship between traditional and progressive styles of teaching and pupil achievement. I was one of the respondents to his call for a telephone interview. What happened was that he read out the names of a number of Primary schools in which we supervised student teaching practice. For each school he wanted to know whether I would call it 'formal', 'informal' or mixed'. I gave obliging top of the head replies. And that was all. Of course, he would have had numerous other respondents and no doubt a large pool of 'data'. All the same, when the book came out claiming, in very general terms, that formal teaching produces better results than informal teaching I couldn't help pondering the old adage 'rubbish in-rubbish out'. Doubts were strengthened by the fact that the most successful school in the sample was in fact categorised as a 'progressive' school. Wouldn't his energies have been better spent explaining how this aberration came about? He had not done so because he was interested only in cause-effect relationships and not the fine grain of educational practice.

The Bennett case also illustrated how educational research merges with politics. When interviewed for a BBC broadcast he affected a naïve innocence. He had 'just told it as it was'. He refused to consider how his results played into the backlash against progressive schooling that was going on.

Other contemporary events were the William Tyndale and Risinghill School scandals. Both these north London schools were depicted by investigative journalists from nearby Fleet Street as chaotic (the latter labelled Raising Hell School) and the teachers as enemies of the public good. 'Panorama' weighed in and In short order Prime Minister Callaghan produced his Ruskin College speech, the first step down Ted Wragg's 'slippery slope to state control'.

The OU experience had strengthened my perspective. It was seriously hard work, meeting publishing deadlines, dealing with a team of contributing academics and BBC egos. There were researches in Milton Keynes itself, in the adventurous campus high schools there; in New York's Urban Coalition and in Yorkshire's progressive Primary schools with Sir Alec Clegg, the charismatic Chief Education Officer.

In the Yorkshire coalfield we filmed entrancing sessions of dance and movement while through the Victorian school windows demolition work was going on, great cranes demolishing the communities to which these graceful ten-year olds belonged. I thought the camera ought to notice this but the producer was too interested in the dance to be persuaded. Nor was Sir Alec Clegg in person and on camera able to reassure me that this curriculum was not a romantic retreat from stark social reality. Something similar happened at the Yehudi Menuhin School in Surrey where the opportunity to capture the classical music eliminated some counter-cultural after-hours rock, the 'hidden curriculum'.

There were flaws in the OU operation, certainly, and I was too junior and unconfident either to contribute well or to benefit to the maximum. What I did take away, however, was the idea of curriculum as 'ideology in action'. This was Malcolm Skilbeck's major input as senior consultant to the course we were developing. The merit of the idea of ideology is that it brings 'fact' and 'value' together in a unified whole, an outlook, an understanding of the world carrying with it a programme of action. Thus, socialism or conservatism as political examples each have their own understanding of history, of social change and, of much, much else like, say, relations between the sexes. They contain also a dynamic towards action.

Skilbeck proposed three 'ideologies of education': classical humanism, progressivism and reconstructionism. Ideologies are understood as clusters of beliefs and values that underpin fundamental outlooks or world-views. The idea is that critique is possible at the level of ideology. The term is used descriptively, not pejoratively. So we can say that progressivism is rooted above all in a view of the child as an autonomous learner seeking personal growth and fulfilment; it offers on the face of it very little in terms of a canon or prescribed syllabus.

By contrast classical humanism emphasises historic human achievement and tradition; 'the best that has been thought and said'. The child here is, in my favourite Oakeshott quotation, 'a postulant to the human condition'. (My Master's tutor Glenn Langford was later to argue for a view of education as the development of 'persons').

Thirdly for Skilbeck, reconstructionism emphasises the social role of education in maintaining and improving quality of life and culture. John Dewey is probably the leading modern advocate of this view.

While it is easy to see value in each of these three broad views, to acknowledge that all have a part to play in any thought about education, it is more difficult to reconcile them in that thought and its implementation. More normally these ideologies are resources for opposition, argument and emphases. Curriculum design can be seen as the balancing of competing claims from these sources. Skilbeck's typology may at best be used as a language for debating curriculum. What it cannot do is to offer any sort of final reconciliation among them. At root they present red lines defending respectively the interests of the learner, the claims of the heritage and the demands of the social context.

This schema I brought to Exeter in 1976. In successive iterations of the BPhil(Ed)/MEd course it served as a hook for much of the teaching. Earlier I have said the disciplines of education look toward academia-and I did contribute to the literature of the philosophy of education, for example when I had something to say about communitarianism, Tony Blair's favourite philosophy at the time. In the main, however, my interest was and remains in the knowledge embedded in professional practice and how it might be supported.

Afterword

The two pieces above by Mary Wilkinson and Mike Golby are written at very different temperatures. Where Mary is passionate, Mike is contemplative. Hers is inflamed by shocking public events that have brought us all to re-examine our educational mission. His is a longer story of a slowly unfolding awareness of the truth in H G Wells' insight that civilisation is a race between education and disaster. No doubt these elements, fervent yet interrogative are present in most minds today.

26 Colin Richards

Three views of the curriculum: a critique of the chief inspector's curriculum commentary

Introduction

Colin offers this brief but incisive paper. It is a critique of the simple-minded version of the curriculum which Amanda Spielman, Ofsted's Chief Inspector, brought to her new role in 2017.

Colin contrasts the broad and inclusive view of the school curriculum ('activities...to promote intellectual, personal, social and physical development of pupils'), which he personally helped to define as an HMI in the 1980s, with two recent and much more restricted views of the curriculum: the so-called 'National' curriculum ('comprising a series of subjects little different from those a century ago') and the even more inadequate 'tested' curriculum which requires Primary schools to focus on only two subjects.

Offering a wide-ranging curriculum to all Britain's schools is an important social justice issue because many children in English local authority schools, where the national curriculum is compulsory are missing out on the benefits of a rounded education compared with all the other children in Britain, where the national curriculum is not compulsory. This unfair advantage applies not just to pupils in Scotland, Wales and Northern Ireland and not just to the 7% of pupils in fee-paying independent schools, but also to all the other English pupils in state-funded 'academies' and the so-called 'free' schools.

The curriculum was once famously described as a ten-letter dirty word. One leading authority asserted 'The curriculum matters but that is the extent of agreement about the curriculum.' Almost thirty years on from the Education Reform Act of 1988 which prescribed a curriculum for the first time since 1926, both statements remain true.

The curriculum is contested, problematic, and value-saturated, though HMCIs recent commentary fails to recognise this. The curriculum is an educational minefield where angels and chief inspectors should fear to tread. Angela Spielman has trod and, seemingly unwittingly, is taking Ofsted with her on a potentially very hazardous journey.

There are almost as many definitions of the curriculum as there are pundits to proclaim them. Let's start with one about which there was a near- consensus prior to the government of the day intervening in what had been 'a secret garden'; I stress 'near-consensus' since unanimity in this value-laden area is an impossibility:

> '*A school's curriculum consists of all those activities designed or encouraged within its organisational framework to promote the intellectual, personal, social and physical development of its pupils. It includes not only the formal programme of lessons, but also the 'informal' programme of so-called extra-curricular activities, as well as those features which produce the school's ethos...*' (HM Inspectorate 1986 *The curriculum from 5 to 16* HMSO)

I believe that view would achieve wide degree of approval among education professionals thirty years on; it is certainly more wide-ranging than HMCI's view of the curriculum as a 'body of knowledge' and 'a set of standards'. That earlier liberal view of the curriculum has been seriously weakened, and is still being undermined, by a politically-inspired narrow view embodied by Gibb and the DfE and not seriously questioned in the chief inspector's commentary. Certainly, in its pronouncements thus far Ofsted does not appear to be endorsing this liberal perspective when it comes to inspecting the curriculum. Perhaps, just perhaps, this will change in the new inspection framework promised for 2019, but I'm not holding my breath.

Then there is the so-called but misnamed 'national' curriculum comprising a series of subjects little different from those listed in the secondary school regulations of a more than a century ago. Of course, the curriculum isn't 'national'; it doesn't exist in three quarters of the constituent parts of the United Kingdom. In England it is restricted to LA community schools; academies and independent schools are not required to follow it — which should raise questions about its value.

As part of the research programme she is undertaking the chief inspector is not proposing to investigate the profession's perceptions of the value and relevance of the present 'national' curriculum. Though supporting the notion of 'a careful balance' in curriculum design, she doesn't recognise the grossly imbalanced 'national' curriculum, especially at primary level, which she wants 'delivered', with an emphasis on learners 'receiving knowledge' rather than acquiring it and making it their own. I suspect this view is far removed from those of the majority of professionals she is seeking to influence. But let's be clear: the 'national curriculum' as currently promulgated is being fully endorsed by the chief inspector without any substantial body of research or inspection evidence to support her claims of its value. It is true that in her role she can scarcely oppose government policy but she could, but doesn't, intend to raise questions about its value and its effects. She should.

Thirdly there is the 'tested' curriculum which in primary schools involves only two subjects. In critiquing this view of the curriculum, the chief inspector is on stronger ground. I strongly suspect, though we don't know for certain, that the vast majority of primary teachers would accept her view that curriculum has been unduly narrowed by test anxiety and preparation. Probably, though we don't know, many secondary teachers would accept her criticisms of the narrowing of Key Stage 3 but like their primary colleagues would blame having to meet the accountability requirements of Ofsted and the DfE for those problems. They would agree with her that the 'tested' curriculum is an impoverished curriculum: but is her endorsed 'national' curriculum much better?

Without any sense of irony the chief inspector criticises schools for 'a weak theoretical understanding of the curriculum', a shortcoming certainly illustrated by her own commentary and by the lack of any theoretical work on the school curriculum by Ofsted since its inception twenty-five years ago. This understanding could well come, not from Ofsted itself but at least in part from those working in academies and independent schools untrammelled by the impoverished 'national' curriculum. Who knows, that theoretical understanding could even be developed by those academics vilified by a previous Secretary of State as 'the blob'!

Afterword

Most professional practitioners would endorse Colin's wide-ranging view of the curriculum, because they see education as contributing to the personal development of learners, whereas Ofsted, under political influence for the past 30 years, has been trying to limit the curriculum to a 'body of knowledge' or a 'set of standards'. This difference about educational purpose is crucially important for all children and for their parents, as well as for teachers. How can it be turned into a public conversation - a great debate?

Teachers are currently leaving the profession in their droves. Is the Ofsted approach to the curriculum one of the causes of their disaffection? Can a consensus be reached that a new approach should be tried?

The editors humbly suggest that the wisdom of senior retired practitioners like Colin Richards ought not to be overlooked but sought out in the great educational debates surely soon to begin.

Philosophical End Piece

Introduction

Here is an attempt to make sense of the review we have undertaken of a generation's work in education. What has been learned for the future? What have been the advances and what the set-backs in the continuous struggle to provide a better future and a better society for our children, our students? Is there progress in education or are we simply doomed to make the old mistakes in new guises?

Retrospective

To look back to the early and later sixties today is to contemplate another country. It feels as an astronomer must when contemplating the early micro-seconds of the universe following the *Big Bang*. From such concentrated energy what an explosive, expanding educational universe we now must deal with. Many of us writing here were at our most energetic then and into the seventies carried along by high potency ideas and optimism. Stella Darke and I entering the primary school full of inspiration; Will Taylor, Paul Niklaus and Gail Parfitt entering secondary and community education with high ideals.

In the main we swam with the tide and looked disbelievingly upon older colleagues slow to respond to progressive ideas: in the primary school times-tables, the kings and queens of England and mechanical reading round the class as holy writ; in the secondary school defensive 'subject-mindedness' opposed to the 'integration' we advocated; whole-class, preferably streamed and setted, teaching; discipline; and getting them through their GCEs.

The school of those days was a closed world ('no parents beyond this point') and each classroom a teacher's private fiefdom. We newcomers sought to overcome all this, convinced that reason and history were on our side. Stella developed deep rapport with pupils and their families, such a positive result of taking their interests seriously. Will too was on his students' side revelling in the privilege of promoting his love of learning with them. Gail and Paul were also close to their students, both of them venturing into territory beyond the school gates, the local community.

To my mind, the effect of government by the market as regulated by the arm's length instruments of the state (Ofsted, the Office for Students etc) has been to iron out diversity in the maintained sector while releasing some wild extravagancies elsewhere. Sameness is the rule where there is close supervision, control and comparison. Experiment is discouraged, compliance is a virtue. This can only be unhealthy for progress which is achieved best by imaginative practical measures carefully monitored and evaluated.

In the universities too these early sixties were a period of growth and optimism based on the traditional assumption that university education was a right of all who could benefit from it. New universities were being created and the decade saw their number grow from 22 to 45, which is still less than one third of their present number.

The Colleges of Advanced Technology created in the 1950s entered the university sector in the sixties but their advent caused no general rethinking of the higher education curriculum. No new purposes for this doubling of the number of universities were proposed. It was more of the same. However, Lord Lindsay renewed the educational vision at Keele as Gordon Brown makes clear. The philosophy behind the four-year degree was explicit. There is depth but there is also breadth. I too had been struck by the wording in gold leaf around the Roborough Library at Exeter university in 1958: *'Wisdom is the principal thing: therefore get wisdom and with all thy getting get understanding'* and I had wondered what bearing my studies had on that ambition. After all, it was something of the kind that I had in mind when applying to read philosophy in 1958.

The trap of elitism

Maurice George speaks in these pages of life at Oxford in the fifties, assuming that its elitism cannot change. Readers will have noticed a strange apparent contradiction within his paper. He decries most of what he depicts. But is grateful for the education it provided for him! It can't then have been all bad? We all live with contradictions and this is a particularly honest admission. A very similar schism sits in the minds of many of us around the eleven-plus. We have benefitted in a flawed past but we think there is a better way for all to benefit in an improved future.

What money can't buy

Paul Ernest considers the impact of the later marketisation of universities on the work of the academic. I am reminded of Elizabeth Anderson's thesis in *Value in Ethics and Economics.* There are certain 'goods 'which undergo transformation if they are the subject of trade. One would be love ('can't buy me love'). Another justice. Another wisdom. You can't buy those either. If you try to, you corrupt the very thing you seek.

Under certain circumstances, however, you can secure the possibility that love and wisdom can be exercised within the competitive turmoil of social living. It is the churches, the hospitals, the judicial institutions, the schools and universities that cost the money. These institutions serve to defend certain key values of our civilisation. Their personnel are of course paid. But their salaries are a subscription of trust in the idea of a service governed by principles, not by the profit motive.

Of course, there are costs in providing anything on the surface of the earth. It is a matter of how far we can defend the cash nexus from contaminating the relationship between provider and client. My (I regret to have to say 'private') dentist does not require cash in advance nor does she personally collect cash from me. That transaction is done formally at Reception. The NHS provides services, it is said, 'free at the point of delivery'. But we do all pay, of course, through our taxes.

Trust: a new covenant

The effect of these delicate arrangements for funding personal services is to emphasise the levels of trust that must exist between the provider and the client. The provider trusts the client to pay. The client trusts the professional to be governed by the knowledge that payment will be forthcoming, and accordingly to provide a standard of service recognised by the professional body that safeguards the conduct of practice.

Allen has stressed the necessity for trust in the teachers and the complex demands of their jobs. It is certainly time to regularise the covenant between teachers, parents and the state-a task to be considered by the new National Education Council we propose. The word 'covenant' has real applicability here. For a covenant is more than a cease-fire, a truce, a contract, a treaty or an agreement. A covenant implies a settlement based on a deep moral commitment, not a mere legal obligation. This feature, this moral dimension is what makes trust the essential quality of both sides. It is, incidentally, the precise reason why breeches of professional trust are taken so very seriously by professional associations and in the courts.

Trust is easily lost and hard-won. Happily, teachers have retained a considerable measure of public respect with the British Social Attitudes Survey reporting in 2016 that 92% of the public expressed 'respect; or 'a great deal of respect' for teachers. Some of this may be attributable to history and some to the empathy of other workers for all occupations are surely highly stressed these days. Whatever, there is a fair wind for positive development based on closer relationships of a non-materialistic kind. Teachers will need to encourage positive views of education as personal development alongside its proper and more tangible vocational aspects. In all this it is vital that teachers themselves retain a broad view of their work as not only 'serving customers' but promoting students' development as persons.

Practical measures

In March 2018 the government announced that in order to reduce teachers' workload and to improve recruitment there would be no changes in assessment or in the curriculum for the duration of the current parliament. This was of course to be welcomed. The sheer quantity of work outside the core activity of teaching had become intolerable. Of course, no one denies there is work to be done outside the classroom. There is planning, preparation and marking. There are budgets to construct and financial control to maintain. There are reports to write, governors to be involved, parents to consult with. There are periodic inspections to be prepared for, which in an ideal world would be taken in the school's stride, but in reality often prove disruptive.

All of these pressures are in principle legitimate and can be managed with skilful leadership, robust systems and dedicated staff. Yet it is vital to remember that the core activities of school are teaching and the learning that ensues from it. At the time of the announcement of a moratorium on change a former teacher who had resigned after three years in school said he felt the whole system 'needed standing on its head'. That is my belief also.

A change of heart

The difficulty we face in the final section of our work in making recommendations for educational change is that what we are calling for really requires a change of heart, a re-conception of education as a social good.

It is not only a matter of a reduction in workload, welcome as that is. While relatively simple reductions in pressure on teachers are welcome, we believe it is time to centre down upon the teaching and learning which is the whole *raison d'etre* of the school as an institution in the first place. Doing so will demonstrate the importance of teachers occupying the centre stage. It is only the inherent quality of the educational interface, the teaching moment, that can answer the question posed above by Will Taylor, 'by what right do we compel children to attend school at all?'

Schools are custodial institutions, but their justification is not simply that they keep youngsters out of the way and off the streets for long periods of time. Even in the case of prisons a moral, ameliorative principle is recognised, even if scandalously and shamefully neglected in practice.

Schools and prisons, while custodial, are also governed by higher principles: in the case of prisons, rehabilitation; in the case of schools, education. It follows that reform in both cases must rest upon a concept of human betterment or flourishing such that the 'product' will be a reformed and better person.

So I do want to see less testing of children, less inspection of schools, less prescription of teaching aims and methods. But I am not opposed in principle to testing, not opposed in principle opposed to

302

inspection, and not opposed, within limits, to a prescribed curriculum.

Rather, I want to see testing, inspection and curriculum re-imagined and understood as contributing in their own ways to the learning which is the stock-in-trade of the school. We should always ask of any new measure or reform 'how does this improve the quality of learning in the classroom and beyond?'

The educational relationship

What, then, characterises a healthy educational order, a proper educational relationship?

I want to explore three very basic principles, respect for persons, respect for enquiry and respect for the teacher.

First, all participants, teachers and students are of equal moral standing and all are due appropriate respect as such.

Second, since school's educational mission is founded on knowledge and knowledge is always provisional, always developing, nothing is unchallengeable.

Third, the teacher will always be the senior person in the educational situation, responsible for its organisation and general conduct but also always ready to meet challenge and questions openly.

As to the first principle: schools are pre-eminently moral communities. For me this means membership is open to both teachers and taught *as persons*. What this means is that the community is essentially that of humankind: school is not an interest group, a supporters' club or a religious, political or any other kind of campaigning organisation. It unifies individuals as persons and sets itself against only those who would capture it for a sectional interest.

I well remember Bob Moon, a Head of House at Stantonbury Campus, Milton Keynes consulting with the youngest, most inarticulate students the structure of the Assembly they were shortly to conduct. His courtesy, patience, interrogative style and listening ear as these young people struggled to express themselves was remarkable. These young people were being treated with non-condescending respect, in fact as *persons* inferior to their teachers only in respect of their inexperience.

The educational relationship is essentially one of moral equality. It is for this reason that schools are our best hope of building community both within and outside their walls. This moral standing must be defended against capture by those who would convert this humanistic purpose to some other end; ploughshares can be turned into swords and students into trainees in no time.

As to the second principle, respect for enquiry: this puts at the centre open-mindedness, the willingness to think, to consider even the loftiest authority, even one's own strongest convictions may be mistaken. Respect for enquiry entails that all participants, teachers and students, participate as scholars, not as supposed 'empty vessels' in the continuing egalitarian conversation which is an educational situation. It applies at every level of education.

The American psychologist Jerome Bruner once asserted that anything can be taught in some recognisable form to anybody at any stage of development. This was a brave hypothesis that need not be tested to destruction to see that the youngest, slowest child can be seen to engage in purposive activity bearing the characteristics of, say science or poetry. The sorting of fallen tree leaves in autumn or the singing of playground songs are examples. Much could accrue from developing these common interests.

As to the third principle, respect for the teacher: this requires, first, that the teacher be herself an educated person, not a robot. There can be no moral relationship with a machine though, quite a different matter, machines can be put to good and bad purposes.

School, then, is not merely a mechanism for social control but at root a community whereby individuals come both to control their own lives and to understand those lives as lived in common. This means that while I do see schooling as part of preparation for working life, I also want it to go further. I want schooling also to equip students to make their own informed decisions about their own adult life and about the society they will live in. Philosophers have expressed this broader aim as the pursuit of 'personal autonomy based on reason'.

I do not under-estimate the challenge this view of education offers to the status quo. The political rhetoric has always been couched in terms of material societal benefits, principally the growth of the economy.

To reiterate: I do not reject that aim but insist that the net of education be cast more widely. Education, I say, is about human flourishing in the round. Citizens are more than workers and consumers. They are also seekers after their own destinies, carrying responsibility for their own lives. This entails that they be given access to all the tools - commercial, aesthetic, moral, political and spiritual- that have been found useful in the pursuit of the good life by our forebears.

In short, in a democratic society all must have the benefit of equal access to our cultural heritage. A broad and balanced curriculum of the kind identified by Colin Richards above will represent that heritage and make access to it possible for all. The school curriculum is the predominant vehicle for that vital task because only schools address the whole population. It is a further question how the 'whole population' may in practice be included. Divisions of schools prematurely into 'types' - tripartite types, 'state', sponsored, public and private school types - specialised academies and 'studios' - all these are potentially divisive if not deployed within a coherent overall framework.

Just as conscription in the two world wars of the twentieth century revealed gross deficiencies in the physical health of the nation, so mass compulsory education has revealed vast discrepancies in access and response to a broad liberal education. These injustices have been remarked upon throughout this collection of papers, notably by Mary Wilkinson and Will Taylor. Despite rearguard attempts to revive the grammar school (which can only benefit the few and deprive the many), a comprehensive education based on a comprehensive curriculum is not only a democratic necessity but also an entitlement for all. Further, we might also ask by what principle any minority should opt out of this entitlement. But we have not made a case against so-called 'independent' or 'private' education in this book. The case is, however, made most eloquently in Green and Kynaston's *Engines of Privilege: Britain's Private School Problem (2019)*.

Afterword

Mike has tried to penetrate the deeper mysteries of teaching, the still centre where real learning occurs. What emerges most evidently from his perspective is that there can be no science for good teaching. It is not a neurologically advanced form of coding. Learning cannot be imposed but can only be presented as an opportunity to be taken up by willing learners, whose interest has been excited.

It follows that respect for the autonomy of the learner must be uppermost. Lead the horse to water, certainly. But make (make?) him (him? him!) drink?

The whole language of 'delivery', whether applied to the curriculum or to other non-portable realities like love or trust is profoundly misleading. In just the same way, talk of 'driving up standards' betrays a cynical mindset, the coercive view of the authoritarian. In that the language of education has been so corrupted by these mechanistic thought-forms, the way to the genuine delights of learning for all will be steep and rock-strewn.

That is why Mike speaks of a covenant between teachers and the wider polity. A covenant is a contract built on trust. Of course, there were excesses amounting to breeches of trust fifty years ago and these are referenced in our Preamble and elsewhere. In many ways, not much has happened since. There are millions who are completely outside the loop of education. Yet we must persist. In the present period of social and political turmoil the privileged educated-and that means us-must extent the opportunities we enjoyed to those less fortunate The National Education Council must have as a top priority the extension of a broad and rich curriculum entitlement to all. More, it must consider how to make lifelong learning a reality for all. We need an educated not an imperfectly schooled society.

V

Conclusions and Recommendations

Conclusions and Recommendations

Collated by Carole Newton

The current crisis in education

In this section we consider key implications of this work and make some practical recommendations.

The Exeter Society for Curriculum Studies is a group of senior retired professional educators, but our concerns are entirely about the future. We do not romanticise the past in this work and we certainly do not believe that educational practices forty years ago were in every respect better than they are today. But we do submit that education is now in crisis. The system needs a radical overhaul in which the 'five big mistakes' identified in Chapter2 are addressed and corrected. Changes are required urgently in the short term, for the sake of our grandchildren, their children and future generations. For the longer term we need new generations of teachers ready to act as cultural critics, thinking people who can stand up for true education not reduced to conformity and subject only to power.

A crisis exists when the march of events reaches a turning point. It separates an unsustainable past from an unpredictable future and, as the papers in Section One make clear, today's educational system is indeed unsustainable. A crisis is also a crossroads where decisive turns must be made.

The decisive turn proposed throughout this work is that education re-align itself with social purposes and justice alongside economic purposes and material prosperity. The outcome of a crisis determines in a fundamental manner the shape of things to come, and we believe that the recommendations we now put forward describe a machinery for that purpose, a just education for all.

In Chapter One we followed the twists and turns of educational policy during our professional lifetimes. The centralisation of power over the curriculum in the 80s was followed by the wholesale marketisation of the education service. Statism and the market are incompatible ideologies in theory and in practice first the one and then the other has predominated. For thirty years the Orwellian nightmare of state control of education, Ted Wragg's *Ten Steps* in Chapter 1, has existed alongside an unjustified belief in the positive effect of injecting private enterprise into every aspect of education provision. This ideological confusion has led directly to the incoherence and injustice found in today's education system.

Among the important things which have been lost to education are local democratic control, a rich public service ethos and the basic concept of fairness for all. That these goals were never fully achieved in practice is no reason not to embrace them anew. Education should no longer be seen as primarily a service industry for the global marketplace, a producer of a 'world-class' workforce. Education has its own intrinsic values around the idea of human potential and personhood. Albeit that these classical values have in the past been the privilege of a few, today they are endangered and must be re-imagined for the many as 'just education'. That is what a 'balanced curriculum' should be seeking, alongside the essential, more material benefits.

The education crisis is closely linked to today's wider societal malaise. It has always been unfair that the rich have had more chance than the poor to obtain a 'good education' for their children, but the increased levels of social inequality in recent decades have embedded this injustice to such an extent that social cohesion is now at risk. The rhetoric of class war is no longer much used, but social divisions between the haves and have-nots are as deep as they were a century ago.

Danny Dorling (2017) has written persuasively about 'peak inequality'. A small, self-serving and often tax-avoiding elite has become ever richer, while another small - but growing - minority of the population is constantly engaged in a struggle to avoid slipping into poverty, or even destitution. Between these two extremes, far too many people in the middle are only 'just about managing'. While money, or the lack of it, is the presenting problem, it is clear that the current crisis has also been created by attitudes of contempt and disrespect widely found across all social groupings.

Recent experience of such phenomena as the MPs' expenses scandal, the banking crash of 2008, the Brexit decision, the election of Donald Trump and the Grenfell disaster have seemed, each in its own way, to point to a deep malaise and a divided nation. These events revealed both a widespread, top-down disrespect and disregard for the people *en masse* from those in power, and also, unsurprisingly, a reciprocal deeply-felt, bottom-up contempt for the mainstream ruling 'establishment'.

Such revelations may well have come as a shock to those who continue to believe in the benefits of a liberal education and in a necessary link between education and democracy. Social cohesion is essential to a flourishing democracy, which is why all politicians claim to be in favour of 'social mobility'. In its present form, the education system is certainly not contributing to social mobility or to social justice in any substantial form. In fact, if anything education has become part of the problem and no pathway to its solution.

Dorling subtitles his book 'Britain's ticking time-bomb'.

Education therefore needs to recover its sense of purpose as a public good if it is to become part of the solution to the problem of a divided nation - rather than a reflection, an illustration and an aggravation of the problem.

The developing climate of opinion

In the past few years, many other experienced professionals have also recognised the crisis in education and called for root and branch reform. In April 2017, for example, Tim Brighouse identified five systemic structural issues urgently needing attention, as follows:

1. The growing crisis in teacher recruitment and retention, noting that teacher supply was one of just three statutory duties of the secretary of state following the 1944 Education Act while the Minister now has over two thousand duties.

2. The unbalanced school curriculum, with an over-emphasis on numeracy and literacy at the expense of other, almost-as-important subjects and the absence of any notion that children deserve a rounded education.

3. The over-centralised system of governance and accountability in which ministers exercise too much power and too little judgement.

4. The false prospectus of 'parental choice' when it comes to school admission arrangements, the reality being that schools effectively choose parents through covert selection and that many schools find ways to favour the rich and well-connected over children from more challenging families.

5. A large funding gap between state-funded schools and the private independent sector, which perpetuates inequality and militates against social mobility - a declared aim of both government and opposition parties.

Brighouse called for an Enquiry to be chaired by education spokespeople from the main political parties, modelled on a

Parliamentary Select Committee and taking evidence from all stake-holders with pertinent views on what the education service should look like.

In the same month Michael Bassey called for a National Educational Council (NEC) to advise on significant issues in educational practice. It would examine critically the state of national education and make proposals for change, with an expectation that the government of the day would act upon them. He suggested that, following this initial Report, the proposed NEC should continue to exist in order to publish non-mandatory guidance from time to time on matters of curriculum and pedagogy. But Bassey emphasised that it is always the schools themselves which should make key educational decisions, in discussion with their communities and from their professional knowledge of their pupils.

In July 2017 Melissa Benn pointed out that 'free' schools and mass 'academisation' can no longer be considered the cure for social and educational inequality. Parents are beginning to rebel against the narrow curriculum, the excessive testing of pupils from a very young age and the increasing number of rogue school admission systems. There is widespread unease about heads of multi-academy trusts receiving two or three times more salary than the prime minister, while teachers' pay has crawled up by just 1%.

We thoroughly endorse her conclusion that the times require a fresh vision for state education, one that is *based on ethical service with the re-professionalisation, and trust, of teachers at its heart.*

In September 2017 the Labour Party announced its intention to create a new **National Educational Service (NES)** drawing on the public's positive regard for the National Health Service. The NES is Labour's umbrella term for a raft of pledged reforms, including the return of the Educational Maintenance allowance for

315

16-19 year olds and the expansion of free adult education opportunities.

Even the Theresa May government, in March 2018, began at last to recognise the seriousness of problems in schools. It announced that, in order to reduce teachers' workload and in the hope of improving recruitment, there would be no more imposed changes in the school curriculum or its forms of assessment for the duration of the current parliament. This announcement was obviously welcomed by a weary workforce, but it offered much too little. The damage has been done over many years and by several different governments. The time has come to seize the day and to insist that education stops being a party-political football. The crisis demands a national debate and a public conversation (this time, a '*really* great debate') that will consider all future directions of educational change. This would need to be led by an independent body, such as Bassey's proposed NEC.

We therefore call for

- An Emergency Brake on all education legislation and the suspension of the implementation of the most contentious of recent policies

- An Enquiry into Future Directions in Education and

- A National Education Council (NEC).

We further recommend, with Tim Brighouse, that the initial enquiry by the newly formed National Education Council should be conducted as an all-party enquiry taking evidence from all stakeholders, along the lines of a House of Commons Select Committee.

We fully understand that education can only be one part of the solution to social disaffection. The wider predicament in society has its origins far from local schools, in the complex problems and politics of international capitalism, globalisation and technological change. But this book has been written in the belief that education can and ought to be a key part of any solution. Where else, apart from in local schools, colleges and adult education contexts, can the nature of the malaise be widely discussed, understood and addressed by the nation's citizens? We are convinced that a more just system of education entails a whole-hearted effort to work towards an *educative society* (see chapter 13) and that this in turn would enhance social cohesion and revive popular faith in the democratic process.

The scope of this work

As a group it has never been our intention to offer a blueprint for the whole system. The recommendations below are far from comprehensive, they are largely confined to numbers two and three on Brighouse's list of five concerns above. Nor would it be appropriate for any small group to attempt to do the work of the proposed National Education Council before it has even met and started its deliberations.

All we want to offer are some considered thoughts and conclusions on what an education system in the 2020s might look like so that it contributes to a healthy, more just society, more at ease with itself.

Our recommendations cover many aspects of the school system in the areas of school governance, professional teaching, curriculum development, school improvement and democratic accountability. They do not cover the important pre-school and further education sectors which have an essential part to play in the creation of a coherent national education service. Nor do we address here in our Recommendations the university sector which is affected by many of the same pressures as the school system (see Chapters 15,16, and 17). The implications of our work for these areas of education are probably apparent but we ground our

Recommendations in our own first-hand experience as practitioners in schools, colleges and the institutions that support them, teacher education, educational research, inspection and administration. Promoting a more general vision will, we hope, be a continuing task for the NEC.

Recommendations

Our first three recommendations below concern the proposed NEC itself, its remit and its way of working.

The National Education Council (NEC)

We recommend that because the crisis in education is manifest in every part of the system the initial NEC Enquiry should have the widest possible terms of reference and its first Report should address issues of pre-school and lifelong learning as well as the mainstream work of schools, colleges and universities.

A basis in research

We also recommend that the NEC when considering the evidence presented to them give priority to research evidence and findings that are themselves in the proper sense educational. That is to say, research in which questions concerning values are fundamental. The NEC must both encompass and transcend simplistic understandings of research. Educational research is of particular value when it recognises complexity, when it organises experience into meaning. There is of course a place for research that seeks causes and effects, that is quantitative and statistical. But this 'scientific' model has been greatly over-rated when applied to classrooms and schools. Research should build up our knowledge of successful teaching, curriculums and organisations on the basis of insider experience, not on accumulated data from tick-box schedules.

We are passionate on this matter for we have seen the effects of 'scientific' research on, for example, the promotion of phonics in the primary school. And we have both conducted and learned from qualitative and case study research, such as, for example, Maurice Holt's account of comprehensive schooling at Sheredes School. (Holt, 1997) No, education is not an applied science. It is about human relations, complexity and subjectivity.

The on-going work of the National Education Council

We further recommend, with Bassey, that following its initial Report the National Education Council become a permanent body to monitor and support schools and teachers in all possible ways.

The NEC should be empowered to make recommendations to government on all matters affecting state-supported learning, whether in schools, colleges and universities or in pre-school and post-school educational institutions. Such a wide remit should include explicit treatment of: the varied aims and purposes of the education system; its organisational structure from pre-school to all post-school sectors, including further education colleges and universities; the school curriculum and forms of assessment; teacher professionalism, including the recruitment, retention and support of teachers; the evaluation and inspection of educational institutions; the role of adult and community education.

We recognise that even this list may not be exhaustive; other parties, stakeholders and agencies will bring their own preoccupations and interests to the table, making the agenda for the Enquiry either fuller or differently focused. NEC's agenda and work will, in practice, have to be set by reaching a consensus on the many initial expressions of interest and concern that its members receive.

An Educational Enquiry

To cope with such a huge brief we envisage that from the start the NEC will need to undertake or commission a very large number of major enquiry projects. Expert evidence from professionals and academic researchers will be indispensable to its work. But we urge Council members not to expect, or want, submitted evidence to take the form predominantly of statistical findings or so-called 'hard' evidence.

Any research that claims to provide proven facts and figures about educational practice should be treated with caution. We have shown in Chapter 10 and elsewhere how figures based on test results and school league tables can distort educational practice, leading to schools 'gaming' the system, or to certain groups of 'average' children being ignored, or to some other unintended, unjust or anti-educational consequences. We have also argued *a fortiori* that that the figures produced in international comparisons and league tables should always be treated with suspicion. (Chapters 11, 18 and 19).

Education overseas

If international experience is going to be sought by the NEC for useful evidence or inspiration, we would suggest that the only countries worth examining are those which explicitly espouse justice and fairness as part of their national education policy and which also have a 'whole person' approach to educational goals similar to the traditional British notion of a well-rounded person. Currently this might mean Canada and Finland, for instance. Countries like the USA, where social and educational inequalities are as rife as they are here, or France, where the education focus has always been solely on intellectual and academic achievement, have less to offer.

Research and Development

Many of us have been engaged in school-based research and curriculum development over many years and have conducted academic research in collaboration with scholars at home and abroad.

One common insight from this collective experience is that subjectivities always matter in educational contexts. The 'facts' seldom speak for themselves, because they can always be interpreted in different ways. Each educational institution has its own particularities. Every practitioner has their own personal experience of - and their own perspective on - issues of teaching, learning, assessment and school organisation. How colleagues work together is governed by their perceptions one of another and of their shared tasks.

How learners learn is a uniquely personal affair, always being done for the first time and in a specific context of time and place. Educational matters are not only complex in themselves, they also involve human beings - teachers and learners - in all their complexity. Qualitative approaches to research are therefore in and of themselves more legitimately educational forms of enquiry, offering more meaningful evidence because they make researchers get below the surface of things and ask the difficult questions.

In our experience human factors always play the main part in any and every successful educational process. For example, the apparently simple, universal and quantitative method, beloved by Ofsted for many years, of target-setting, measuring outcomes and issuing numerical grades has never been more than a very small part of an effective curriculum development strategy or a successful school improvement process. There are no '*off the shelf*' answers to school improvement based on metrics or algorithms.

By the same token, we urge NEC members not to be seduced by the claims of Artificial Intelligence or Robotics pioneers. Good education, as we have argued above requires good teachers (see Chapters 20, and 21). Teachers cannot be replaced by machines.

Other Recommendations to the NEC

The recommendations below cover three areas of the system which many of the authors have experienced at first hand, specifically: *governance* which is in disarray; *the curriculum* which is unbalanced and over-prescriptive, and *school inspection and evaluation* which for many years has been superficial and too mechanistic.

We recommend a return of schooling to local democratic accountability and that a new designation of 'community school' be created, with the premise that all schools are potential centres of lifelong educational opportunities.

Having been freed from local control, the new system of academies and multi-academy trusts have in many cases lost contact with their clientele in local communities. This, rather than the many troubling, documented cases of mismanagement and criminality in the demi-monde of the academies, must provide the main argument against further academisation. Local schools are in the right position to promote social cohesion and expand educational opportunities for young and adult learners alike. Closer and democratic regulation of the market for education could promote community development and provide life-long educational and educative activities for all. In nourishing the cultural life of their communities, local schools could simultaneously enrich the school curriculum and serve the ends of social justice and reducing inequality.

The National Education Council should as a foundational task investigate and promote a robust curriculum structure in which existing disciplines are seen as resources for learning, not bundles of knowledge divorced from educational purposes

There is widespread agreement that in the past 30 years the curriculum has been prescribed in too much detail leading to robotic teaching. Also, that an excessive emphasis on the 'basics' has narrowed pupils' experience. This compression has happened at a time when schools are being asked to deal with more issues in the curriculum because of urgent social concerns.

Examples of social concerns that have been the subject of periodic moral panic, but which remain to be systematically integrated into the curriculum, include:

- obesity and health

- drugs and drug culture

- citizenship, democracy and the social order

- terrorism

- multi-culturalism

- personal financial management

- the cyber revolution

- the threat to the environment ('green' issues)

- education for resilience in the face of the uncertainty and rapidity of social change

None of these sits squarely and comfortably within the received framework of curriculum 'subjects'. They have been largely ignored by a national curriculum which was derived from the nineteenth century, was fit for some aspects of the twentieth century but has become increasingly redundant for the twenty-first. Yet such themes demand a rightful place in the awareness of young people who will confront issues and situations we cannot predict.

Our view of the curriculum has been signalled many times in these pages. Every school curriculum is much more than a comprehensive set of syllabuses. The curriculum comprises all the learning for which the school is responsible, whereas the syllabus consists merely of a content list of the subjects or topics to be studied together with the tests to be taken, or other indicators of performance. The syllabus is a paper exercise, while the curriculum is the lived experience of the learners who are subjected to it.

What we have had for the past thirty years might more accurately be called a National Syllabus than a National Curriculum. What we have long needed is a national conversation, led by educationalists and politicians working together with a shared agenda, about how the school curriculum should contribute to personal, social and political identity in the 21st century.

The NEC should establish regional and local communication networks among schools and foster curriculum development among them.

We believe that the curriculum should reflect and consolidate regional or local identity. Schools need to serve and be accountable to a meaningful community. Young people are made well aware of their national identity in many ways, for example via international sport, military events, the Royal family and the BBC. Regional and local identity, by contrast, are much overlooked.

There is a danger that much of the current school curriculum has no connection with younger people living in a virtual, wired world and communicating via social media. The school versions of history, geography, science, literature, religious education, the creative arts and even physical education often seem to come from places and times that are remote from today's young and their interests. For a long time schools have been expected to present universal and cosmopolitan values of a highly generalised nature in an outdated curriculum framework about which even some teachers find it hard to enthuse. These values came originally from university professors focusing on scholarship rather than on rounded personal development, with '*the child regarded as a gradually increasing fraction of a professor in each branch of study, doomed to swallow with or without cramming and at stated times to regurgitate for inspection those logically perfect but psychologically indigestible gobbets of erudition*'. (Zilliacus,1934). More recently, Stuart Hall spoke of inner-city teachers as lost souls travelling from suburbia to the inner city, there to offer learning to which they themselves did not fully subscribe.

Their degrees and their teacher-education courses will make teachers representatives to some extent of the universal among the particular. There is an important place in the education system for the promotion of scholarship which may tend to take some people out of their local community and neighbourhood into a world of academic and intellectual discovery. The country will need its professors and its world-class subject experts in the future. But the school system and the school curriculum as a whole should no longer be directed or dominated by this requirement, or by narrow, cognitive forms of knowledge. The problem for most teachers in schools - and for curriculum developers - is to find appropriate ways to make a much broader set of educational values relevant in ever-changing contexts and then to transmit them effectively to the vast majority of young people. This task is clearly harder in a culturally diverse society. The need is for a richer and more locally relevant curriculum which would allow all school teachers to be authentic models for their pupils, as exemplars of a life worth living.

We recommend that the NEC conduct a thorough investigation of school culture with a special regard to the mental health of teachers and students. A good start may be in the 'slow school' movement.

Another symptom of problems with the current school curriculum is the increasing level of stress throughout all levels of education. When schools, colleges and universities are made to operate as businesses in a competitive market there is inevitable strain on all parties. An ethic of constant aspiration may be integral to competitive sport, from where so many of our 'heroes' emerge. But it is of limited value in education where the virtues of co-operation, care and community cohesion are more important. The reports of ubiquitous self-harm and increasing numbers of suicide among the young provide dreadful evidence of this modern malaise.

The NEC should promote the study of teaching. It should establish a Resource Bank of successful teaching based on case study and the first-hand accounts of practitioners. It should liaise with the academic research community in developing rigorous methods of grounded educational enquiry about teaching and learning.

In this book we have expressed an understanding of teaching as a set of activities which is frequently misrepresented as the transmission of messages (or of knowledge or of information) from one location (person) to another. We reject this 'delivery' model of teaching. Good teachers are always more than messengers. Teaching is a complex social activity, not one end of a signalling system.

Very little of effective teaching consists in passing on information. It consists in activities designed to promote learning. In presenting such activities, say a group project or a field trip, teachers are involved in negotiating meaning with pupils. Both teachers and pupils will inevitably interpret what is before them and many constructions of the same situation will exist. Good teaching is therefore much more accurately described as continuous conversation and a mutual search for meaning than as 'stand and deliver'. Teachers will often say that they come to understand more of their subject in the process of teaching it even to the youngest pupil. The never-ending struggle with numbers, words and meaning is what makes teaching so interesting and so demanding; and the same is true of learning.

Teacher Education

It is a given that teachers should themselves be educated people. This in itself means not seeing themselves as just messengers or conveyors of information; teachers need a sophisticated understanding of teaching as a social process. Teachers must also have some detailed understanding of the educational process and of the choices open to them as teachers. Otherwise they will be hapless victims of circumstance, with their practices falling in with whatever is convenient and fashionable. They would become 'knowledge workers' (Chapter 16) Such workers' relationship to wisdom would be roughly comparable to 'sex workers' relationship to love.

Teachers need an awareness of educational values and of the fact that education is 'essentially contested', and open to question. Teachers have to find their own way on the difficult path between knowing the various alternatives and making a personal commitment. Because it is such a difficult and complex job (see Chapters 20 and 21), our view is that teacher education demands space outwith the school as well as 'on the job'. Teachers throughout their career need to bring disciplined thought to the daily questions, great and small, which arise from, and in, practice. This cannot well be achieved while carrying a full teaching timetable. Time and space must be made for critical reflection.

We recommend that the proposed NEC should explore methods of school inspection alternative to those employed by Ofsted.

No-one loves inspectors. Life as a teacher would be easier and quieter without them. But it would also be prone to outdated routines, convenient inefficiencies and unrealised potential in both teacher and taught. We appreciate, therefore, that inspection has an entirely legitimate place in any professional regime. But it can take many forms and can have many purposes, some of which are inappropriate in educational institutions either because they are over-politicised or because they are epistemologically mistaken. Colin Richards has provided in Chapter 22 a taxonomy of approaches. He makes a strong case against the pseudo-scientific approach of the check-list and in favour of the qualitative approach of detailed observations, respectful conversations and professional judgements.

Ofsted has been particularly disappointing for many years. In September 2018 the House of Commons Public Accounts Committee reported in considerable detail on Ofsted's work and found a depressingly large number of shortcomings. It is clear that Ofsted is not ensuring quality in any way. Headlines from the Report included:

- Ofsted is not meeting its statutory target for re-inspecting schools every five years. It is unacceptable that many schools (and Further Education Colleges) have not been inspected for over six years (in some cases over 10 years).

- Ofsted's short inspections do not allow inspectors to make a meaningful assessment of a school's performance or to help schools improve.

- Ofsted does not involve parents enough in school inspections.

- Ofsted does not make the most of its unique position to use intelligence from inspections to lead change and be a force for school improvement.

- The system for school accountability and school improvement is muddled, with overlapping roles leading to inefficiency and confusion for schools and parents. There is uncertainty about who is responsible for school improvement in schools labelled 'inadequate'.

After these damning criticisms, we simply make three observations.

Firstly, while Ofsted may seem expensive, it is grossly underpowered in financial terms considering the large ambition of its brief.

Secondly, it is still seen by many teachers, rightly or wrongly, as having an agenda that is not 'just education' but also political. Teachers have suffered enormously from badly-managed Ofsted inspections for over twenty-five years. The age of shaming schools and attacking teachers and 'experts' should be past. For the next twenty-five years politicians and educators must work together on shared goals.

Finally, it is in the matter of methodology that we most profoundly dissent from the Ofsted approach.

School improvement is a much greater undertaking than school inspection. While inspection in some form should certainly be a part of the improvement process, as currently conducted by Ofsted it is likely to disrupt it.

Envoi: The crisis revisited

We have referred to education in crisis and asserted that decisions must be taken lest something even worse than Ted Wragg's Ten Steps befall us all. His was a vision of Orwellian state control. What we are faced with now is a system spinning out of control and even intelligibility, forever destined to separate us centrifugally one from another.

The gravity of today's crisis in education is different in kind to crises elsewhere. Arguably, critical situations in, say medicine, social services, defence etc, could largely be met by increased funding. That is the predominant message from professionals in those areas, as witness the periodic campaigns for an hypothecated tax in aid of the NHS. Of course, there are radical challenges to existing practices in health, social services and elsewhere. But none we believe more fundamental to the success of our society than in education.

'More of the same' is not what is required in education. Who wants a still more highly prescribed national curriculum, an intensified inspection regime? Who wants a complete denationalisation of the education service, a sell-off to the private sector? Those are the polarities around which education crisis rotates.

All of this is another way of saying that the aims of education are strife-torn.

- education as the transmission of approved knowledge or education as the search for meaning between generations and cultures?

- education for the status quo or education for a problematic future?

- education for employment and productivity or education for personal fulfilment?

- teachers as 'knowledge workers' or teachers as cultural critics and key figures in cultural change?

The complexity of these choices, which is grossly over-simplified as they stand here on paper, makes great work for the armchair theorist. But where it counts is on the ground in the daily professional work of teaching. It is not too late to learn the lessons of the recent past and to build upon them towards a better future.

Select Bibliography

Anam, T. (2015) *The Rohinga Crisis is not an isolated tragedy - it's the shape of things to come*, The Guardian 19 May 2015.

Anderson, E. (1993) *Value in Ethics and Economics*, Harvard University Press, Cambridge, Mass.

Attali, J. (2006) *A Brief History of the Future: A Brave and Controversial Look at the twenty-First Century*, Arcade Publishing, New York.

Auden, W.H. (1991) *Collected Poems*, Penguin Random House, New York

Ball J. and Greenway A. (2018) Bluffocracy Biteback

Bassey, M. (1991) *Creating Education Through Research: Presidential Address to the British Education Research Association(BERA)*, 29th September BERA.

Bassey, M. (2011) *Education for the Inevitable*, Book Guild, Kibworth

Bauman, Z. (2000) *Liquid Modernity*, Polity Press, Cambridge

Becker, H., Geer, B. , Hughes, E. (1968) *Making the Grade: The Academic Side of College Life*, Wiley, Hoboken, New Jersey

Bell, D. (1993) *Communitarianism and its Critics*, Clarendon Press, Oxford

Benn, M. (2018) *Book Review of Cleverlands*, in Forum, Vol 60 No 1 pp 137-142

Bennett, S.N. (1976) *Teaching Styles and Pupil Progress*, Open Books

Bernstein, B. (1971) *Class Codes and Control*, Routledge and Kegan Paul, London.

Booth, T and Ainscow, M (2000) *The Index of Inclusion: developing learning and participation in schools*, Centre for Studies on Inclusive Education, Bristol

British Educational Research Association (2018) *Quality in Close-to-Practice Research*, Research Intelligence 137 Autumn

Brink, C. (2018) *The Soul of a University: Why Excellence is not Enough*, Bristol University Press.

Bullock Report - A Language for Life (1975), UK Government Ministry of Education Report

Campbell, D.T. (1979) *Assessing the impact of planned social change*, in Evaluation and Program Planning, Vol 2, no 1 pp 67-90

Churchill, W. (1954) Quotation from the Ashby Report cited in Bynner, J. *Whatever happened to lifelong learning? And does it matter?* Journal of the British Academy, Vol 5, pp 61-89.

Club of Rome (1972) *Limits to Growth*, Potomac Associates Universe Books New York

Collini, S. (2012) *What are Universities For?* Penguin, London

Crehan, L. (2016) *Cleverlands: the secrets behind the success of the world's education superpowers*, Unbound: London

Delors Report (1996) Delors Commission UNESCO, Paris

Deming W.E. (1994) *The New Economics for Industry, Government, Education* MIT Press

Department of Education and Science (1965) *Circular 10/65* HMSO, London

Department of Education and Science (1977) *Education in Schools (Green Paper)* HMSO, London

Department for Education (2016) *Education Excellence Everywhere (White Paper)*, Government Publication, London

Didau, D. (2016) *What if everything you knew about education was WRONG?*, Crown House Publishing, Carmarthen

Dorling, D. (2017) *The Equality Effect: improving life for everyone*, New Internationalist, Oxford

Dorling D. (2018) *Peak Inequality* Policy Press

Eberl, U. (2010) *Life in 2050*, Verlag, Beltz and Gelberg, Weinheim

Edgerton, D (2018) *The Rise and Fall of the British Nation: a twentieth century history*, Allen Lane, London

Eisner, E. (1983) *The Art and Craft of Teaching* in Educational Leadership, Volume 4 No 4 pp 4-13

Elsdon, K. (1991) Speech to *Educational Centres Association September Conference*

Fish, D. (1995) *Quality Mentoring for Student Teachers: A Principled Approach to Practice,*

Fish, D. (2004) *The educational thinking behind the Royal College of Surgeons of England's first curriculum framework* in Annals of the Royal College of Surgeons of England, August

Flanders, N. 1967 *Teacher Influence in the Classroom. Interaction analysis: theory, research, and application* Addison-Wesley.

Flanders, N. 1970 Analyzing Teacher Behavior. Addison-Wesley

Flude, R. and Parrott, A. (1979) *Education and the Challenge of Change,* Open University Press, Milton Keynes

Friedman, M. (1982) *Capitalism and Freedom* University of Chicago Press

Freire, P. (1968) *Pedagogy of the Oppressed,* Seabury Press, New York

Gardiner, H. (2006) *Frames of Mind: theories of multiple intelligence,* Basic Books, New York

Garland, R (1980) *Department, Inspectorate and the Agenda for Change* in Golby,M (1980) *The Core Curriculum Perspectives 2,* University of Exeter School of Education

Giddens, A. (1991) *The Consequences of Modernity,* Polity Press, Cambridge

Gipps, C. (1990) *Assessment: A Teacher's Guide to the Issues,* Hodder and Stoughton, London

Golby, M at al (1975) *Curriculum Design and Development* Croom Helm

Golby, M. (ed) (1980) *The Core Curriculum Perspectives 2,* University of Exeter School of Education

Golby, M. (1992) *School Governors: Conceptual and Practical Problems* in *Journal of Philosophy of Education 26 (2)*

Golby, M. and Schnur, J. (1995) *Teacher Education: A University Mission* in *Journal of Teacher Education Vol 46 No1 for the American Association of Colleges for Education*

Goldacre, B. (2012) *Bad Pharma,* Faber and Faber, London

Goldberg, S. (2013) *Secret funding helped build vast network of climate change denial thinktanks,* The Guardian February 14th

Gould S.J. (1980) *The Mismeasure of Man,* W.W. Norton and Co., New York

Grayling, A.C. (2017) *Democracy and its Crisis,* Oneworld, London

Green, F. and Kynaston, D. (2019) *Engines of Privilege: Britain's Private School Problem,* Bloomsbury, London

Habermas, J. (1974) *Theory and Practice,* Heinemann, London

Hayek, F. (1944) *The Road to Serfdom,* Taylor and Francis, Abingdon

Hirst P.H. and Peters R.S. (1970) *The Logic of Education,* Kegan Paul, London

Holt, M. (1978) *The Common Curriculum,* Routledge, London

Holt, M. (1985) Practical *and Moral Aspects of Curriculum Change* unpublished doctoral thesis, University of Exeter

Holt, M. (1987) *Judgement, Planning and Educational Change,* Harper and Row, New York

Hoyle, E. (1969) *The Role of the Teacher* RKP London

Hutton, W. (2015) *How Good We Can Be: Ending the Mercenary Society and Building a Great Country* Little Brown, London

Illich, I. (1973) Tools *for Conviviality*, Harper and Row, New York

IPPC (2014) *AR5 Synthesis Report on Climate Change* Intergovernmental Programme on Climate Change Geneva

Kellaway, L. (2017) *The last word* in The Week, 2nd December 2017, p.61

Kelly (2004) *The Curriculum: Theory and Practice*, Sage Publications, New York

Kemmis, S. and Carr, W. (1986) *Becoming Critical*, The Falmer Press, London

Kline, P. (1994) *An Easy Guide to Factor Analysis*, Psychology Press, London

Kolbert, E. (2014) *The Sixth Extinction: An Unnatural History*, Henry Holt and Co., London

Koretz, D. (2017) *The Testing Charade: pretending to make schools better*, The University of Chicago Press, Chicago and Oxford

Kossenniemi, M. (1982) *Twenty-two years after becoming a teacher* Helsinki Suomalainen Tiedeakatemia

Langford, S. G. (1978) *Teaching as a Profession*, Manchester University Press

Langford, S.G. (1983) *Education, Persons and Society*, Macmillan, London

Larmer, B. (2016) *The Long March from China to the Ivies*, The Economist 1843, April-May, pp 84-89

Lave, J. and Wenger, E. (1991) *Situated Learning: legitimate peripheral participation*, Cambridge University Press

Letwin, O. (2017) *Hearts and Minds: the Battle for the Conservative party from Thatcher to the Present*, Biteback Publishing, London

Lindsay, A.D. (1943) *The Modern Democratic State*, Oxford University Press

Mansell, W. (2007) *The Tyranny of Testing*, Politicos Publishing Ltd, London

Molnar, A. (2017) *Dismantling Public Education: Turning Ideology into Gold*,

Montacute, R (2018) *Access to Advantage* The Sutton Trust

Morgan, N. (2017) *Taught not Caught: educating for 21st century character*, John Catt Educational, Woodbridge, Suffolk

Morris, H. (1925) Internal Cambridgeshire Memorandum in Ree, H. (1984) *The Henry Morris Collection*, Cambridge University Press

Mountford, J. (1972) *Keele, an Historical Critique*, Routledge and Kegan Paul, London

Muller, J.Z. (2018) *The Tyranny of Metrics*, Princeton University Press, Princeton and Oxford

Myatt, M. (2018) *The Curriculum: Gallimaufry to coherence*, John Catt Educational, Woodbridge, Suffolk

Newfield, C. (2008) *Unmaking the Public University*, Harvard University Press, Cambridge, Massachusetts

Newman, J.H. (1852) *The Idea of a University* Aeterna Press (2015)

Oakeshott, M. (1989) *The Voice of Liberal Learning*, Yale University Press, New Haven, Connecticut

O'Connor, D. (1957) *An Introduction to the Philosophy of Education*, Philosophical Library, New York

Olssen, M. (2010) *Liberalism, Neo-liberalism and Social Democracy*, Routledge, New York and London

Peters, R.S. (1966) *Ethics and Education*, Routledge, London

Plowden Report (1967) Children and Their Primary Schools Central Advisory Council (England) HMSO

Popper, K. (1945) *The Open Society and its Enemies*, Routledge, London

Price, D. (Ed) (2017) *Education Forward - moving schools into the future*, Crux Publishing, London

Reay, D. (2017) *Miseducation: Inequality, Education and the Working Classes*, Policy Press, Bristol

Roffey, S. and Perry, J. (2014) *Special Needs in the Early Years*, Taylor and Francis Group, London and New York

Rose, J. (2001) *The Intellectual Life of the British Working Classes*, Yale University Press, New Haven and London

Rusk, R (1957) *Doctrines of the Great Educators* Macmillan New York

Russell, B (1926) *On Education* Routledge

Sahlberg, P. (2011) *Finnish Lessons: What can the world learn from educational change in Finland?* Teachers College, Columbia University, New York and London

Sandel, M (2018) *How to save democracy*, New Statesman 18-24th May

Schumacher, E. (1993) *Small is Beautiful* Vintage

Schon, D. (1987*) Educating the Reflective Practitioner* San Francisco Jossey-Bass

Schulman, L. S. (2004) *The Wisdom of Practice: Essays on Teaching, Learning, and Learning to Teach,* Jossey Bass, San Francisco

Seymour, J. (1976, 1997) *The Complete Book of Self-sufficiency* Corgi

Sicart, M. (2014) *Play Matters,* Massachusetts Institute of Technology (MIT) Press

Skilbeck, M. and Reynolds J.B. (1976) *Culture and the Classroom,* Open Books Publishing, London

Smith, J. (2001) *The Learning Game: a teacher's inspirational story,* Abacus Press, London

Smith, L. (2011) *The New North: The World in 2050,* Profile Books, London

Stenhouse, L. (1975) *An Introduction to Curriculum Research and Development,* Heinemann, London

Sutton-Smith (2001) *The Ambiguity of Play,* Harvard University Press

Tibble J W. (ed) (1966) *The Study of Education* RKP

Tomlinson, M. (2004) *14-19 Curriculum and Qualifications Reform ('The Tomlinson Report'),* Government publication, London

Vickers, G. (1983) *The Art of Judgement: Study of Policy-Making,* Longman, London

Wegerif, R. (2013) *Dialogic: Education for the Internet Age*, Routledge, London

Weinstein, B (2009)*Is it still cheating if I don't get caught?* Roaring Book Press, New York

Whitehead A N. (1929) *The Aims of Education* Macmillan,

Wilkinson R. and Pickett, K. (2009) *The Spirit Level: why more equal societies almost always do better,* Allen Lane, London

Wilkinson, R. and Pickett, K. (2018) *The Inner Level: how more equal societies reduce stress,* Allen Lane, London

Willetts, D. (1918) *A University Education,* Oxford University Press, Oxford

Williams, R. (1961) *The Long Revolution Chatto and Windus*

Wilson P S (1971) *Interest and Discipline in Education* RKP

Wittgenstein, L. (1980) *Remarks on the Philosophy of Psychology,* Blackwell, Oxford

Wragg E. C. (1993, 1999) *An Introduction to Classroom Observation* RKP

Yeaxlee, B. A. (1929) *Lifelong Education,* Cassell, London

Young, M.D. (1958) *The Rise of the Meritocracy,* Thames and Hudson, London.

Zilliacus, L.(1934) *Examinations* New Era, p 61